P9-BHW-357

neileengraybeanbagsco
rderichardrogersabsolutVodkacutler
westcoca-colapetergreenawayalvar
penssalvadordalitheminidesignmuseumdunlc
cristobelbalenciagagripsaulbass
breuerhabitatcharlesandrayeameskoda
slegotiziosupermanroadsignsmichelin
olourettoresottsasstupperwaretypograph
hecitycecilbeatonapplemacin
abethdavidcafesvwbeetleisseymiyakelacoste
aliburtonpackagingandygolds
ewylondonundergroundaldoros
labelssainsbury'sthepaperclip
dcarsonalessiellenvonunworthedwardjohnstor
arlesrenniemackintoshfunfairs
mercedesraymondmeier

6/78

TERENCE CONRAN ON
design

TERENCE CONRAN ON
design

THE OVERLOOK PRESS
WOODSTOCK • NEW YORK

New York architects at the Beaux Arts Ball (1931)

To Coco, in celebration of her birth on the day this book was finished

First published in the United States in 1996 by
The Overlook Press
Lewis Hollow Road
Woodstock, New York 12498

Copyright © 1996 Conran Octopus Limited

All rights reserved. No part of this book may be reproduced or transmitted in any form or by any means, electronic or mechanical, including photocopying, recording, or any information storage and retrieval system now known or to be invented without permission in writing from the publisher, except by a reviewer who wishes to quote brief passages in connection with a review written for inclusion in a magazine, newspaper or broadcast.

Library of Congress Cataloging-in-Publication Data
Conran, Terence
Terence Conran on design / Terence Conran with Elizabeth Wilhide.
1. Design — History — 20th century. I. Wilhide, Elizabeth
NK1390.C65 1996
745.4'442—dc20 96-18134 CIP
ISBN: 0-87951-686-0
Printed in Hong Kong
10 9 8 7 6 5 4 3 2 1

Author's acknowledgements
This book would not have happened without my brilliant collaborators, Elizabeth Wilhide, Helen Lewis and Simon Willis. It has been a joy to work with them.

Art Director Helen Lewis
Assistant Designer Amanda Lerwill

Commissioning Editor Denny Hemming
Consultant Editor Elizabeth Wilhide
Project Editor Simon Willis

Picture Researchers Nadine Bazar
                     Gareth Jones
                     Clare Limpus

Production Controller Jill Beed

page 2: Jean Nouvel, Pierre Soria &. Gilbert Lezénès, Arab Institute, Paris (1988)

page 3: Adirondack chairs, Blue Mountain Lake, America

745.4
CON
1996

Contents

8   **INTRODUCTION: DESIGN AND THE QUALITY OF LIFE**

24   **FURNISHINGS AND THE INTERIOR**

60   **HOUSEHOLD**

88   **CLOTHING**

126   **FOOD**

158   **TRANSPORT**

192   **WORK**

220   **FREE TIME**

252   **OUTDOORS**

282   INDEX

287   ACKNOWLEDGEMENTS

design and the

believe to be good design, or is it something that can be measured or scored objectively? Does the concept of good design change according to social, political or economic circumstances, or are there constant factors that enable us to evaluate any object made at any time in history? Why should one person's judgement be any more noteworthy than another's? What do we mean by 'good'? What do we mean by 'design'?

quality of life

People have tied themselves in knots trying to define the whole concept of 'good' design, and filled many pages with dense critical theories in the process. This book does not seek to follow that example, although it does represent an attempt to answer the same basic question. In the following chapters I will be setting out some of the things I enjoy and explaining why I believe they merit attention. You may agree with me; you may even own some of the examples I have chosen. But I cannot pretend that my selection entitles me to come up with a conclusive definition of good design, or, indeed, that anyone's selection would. All I can demonstrate is the process of evaluation that is implied when we choose one thing over another, and explore some of the common criteria that inform these choices. I also hope the book might encourage you to view a little more carefully the everyday objects that surround us.

If defining 'good' design leads us into a philosophical minefield, defining 'design' full stop is not much easier. In one sense, every single thing that has ever been made by man or woman has been designed. This is a fundamental truth but it is one that many people find difficult to grasp, perhaps because it is so obvious.

We are quick to recognize the designer's imprint in the cut of a couture dress, in the façade of a landmark building or in the shape of the latest motorcar. Less visible, but no less significant, are those designs that shape our everyday world, from the humble paperclip to the supermarket label. Design is all around us, in the shape of our houses and the arrangement of interior space, in the way we shop and entertain ourselves, and in the ease with which we move from place to place.

This has always been the case. Design is not a new discipline at all, despite its recent identification with the 1980s, the so-called 'designer decade'. The milking stool is every bit as designed as the Jacobsen 'Egg' chair. There may have been no single designer responsible for the milking stool, but it is designed none the less.

By the same token, we are all, to some extent, designers. It is not necessary to have received formal training, nor to reside in a creative ivory tower, to engage in the process of design. If you have ever redecorated a room, chosen a colour scheme, arranged

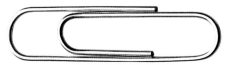

Lightweight, cheap and easy-to-use, the paperclip is so brilliantlly designed we take it for granted.

the furniture or hung pictures on a wall, you have exercised design skills by altering the layout and appearance of a room to make it fulfil the functions you require and to express your personal taste. If you have ever practised your signature, you have designed an image of yourself that you wish to present to the world. In these simple ways, we all make statements about ourselves which influence the manner in which others perceive us.

In choosing these analogies, I do not wish to demean the role of the trained designer. Instead, what I hope to show is that design touches all our lives each and every day, and it is something with which we can engage intuitively.

The whole issue can perhaps be most starkly appreciated in its negative form. Even those who quake at the prospect of defining good design can spot bad design a mile away. Everyone has encountered the restaurant where the tables are so close together you cannot negotiate a path to the loo, the pen with erratic inkflow, the chair that gives you backache. These are all examples of bad design, and we would all recognize them as such.

These designs fail to make the grade because they do not work. Fitness of purpose, then, provides an important starting-point for

'Design is important because if it was not designed it could not be made'

Edward, aged 10

distinguishing good design from bad. It is reassuringly stable ground: either something works or it doesn't; personal taste and opinion do not really come into it. If you know what you require from an article of clothing, a piece of furniture or a form of transport, you can judge for yourself whether the item in question functions as it should: whether it is durable, safe, comfortable, easy to operate or meets any of the myriad physical parameters implied in the notion of function and practicality.

A large part of what design is all about is concerned with precisely this type of problem-solving, tempering technology and material to serve basic human needs. If a design fails to function, it is often glaringly obvious. But even in cases where the technology is more complex and the demands are subtler, the distinction between something that works well and something that does not is still one that can be more or less objectively assessed. You can be taught to judge designs on performance and suitability, and in one sense this is what everyone does when they study a list of specifications or features, test-drive a new car or try on clothes. This element of practicality is a useful definition of the distinction between 'design' and 'art'.

On the functional side, however, it can be difficult to draw the line between design and technological innovation or invention. In the real world, the inventor and designer are rarely the same person. One recent example which demonstrates the difference between these two very similar sides of the same coin is the development of the Freeplay clockwork radio.

The radio is the invention of Trevor Bayliss, a former champion swimmer and underwater escapologist who lives on Eel Pie Island on the Thames. His inspiration was to identify a need which had barely been articulated; and his invention has the 'why-hasn't-anyone-thought-of-that-before?' simplicity which characterizes so many good ideas.

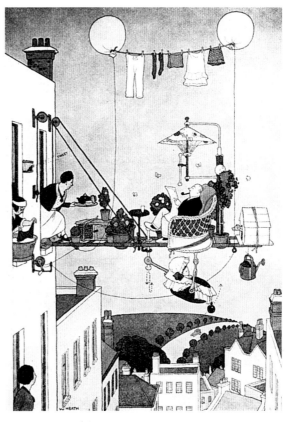

Problem-solving by W. Heath-Robinson, from *Absurdities* (1934).

The sequence of events began when Bayliss was listening to a radio programme about the problems of health education in Africa, where the spread of AIDS has caused an escalating and urgent crisis. Radio was seen as the best medium to convey the healthcare information to help counteract the growing epidemic, but those most starved of information (and therefore at great risk) tended to live in areas where there was no electricity supply. The villagers in such remote parts of the continent were equally unable to rely on a constant supply of batteries to keep a radio powered, or, indeed, to afford the expense of batteries.

DESIGN AND THE QUALITY OF LIFE

11

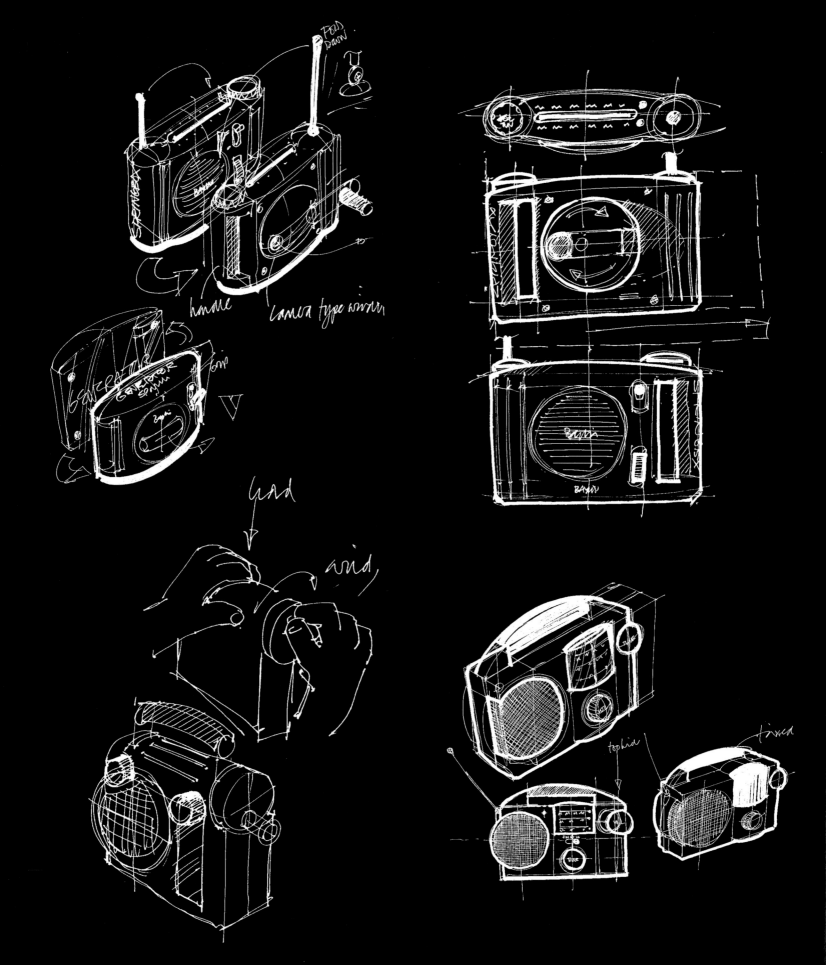

Development sketches (left) for the 'Freeplay' clockwork radio (above, 1995).

The idea of a clockwork radio, run from energy generated by a winder, sprang to Bayliss's mind, and after considerable trial and error he came up with a prototype that actually worked. After an even more protracted period, and with the help of an entrepreneur, he managed to attract interest from a South African company keen to put the radio into production.

Yet, while the Bayliss radio fulfilled its primary function, on other levels it did not work at all. The principle – of powering a radio by a clockwork motor – had been proven, but in practice there were significant hitches. For the radio to succeed as a product, it also needed to be affordable and attractive in its designated market. Research had identified that the type of radio that would have the greatest appeal would be one that was loud, big, and cheap enough to provide an economic alternative to the cost of replacing batteries at regular intervals for a standard radio.

Another factor was the length of time between windings. Bayliss's radio worked as a prototype, but not yet as a product.

The task of ironing out the technical difficulties fell to the Design and Technology department at Bristol University. Eventually, they succeeded in coming up with a design where the volume could be increased without also increasing background hum and where a single winding of 20 seconds could provide 40 minutes of playing time. At the same time, Andy Davey of TKO, a London-based product design consultancy, was working on a design that could be produced for the right amount of money and that looked attractive, too, shedding the endearing but unmarketable Heath-Robinson appearance of the original prototype.

The point of this story is to show how invention and design, while intimately related, are not necessarily the same. Having the idea, proving the principle, or inventing the process are key creative activities. But applying the principle, invention or process so that it works on all levels is equally important. There was more than an element of design thinking in Bayliss's original conception and in his entire approach to the problem, but, like many inventors, he was able to take the idea only so far. The process of turning his invention into a product demanded another set of skills. Inventors need designers and vice versa.

Bayliss was able to identify a need and devise a solution to meet a specific problem. Many inventors, however, do not fully envisage the uses to which their products will be put. It is said that Alexander Graham Bell believed that the principal use of the telephone would be for playing music to those who subscribed to listen, failing utterly to foresee the pivotal role of telecommunications in shaping life this century.

Equally often, a material, technique or system devised for one application ends up achieving its greatest success in a widely different arena. Teflon, for example, originated as a coating in space

'Design is the tribute art pays to industry'

Paul Finch, *Architects' Journal*

technology, but found a much more widespread use in the home, as a non-stick lining for frying pans and as a friction-free coating for the thread of corkscrews. The technology which makes possible the Internet was developed in response to the need to design a bomb-proof network of mainframe computers. Scores of products from the Burberry trenchcoat to the Zippo lighter owe their origins to the exigencies of wartime.

To borrow the advertising slogan, design is 'the appliance of science'. In other words, it is largely to do with common sense. It is common sense to design a tool to fit the hand, a desk to provide comfortable working height, clothing to fit the human body. In the time-honoured phrase, we largely expect form to follow function. But if design were merely a means of applying invention and technology to create people-friendly products, there would be no need to argue about it.

I like to think that design is 98 per cent common sense. What makes design so interesting and challenging is the other two per cent; what one might call 'aesthetics'. At this point the murky waters begin to rise. Many products which achieve 98 per cent are demonstrably good; but those with the extra two per cent have a magic ingredient which places them in another category altogether. That two per cent makes the difference between something which is perfectly acceptable and something which is so special that everyone wants to possess it. When the magic ingredient is present, the quality of life is improved. People are happy and pleased to use the product, not merely because it works well but because it lifts their spirits, and gives positive pleasure rather than simply offering absence of frustration. If something is aesthetically pleasing – if it strikes a chord, creates excitement or a surge of desire – people are often willing to overlook or overcome less-than-perfect performance in other areas. No one would call the Citroën DS an easy car to drive, but for those who love the way it

looks, learning how to handle its idiosyncrasies is a small price to pay for aesthetic pleasure. Indeed, the quirks of the car lend it character, and learning to deal with them elevates the driver, in his or her mind, into a connoisseur's club of DS-lovers.

One of my favourite designs, Concorde (launched 1976) has the magic of the truly special.

The magic ingredient, of course, is an extraordinarily complex phenomenon. You can test a product to determine whether it can be made economically, whether it fulfils a given set of objective standards, whether it can be marketed and sold to its designated consumers at a price they are prepared to pay. You cannot, however, quantify the magic ingredient; you can only recognize it when you see it.

In matters of taste, it is usually impossible to get a consensus of opinion. I can think of only a few examples where the majority of people would agree on aesthetics. Concorde is one design which seems to attract universal approbation. I have rarely met anyone who has not been inspired by the sight of Concorde in flight. What creates the magical effect? Is it the fact that this supersonic jet resembles a perfect paper dart, or that it symbolizes power, luxury and instant gratification? Or does Concorde merely provoke an irresistible sense of optimism and faith in the future?

DESIGN AND
THE QUALITY
OF LIFE

14

Flamineo Bertoni's Citroën DS (1957) drew just a few adoring fans to the Paris Motor Show.

While I am not a theorist, I think it is worth pointing out that centuries of debate about design and taste have skirted round the same issues without really pinning them down. 'Have nothing in your houses which you do not know to be useful or believe to be beautiful': William Morris formulated what he called his 'golden rule' for good design over a century ago, although he was by no means the first or last to express such ideas. 'Beauty' and 'utility' were the twin notions to which the classical designers and architects of the eighteenth century subscribed. They, in turn, based their definition of good design on a much more ancient formula. Writing in the first century AD, Vitruvius advised that 'commodity, firmness and delight' were the fundamental qualities of good architecture. We might translate these today as 'fitness of purpose', 'structural integrity' and ... delight.

These appealingly simple guidelines, however, leave us just where we started. We can apply certain objective criteria to determine whether a product is useful or not: whether a building keeps out the weather, or whether clothing is warm and comfortable; but beauty is another matter, remaining resolutely in the eye of the beholder. William Morris, for example, utterly detested those elegant Georgian squares and terraces in which eighteenth-century architects expressed their ideals. Robert Adam, had he been alive in the late nineteenth century, would have been mystified by Morris's championing of humble cottage furniture and craftwork. Tastes change, from era to era, and from person to person.

Is there nothing objective about beauty, delight or the magic ingredient – call it what you will? Does this subjectivity matter?

There are undoubtedly certain common notions of form and proportion, and certain shared responses to material, colour and pattern which help to shape our collective tastes. Nature may well be the ultimate touchstone. An instinctive appreciation of the living world is evident in the oldest design concepts. The form of the tree is expressed in ancient temple façades, while the proportional blueprint of the classical Greeks – the Golden Section – is based on the same ratio that naturally occurs in the process of growth, in the spiral forms of shells and galaxies and even in harmonic relationships in music. Our response to nature is so innate and so deep rooted that its origins are largely irrelevant.

Certain colours inspire common reactions in people, a shared language of association which designers use to communicate values. Red, nature's warning, is bold, arresting, dangerous and exciting. Think of the shop window sign which screams 'SALE' at passers-by. Technically, the red end of the spectrum is warm and 'advancing', which means it draws the eye and stands out from its surroundings. Blue, on the other hand, is traditionally cool and soothing; a blue bottle promises that the water it packages will be refreshing, thirst-quenching and pure, simply by drawing on the way most people respond to the colour.

Some of these associations are age-old; others are shaped by more immediate contexts. The sum total of cultural influences gives us period 'styles', epochs of design which are instantly recognizable within their own time-scale. Even when one period is self-consciously recreating another, the context always wins through. Those Victorian Gothic interiors, so scrupulously medieval, remain Victorian rather than Gothic.

On a more ephemeral level, you can see a similar effect in the styling of period drama for television or cinema. *Gone with the Wind*, despite its antebellum trappings and crinolines, is unmistakably Forties in appearance; *Far from the Madding Crowd* transported the

The blue of the Ty Nânt bottle spells out a message of purity and refreshment.

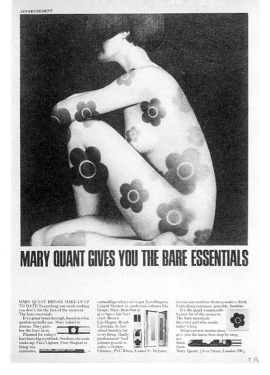

MARY QUANT GIVES YOU THE BARE ESSENTIALS

MARY QUANT BRINGS MAKE-UP UP TO DATE! Everything you need, nothing you don't, for the face of the moment. The bare essentials

It's a great breakthrough, based on what models actually use. Mary talked to dozens. They gave her the bare facts.

Planned for today's bare bony big-eyed look. Starkers, the nude make-up. Face Lighter, Face Shapers to bring out, minimise,

camouflage what you've got. Eye-Shapers, Liquid Shadow in unobvious colours like Grape, Slate. Blot-Out to give lips a fair bare start. Brown Lip Shaper. Brush Lipsticks. In fact chisel brushes for everything. Madly professional! Nail colours geared to today's clothes: Chrome, PVC White, Camel+. In pairs,

so you can combine them to make a third. Everything compact, portable, fussless.

It's the quick commando beauty kit of the moment. The bare essentials for every girl who wants today's face.

Strip-cartoon instructions give you the know-how step by step; get them from Mary Quant, 3 Ives Street, London SW3.

7 A

Mary Quant's 'Bare Essentials' advertisement (1966) for a range of fun and fashionable cosmetics.

swinging Sixties of the King's Road to Hardy's Wessex. The fashion – or style – of a particular period is always most clearly crystallized when it is trying to ape the past.

The same study of any historical period quickly reveals that very little is truly new. Originality is a modern obsession, where the term 'new' promises instant value. Design is sometimes criticized for failing to reinvent the wheel, a point of view which ignores the fact that humans are essentially adaptive creatures, refining and adjusting the world to suit their changing needs. No designer cannot afford to ignore what has gone before.

If design is rooted in historical context, it also reveals social strata, not so much 'you are what you eat' as 'you are what you buy'. People signal their differences and similarities in every conceivable way – in the cars they drive, the furnishings they choose, the clothes they wear – following complex purchasing patterns to assemble a composite image that suits the way they perceive themselves. Television programme-makers, novelists, and feature writers have a lot of fun with the minutiae of consumer choice. 'Through-the-keyhole' is a game everyone likes to play.

Neither taste, nor design, exists in a vacuum. However hard you try, in selecting one thing over another you label yourself. As choice expands, the nuances become ever-more important. Design is one of the most critical ways in which these nuances are expressed.

At the end of the twentieth century, putting the case for design is not a comfortable position. Every decade passes with a backlash; the end of the 1980s saw 'Design' with a capital 'D' thrown in the dustbin. Design, if not actually responsible for the worst excesses of the preceding years, has at least become synonymous with them. Greed, materialism, unfettered markets, yuppies – and design – have been tarred with the same brush.

You would think there can be no worse contemporary epithet than 'designer': 'designer water', 'designer jeans', even 'designer drugs'. The adjective has come to imply spurious value, cynical manipulation, the justification of inflated price through a false impression of status and exclusivity.

Design can and should add value, but the value must not only be real but be seen to be real. In my view, design has little to do with applying a 'designer' logo to a perfectly ordinary polo shirt: that is marketing. Nor has design got much to do with changing the trim and bumpers on the latest Ford or Toyota: that is styling. Marketing and styling have their place, but these highly visible aspects of consumerism have only confused the issue where design is concerned, obscuring its fundamental value.

I believe that choice is empowering. It is often forgotten that people can only buy what they are offered. If people are not offered new ideas and new products, they cannot make a decision about them. A world where we all drive the same car, watch the same programme on the same television set, wear the same clothes and eat the same food may appeal to multinational moguls and political dictators, but for most of us it is a frightening and depressing prospect.

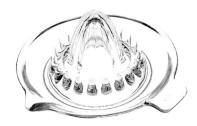

How can design add value? During my student years I became quite convinced that there was a strong social purpose to design, that it is the opposite of elitist. I believed, and still do, that if something is well designed it can improve the quality of life of the user. I also believed, and still do, that something which is well designed should not necessarily cost more than the equivalent object which has been designed without care, thought or professionalism. To this end, the professional designer must fully understand manufacturing, marketing and selling processes, and ensure that the product he or she designs can be economically and efficiently made, and competitively priced.

If you look at it this way, you can see that good design is as fundamental to the success of manufacturing and retailing as it is to the well-being of the individual. It is not an added extra, a superficial styling twist, or a marketing con foisted on a gullible public. It is not about pushing up price or creating elite brands through the mystique of a label. Some of the most 'luxurious' products that money can buy have the opposite effect to those which are well designed: they can be alienating, even insulting. The identification of design with elite goods and snob value has helped to bring about its poor profile today, a misrepresentation of its true purpose to producers and consumers alike.

Yet while choice allows consumers to vote with their wallets, it can also be confusing. Faced with a range of similar goods at similar prices, many people react with uncertainty and choose the 'safe' option. In turn, manufacturers and retailers reinforce this lack of confidence, avoiding innovation and quality in favour of the lowest common denominator. Products inspired by sales graphs are every bit as cynical as so-called 'designer' goods and it is

a cynicism which is sadly pervasive in the high street. That dreary cry 'give the public what they want' (which means 'what they bought last year, and the year before that') effectively rules out offering consumers what they never knew they might like until they were offered it. It rules out joy in design, and it diminishes the potential quality of life.

The remedy, I believe, is not to hive off design into ever-more esoteric areas, but to integrate it more fully in the entire process of product development, manufacturing and retail. Design can and should add value through choice, but it can only achieve this if it is combined with good business sense.

When I began work as a newly trained designer in the Britain of the early 1950s, the business climate was deeply conservative. There were shortages of practically everything; no one was prepared to experiment with new ideas, particularly in view of the fact that factories were unable to cope with the current level of demand.

For young designers like me, the Festival of Britain in 1951 offered a beacon of hope for the future. The public flocked to see the exhibits and people were charged with enthusiasm for the new ideas on display. They relished the image of a bright, forward-looking country shaking off its rationed, wartime past. Like many other designers who displayed their work, I believed that commissions would soon start to pour in.

Both lemon squeezers do their job, but Philippe Starck's Juicy Salif (1989) has an irrepressible sense of fun.

When several months had gone by without a single new job coming my way, I realized we had all seriously underestimated what we were up against. The retailers and manufacturers had full order books and saw no reason to take risks. All this left me frustrated and very poor.

Taking matters literally into my own hands, I began by setting up a small workshop to make my own designs. By the end of the 1950s, this had grown into a sizable manufacturing business, producing contract furniture to order for offices, universities and hotels. Moving the business to a new, mechanized factory in 1962 provided me with the opportunity to explore the market for domestic furniture.

Our furniture was simple and moderately priced but revolutionary in concept for one reason: all of it was supplied packed flat for home assembly, an utterly alien idea for many retailers at the time, who expected customers to wait three months for delivery. We offered the thrill of instant gratification, but overcoming retailers' preconceptions was an uphill struggle. What was equally disappointing was that those retailers who did take our collection failed to display the pieces with any flair, but simply added them to the jumble of traditional reproductions, Scandinavian imports and middle-market lines set out haphazardly on the showroom floor. Indeed, some shops utterly failed to see the selling point of take-away, flat-pack furniture, and agreed only to stock the pieces if we assembled them prior to delivery. It did not take me long to realize that our furniture would not sell in such surroundings.

The solution was Habitat. With Habitat, we sought to create a shop that was simply and intelligently designed, and that was laid out to display the merchandise to the best effect. By creating an exclusive line of products, we protected ourselves from rivals undercutting us while reinforcing and promoting our company image. Every aspect of the shops was designed to the same end – from the merchandise on sale to the way it was displayed, from graphics and ticketing to way in which staff were trained. Every element complemented and enhanced the others, and it was the combination of all these factors which 'added value' to what we were offering and made the idea stand out.

Habitat was quickly perceived as selling a 'lifestyle'. There is nothing new about such a concept today, but in 1964 it represented a breakthrough. And the role of design in the creation of Habitat was at the heart of its success.

In the case of Habitat, design meant applying a set of values through every stage of a product's development, planning every detail from the outset. The ambience of Habitat was entirely artificial – artificial, that is, in the sense that we deliberately and systematically created it. But it was an image rooted in the reality of the market we had identified and in our passionate belief in our products. The store was designed to appeal to customers whose needs were not being met elsewhere – specifically young, newly married, middle-class people setting up home for the first time. These people were happy to assemble their own furniture using a few screws and an allen key if it meant they could take it away with them. Habitat's core customers would have travelled a bit and broadened their horizons, and had a positive allegiance to their own generation rather than a desire to follow blindly in their parents' footsteps.

With this customer-base in mind, we determined that the store would stock not only furniture but other household goods needed to furnish the home, with particular emphasis on the kitchen and tabletop. This policy, designed to keep the stores busy and cheerful, also emphasized the idea of instant availability. Smaller merchandise was stocked in depth as if it were displayed in a warehouse or market stall, transforming simple objects through the sheer impact of quantity. Larger items were arranged in abstract room

Albuquerque Academy Library

Making a mark: Blade ident for BBC2 (creative director, Martin Lambie-Nairn; 1991).

sets, to suggest their eventual use. The tension between the two forms of display created a buzz of excitement in the stores which proved to be irresistible.

Much of what we sold was designed by me and the Habitat buying team; all of it was selected and presented as if by one pair of eyes. This consistency not only displayed our faith in our own vision and taste, it helped to support and direct the choices of our customers. We offered choice, but within the supportive framework of a selected collection. And the consistency extended to the positive attitude of the staff, the ticketing, signage, catalogues and all the other ancillary material which was overseen by our in-house design team, all of which helped to spell out the message.

The creation of Habitat is an example of the use of design as an integral part of a planning process. Habitat's magic ingredient was our passionate belief in what we were doing, an enthusiasm which we successfully conveyed and to which the public in turn enthusiastically responded. Design could also be described as the art of reconciling function, cost and appearance. Either way, design occupies a unique space between art and science. Designers must be sensitive to what is technically possible and what is humanly desirable.

In Britain we are very good at producing designers, and our designers – in every field from fashion to architecture, graphics to product design – are acknowledged throughout the world for the quality and vision of their work. Lamentably, we are sorely lacking in the ability to nurture our designers on their home ground. The talented fashion graduate forced to work abroad and the award-winning architect who must turn to foreign clients for commissions are so commonplace as to be almost clichéd. Unlike other countries, design in Britain receives next to no funding or investment and has an abysmally low political profile.

In my opinion, this is extremely short-sighted. Design is essential for economic success. There are many instances where design has played a key role in a company's profitability; few instances where a profitable company has succeeded by ignoring design.

Take one example. Paul Smith, the British clothes designer, had the enviable turnover of £70 million in 1994. His sales to Japan are greater than any other European fashion designer. This degree of success has not been achieved overnight; expansion of the company has been slow and steady, allowing Paul Smith to retain control and remain involved in every aspect of the business.

The core of Paul Smith's success, I would argue, is the fact that his lines of clothing, while changing with each season's collection, adhere to certain constants. All of his clothes are well made, from good-quality fabric, with an eye to detail. For every maverick fashion item he produces, there are beautifully cut suits, classic casuals and reliable basics.

Yet the fashionable items – the risky part of his venture – are intrinsic to his success, complementing the company's strengths and image. The fashionable items draw younger customers into the fold, the suit-buyers of tomorrow. The suit-buyers of today, meanwhile, feel they are in touch with the cutting edge of fashion, sharing an aesthetic with movie stars and pop heroes.

The image Paul Smith sells along with his clothes is reinforced by the design of his shops. At first glance, they appear to embody the aesthetic of a traditional gentlemen's tailor: the acres of wood, glass counters and hushed sobriety. Venture inside, and the formality is undercut by wit and irreverence. The counters display quirky products alongside the clothes, unusual items – new, second-hand or antique – that Paul Smith has trawled on his travels. Humour, fun and quirky spontaneity enhance the solid virtues of quality, cut and craftsmanship.

It will not, perhaps, surprise many people that design can play a key role in the success of a clothing retailer. Another example may prove more telling. Throughout the unhappy history of British Leyland, in itself a case study in what has gone wrong with British industry, one marque has remained consistently design-led, innovative and focussed: the Range Rover. Adapting the principle of four-wheel drive to the domestic market, the Range Rover represents a brilliant leap of the imagination, a leap which rival manufacturers took years to wake up to.

Over the last five years, and through two changes in ownership, British Leyland has reconsolidated itself under the Rover name, refocussing its attention, analysing its assets and renewing its commitment to design. In 1994, the Rover 600 series won a British Design award for 'superb exterior styling, which combines a modern look with traditional 'Britishness' and a clear Rover identity'. The exterior styling is defined by the Rover grille, harking back to the tradition established by the company in the 1950s. The

Paul Smith designs classics with a twist, such as this wildly floral, beautifully tailored man's shirt.

designers' brief recommended that they look for inspiration from the older Rover cars in the company's heritage museum. The way forward may take its lead from the past, and I see nothing wrong with building on tradition where that tradition is a good one.

Awards are all very well, but what of sales? The strategy appears to be working. Ever since Rover set about reestablishing the pedigree of its name, sales have risen. The commitment to design has given Rover impetus and a vision for the future. No wonder first Honda invested, then BMW bought the company.

Design can offer something beyond the chink of coins in the till or the rising curve of a sales graph. As well as promoting turnover, good design can be a progressive force, creating a momentum of confidence and a 'feel good' factor which bolsters a society's – or a company's – image of itself.

In Britain, there is a tendency to view design as diametrically opposed to tradition, as a threat to 'heritage'. 'Heritage' tends to win hands down and the result, all too often, is a stagnant pastiche of the past. As the Rover example demonstrates, good design can direct attention to those aspects of tradition which are worth retaining: not pastiche, but a reworking of forms in new contexts to keep them fresh and alive.

As the rate of technological advance quickens, the role of the designer will become ever-more important. How do we interpret scientific achievements in a human way? How do we ensure that we are liberated rather than enslaved by technology? Most of us, at one time or another, have been outsmarted by our video recorder or car radio, machines of such complexity they practically rule out the relatively simple purposes for which they were created. By making technology accessible to ordinary human needs, the designer can play a crucial and enabling role. Without this essential interface, technology is a source of frustration and alienation that leaves us longing for the good old days.

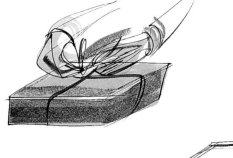

'All beautiful things belong to the same age'

Oscar Wilde

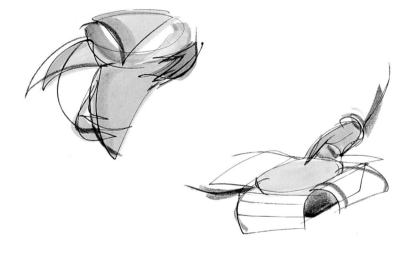

However simplistic it sounds, I believe that the designer's true role is to better the things that surround us. Better them in terms of function, appearance, cost and material; but better them also in terms of aspiration and desire, in the dream of how life might be.

One hundred years after the death of William Morris, perhaps his theories have relevance and resonance as never before. With electronic, robotized factories supplying an increasing number of our needs – and at a price no man-made equivalent can compete with – we should be looking to more crafts-based manufacturing to satisfy our desires. One of my most treasured possessions is a bowl made by the Japanese ceramicist, Shinobu Kawase. Everything about the bowl is quite beautiful: its exquisite delicacy, its sensual curves, the almost translucent glaze. And it is presented with equal care and attention, wrapped in cotton, covered with tissue paper and housed in a box that fits the bowl perfectly, its lid an exact fit, and the box tied with ribbon. I keep the box on a shelf at home, and from time to time I take it down and unwrap it to look at the bowl, to remind myself that there is such beauty in the world.

By anyone's standards, the bowl is a luxury, an expensive item that lies on the cusp between craft and art. It is not something I cannot live without, yet it improves the quality of my life. It thrills and excites and it lifts the spirits.

In this book, I make no bones about offering what is my personal choice, my view of 'good design'. I care about function and practicality, about fitness of material and form for use. As a retailer, I care about price. But the first thing I look for, in any design, whether it is a car or an airport terminal, a suit of clothes or a restaurant, is the excitement that comes when something touches a chord, reawakens the memory, or pleases the eye.

This amorphous, aesthetic, spiritual dimension is just as essential to life as shelter from the elements or food on the plate. It simply makes life worth living.

Having been a potter, I know how difficult it is to produce something as perfect as Shinobu Kawase's ceramic bowl.

Vibrant food packaging brings colourful graphics to the kitchen shelf.

SAUCE PIQUANTE SALSA PICCANTE
Harissa
FERRERO
PIKANTE SAUS PIKANTE SOSSE
HOT SAUCE

ORTIZ
El Velero
BONITO
EN ACEITE DE OLIVA

SWEET CHOCOLATE
IBARRA
MADE IN MÉXICO
INGREDIENTS: SUGAR, COCOA NIBS, ALMONDS, CINNAMON AND LECITHIN.
NET WT. 12.6 OZS.
MANUFACTURED AND PACKED BY
C. GOMEZ IBARRA, SUCS.

A la PERRUCHE
PURE CANNE
Béghin Say

PIGINO
EXTRA
GRAN RISOTTO
RISO SUPERFINO ARBORIO

ORTIZ
El Velero
BONITO
EN ACEITE DE OLIVA

CORTAS.
ORANGE BLOSSOM WATER
EAU DE FLEURS D'ORANGER
AZAHER
10 FL. OZ - 300mL

PIMENTON
"LA DALIA"
JOSE Mª HERNANDEZ, S.L.

YELLOW
CORN MEAL
(POLENTA FLOUR) 1 lb NET 453g.
TO MAKE CORN BREAD

Method:
1. Preheat oven to 425°F.
2. Sift dry ingredients into a bowl.
3. Mix egg and milk and add to dry mix, stir well, fold in melted butter and beat.
4. Grease and flour 6" pan (square) or 9" (round).
5. Place batter in pan and bake 20 - 25 mins. until golden brown.
Packed by
G. COSTA & COMPANY LTD.
Staffordshire Street   London S.E.15

COSTA

COUSCOUS
MITTEL MEDIUM
"HALB VORBEREITET" "PRECOOKED"

FERRERO
FERICO - Z.I. 13127 VITROLLES - FRANCE

PIMENTON
"LA DALIA"
JOSE Mª HERNANDEZ, S.L.

HARISSA
DU CAP-BON
TUNISIE

HARISSA
Dea

PENINSULAR
SARDINES PORTUGAISES
À L'HUILE VÉGÉTALE

CALYPSO QUEEN
Jamaican Curry Dill
Sun Sauce
Net Wt. 12 oz

CORTAS.
ROSE WATER
EAU DE ROSE
ING. Rose water
10 FL. OZ - 300

Le Moulin de Daudet
OLIVES A LA GRECQUE AROMATISÉES
GREEK STYLE WITH AROMATIC HERBS
PRODUCT OF FRANCE
VIEILLE EN PROVENCE
NET WEIGHT 17.64 OZ (1 LB 1.64 OZ)

HARISSA
Dea

HUILE D'OLIVE VIERGE EXTRA
NICOLAS ALZIARI
HUILERIE de LA MADELEINE
VENTE ET EXPÉDITIONS
14, Rue St FRANÇOIS de PAULE
NICE
MARQUE DE FABRIQUE

HARISSA
Dea

PIMENTÓN
La Chinata

PIMENTÓN
PICANTE
La Chinata

Time Saving
KRUCKS
natura
NATURAL BREAD CRUMBS

BREADCRUMBS
CHAPELURE PANIERMEHL BRØDKRUMMER
made from REAL Bread
de pain 100% Aus echtem Brot Lavet af rigtigt brød
FREE OF COLOURING MATTER.

INVALUABLE FOR PUDDING CRUMBS, FISH CAKES, TREACLE TART,
APPLE CHARLOTTE, MEAT LOAF, BREAD SAUCE, BAKEWELL TART,
STUFFINGS, HAM & FISH DRESSING.

furnishings and

'A house is a machine for living in. Baths, sun, hot water, cold water, warmth at will, conservation of food, hygiene, beauty in the sense of good proportion. An armchair is a machine for sitting in and so on'

Le Corbusier, *Towards a New Architecture* (1923)

the interior

I have begun this chapter with a quotation which many will find familiar, at least in its more commonly abbreviated form. Corbusier's famous statement is intriguing for two reasons: for what it says, and for what many believe that it says. For those who blame modern architecture for all manner of social and aesthetic blights, Corbusier's ringing declaration appears to advocate a brutal, mechanical world where even the home has become a grim, planned featureless cell

The urban loft provides the ultimate modern luxury – sheer space – along with the potential to arrange it any way you choose.

In describing the house as a machine, Corbusier seems to suggest a kind of monstrous denial of personality, character and individuality. However, this view misreads the architect's intentions. If you examine the passage in detail, it seems clear that what Corbusier was proposing was that the house should work. In other words, it should provide an infrastructure to support basic human needs – for warmth, light, hygiene, cooking, and so on – just as, he goes on to say, a chair should function as a place for sitting. He was not saying that this was all that a house should be, but that it was one thing that a house *must* be.

Corbusier was writing and working at a time which saw great technological change. Electrical light and power, efficient drainage, labour-saving appliances, changing constructional methods and new materials had the potential to transform domestic life, not merely for an elite, but, finally, for the majority. To Corbusier, these technological developments offered the opportunity to design living space anew, free from historical precedent and tradition. Better living spaces would mean better lives, and not merely in the material sense.

In common with many of the designers, artists and architects of the Modern Movement, Corbusier's pronouncements had a distinctly moral tone. Adolf Loos, for example, famously stated that 'ornament is crime'. This is pretty strong stuff. The fervour of these early modernists and their mission to remake the world can seem at best laughable today, at worst rather frightening. But it is important to remember the conditions against which the modernists were reacting.

The Industrial Revolution which initiated mass-production had also brought about an appreciable decline in the quality of what was produced. More people could afford more goods than ever

'The house that would please me would be some great room where one talked to one's friends in one corner, and ate in another and slept in another and worked in another'

William Morris in a letter to W.B. Yeats

before, but the goods they were sold were often distinguished not in terms of real material value but through applied 'style' and decoration. The great mass of the population, unsure in matters of taste and hidebound by class distinctions, aspired to decorate and furnish their homes with an imitation of the furnishings of the rich. Ersatz materials, poorly copied designs and over-decoration prevailed. 'Shoddy is King,' observed William Morris. 'What's new?' we might concur.

Like their forerunners in the Arts and Crafts Movement, the pioneer spirits of the Wiener Werkstätte and, later, the Bauhaus, sought to redress the situation by directing attention back to the functional, practical nature of things rather than the superficialities of appearance. 'Art is not a special sauce applied to cooking, it is the cooking itself if that be good,' wrote W.R. Lethaby, an Arts and Crafts theorist.

How this was all to be achieved was another matter. To the Arts and Crafts followers, hand-made goods restored dignity to work and natural beauty to objects. Yet hand-made goods were expensive, beyond the means of ordinary people. To the Bauhaus disciples, industrialization provided a more democratic answer. The machine aesthetic, where form was dictated by function, was a rejection of the stick-on styles and superfluous decor of the Victorian period. In the Victorian home, status was upheld by the conspicuous display of drapery, ornaments and trimmings and the practical side of life was scrupulously concealed. The modernists wished to sweep all of these trappings away in favour of an honest use of materials and a direct expression of function.

As we all know, the Brave New World did not turn out quite the way it was planned. Technology has indeed brought great social changes in its wake. It has changed and is changing the way we live. But has it really changed the way our homes look? Over 80 years after Corbusier wrote his provocative words, the majority of people today are still frightened of, even chilled by, modernity. This fear can be seen most obviously in the way people decorate and furnish their homes.

The design of a home should reflect the way the individuals concerned will be using the space, not some received notion of what is right or a stylistic hand-me-down from a bygone age. When people first began eating and even entertaining in their kitchens it was daring and unconventional; in some quarters, even a little shameful. Maintaining a separate formal dining-room kept one's options open, and was a nod in the direction of traditional notions of propriety. But arranging your home to fit in with an Edwardian ideal of genteel living makes even less sense nowadays and stands in the way of using all the space in your home to its full potential. Modern design, by directing people to analyse what they need from a space, provides an innate simplicity and efficiency which is pleasing in itself.

Few people now would willingly forego the benefits of technology in their homes. Not many of us would be prepared to live in rooms heated by a single coal fire, read a newspaper by the light of a spluttering candle, or cook over a smoky range. Even fewer, I suspect, would tolerate nineteenth-century standards of sanitation. Yet many of the same people who welcome all the advantages of twentieth-century life go to considerable lengths to conceal the presence of technology in their homes. Electric lights are shaped to look like candle sconces or gasoliers. Neo-Georgian or pseudo-Victorian decoration in the form of mouldings, fake plasterwork trim, pastiche prints and little bowls of pot-pourri decorate the interiors of brand new homes. Televisions and videos are hidden in reproduction armoires.

I can understand some of the reasons why this should be so, but I must confess to finding the results fairly repellent. As school children before the war, we were taken from time to time to visit stately homes in the vicinity. What always intrigued and inspired me were the working parts of these great houses, the below-stairs domain of dairy, kitchen, pantry, cellar and larder. It is difficult to find anything ugly or superfluous in these seventeenth- or eighteenth-century workplaces. I always felt, and still do, an irresistible attraction to those areas of the house which were designed to work, while the grand state rooms whose purpose was to demonstrate wealth and status left me bemused by their pretension.

Later on I could relate this basic sympathy with modernist principles, with the idea that good design always meant ensuring that an object, or place, functioned properly. If something was designed to function properly, it ought to provide aesthetic pleasure, too. The dishonesty of concealing the true functional purpose of things, and the timidity of blindly copying the past have always made me uneasy.

On the other hand, modern design has often provided people with good reason to be fearful. 'Less is more', another well-worn modernist saying, was a heartfelt cry for purity and simplicity in design, for less applied decoration, less style, less redundant cultural baggage. But the conspicuous failures of post-war housing projects, and other attempts to put modernist ideals into practice, have left many with the conviction that 'less' (in the words of a *New Yorker* cartoon), is sometimes merely 'less'.

High-rise tower blocks thrown up in the 1960s in a commendable attempt to clear slums and provide decent housing for ordinary people are now being torn down with equal fervour. By imposing a sterile sameness, these 'machines for living' have resulted in alienated communities marooned in urban wastelands, a concrete jungle which has hardly been an improvement on the old poverty-stricken terraces of the pre-war period. Broken lifts, graffiti scrawled on concrete and stinking stairwells have become the public face of modernism.

It is possible to argue, however, that such failures arose more out of the way modern ideals were put into practice than any deficiencies of the ideals themselves. Schemes such as Corbusier's Unité d'Habitation, which provided the model for many post-war projects, included a wide range of communal facilities to serve the needs of their inhabitants, from creches to laundries to proper maintenance. In Britain, after the war, similar schemes were given the go-ahead, but minus these essential humanizing elements.

The Dessau Bauhaus (1925-6) was home to the most influential design movement this century.

'Teach your children that a house is only habitable when it is

Poor standards of construction, lack of maintenance and cost-cutting at every turn set the seal on their failure. It is interesting to note that where attempts have been made to salvage some of these tower blocks, the simple expedient of installing a 'concierge' at the entrance – putting a human face on the building – has brought about remarkable improvements, and made them desirable places to live for young people and empty-nesters alike.

At the other end of the spectrum, modernism is often equated with minimalism, the most extreme version of 'less is more'. Taking the modern ideal to its final conclusion, minimalists attempt to live life in surroundings which are as empty as they can possibly be designed to be. What is left on view – and there often is not much – must, of course, be perfect, and it is one irony among many that such spaces are extremely expensive to construct. It seems to me that the essential dishonesty of this approach is that it encourages people to believe that the spare emptiness actually reflects how the room functions, when the reality of the situation is that the accessories of everyday life are simply stowed behind almost invisible cupboard doors. Minimalists must eat, dress, cook, work and play just like the rest of us and need things with which to carry out these activities.

I can marvel at the discipline it takes to maintain life in an empty space, but I cannot see this as a way of fostering simple living. It may be simple, but to me it is a simplicity without charm. I suppose my antipathy to minimalism is not so different from others' antipathy to modernism in its broader manifestations.

I am a great admirer of much of the work of the American architect, Philip Johnson. Yet I recall a story Hugh Casson told me of a visit he made to Johnson's house. Hugh was warmly welcomed by Philip Johnson, who showed him to the living-room and offered him a book to look through. It was only when Hugh sat down, book in hand, that the artful composition of the room truly struck

The walls of Philip Johnson's Glass House, New Canaan (1949) merge interior and exterior.

him – everything was so perfectly positioned, that it was clear there would be a right and a wrong place to put down the book. Hugh thought hard about where to put the book, and chose an appropriate spot on the table. Later, when Philip Johnson offered to show Hugh the rest of the house, the first thing Johnson did was to return the book to a cupboard!

Given such cautionary tales, it is perhaps no wonder that, in Britain at least, modernism has never caught on in a big way, nor that there remains a suspicion that 'less is more' really translates as throwing the baby out with the bathwater. Britain, of all Western countries, was slow to adopt technological improvements in the home, reluctant to abandon open fires in favour of central heating, late to embrace most modern conveniences, from refrigerators to washing machines to dishwashers. Technology, when it

full of light and air, and when the floors and walls are clear' Le Corbusier

arrived, was often viewed with mixed feelings and treated rather like an intruder. At the same time, a great deal of thoughtless 'modernization' went on, displaying an equally misguided attempt to keep up with the times. Old Victorian and Edwardian terraced houses saw their interiors virtually gutted of all architectural detail and distinction; cornices, fireplaces and mouldings were stripped out, sash windows replaced, and panelled doors boarded over, with little or no thought given to the quality of the fixtures and fittings that replaced them.

another to kit out a newly built suburban house with scaled-down fixtures and fittings more appropriate to a stately home. I am no advocate of architectural vandalism, but I do find it dismaying that a common response to the challenge of modernism has been a retreat into the cosy fantasies of the past, into the ill-proportioned, mock-Georgian estates with their coach lamps and scaled-down ruched blinds. I would agree with William Morris that for traditions to be kept alive, they must not simply be copied, but adapted and reworked in a new spirit.

Philip Johnson's Monster House (1995) lies in the grounds of his Glass House in Connecticut.

The backlash, predictably, was not long in coming. Today's booming trade in architectural salvage, absorption in the minutiae of period styles and fascination with historic interiors of just about any age may show a commendable respect for context and heritage but also provide another means of backing away from the present. It is one thing to unblock a boarded-up fireplace, quite

Loft living seems to me a perfect example of how the old can be reconciled with the new without compromise or fakery. Recycled warehouses, commercial properties, even churches or schools offer exciting spatial opportunities, unusual scale and proportion, and tough functional surroundings that provide scope for a wide range of interpretations, broadening the notion and expectations of what a 'home' can be. Reusing redundant industrial or commercial buildings can help to breathe new life into the neglected areas of the city, encouraging mixed-use developments and breaking down the alienating separation of home and work.

When I was a student, I liked to walk the streets at night, looking through the lighted basement windows. This was not the activity of an incipient Peeping Tom, I hasten to add, but was done out of sheer curiosity about how other people lived. In those days, everything looked pretty much the same. People were brought up to reflect their parents' values and more or less indoctrinated into a certain aesthetic which went along with their own position in life. Occasionally, however, I would suddenly see something completely different through one of the windows I was passing – a different way of arranging things, a splash of colour or a terrific collection of original furnishings. Those were the places that attracted me, not necessarily as places to live, but because I would have liked to meet the people who lived there.

Modern paint manufacturers provide home decorators with a vast opportunity for self-expression.

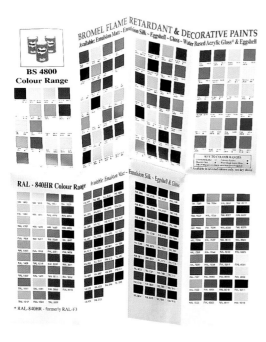

Self-expression still seems perhaps the most important part of what creating a home is all about. As Christopher Alexander points out in his book, *A Pattern Language*, '"Decor" and the conception of "interior design" have spread so widely that very often people forget their instinct for the things they really want to keep around them.' The negative examples I have described – the soulless high-rise, the pastiche estates and the minimal shells – seem to share the same basic lack. For whatever reason, they are not very human.

Within the basic framework, there should be room for the expression of personality. Although I have often been accused of being dictatorial in matters of style, I have not the least interest in laying down the taste law. The interiors which really excite me are those which reveal genuine passion and flair – the courage to be different. Provided the technological element does not dominate, the foreground of any interior can change like a theatre set. I like order and arrangement, but I equally enjoy the transience of clutter, rooms where every little object hasn't got a place, but where things come and go in a constant panoply that reflects life.

The opportunity to create interiors that express our individual tastes has never been greater. For those accustomed to choosing paint colours from a staggering range of shades, it is almost inconceivable that a reliable bright yellow was not invented until the 1820s; as late as the mid-nineteenth century, new pigments were still being discovered: the name 'magenta' commemorates a Crimean battle. Technology in the service of mass-production has advanced so far to make choice almost boundless. Mass media, from film and television to books and magazines, bring us styles from around the world, and relate in minute detail how they can be reproduced. Retailers scour the world for interesting artefacts that were formerly the eccentric souvenirs of a global trek. The media, thirsty for novelty, and retailers, with a beady eye on turnover, have transformed home furnishings into another form of fashion.

In a striking convergence, many fashion retailers have branched out into home furnishing lines to reinforce the lifestyle image they promote. Ever since Pierre Cardin pioneered the concept of licensing a brand, mundane household goods such as sheets and towels have become part of the fashion parade. The supreme exponent of the 'living' concept must be Ralph Lauren, who has built an entire design image on the seamless integration of clothing, lifestyle and interior fashion – shirting-pattern sheets, tartan blankets and all. The latest fashion designer to enter the home furnishings market is Calvin Klein, who is claiming the puritanical high ground.

If the opportunities for choice are boundless, so is the scope for confusion. Living is not a simple business any more, but a marketing concept used to sell videos, magazines, products, information and personalities. 'It's not just home furnishings. It's the clothes you wear, the cars you drive, the foods you eat, the perfume you wear,' notes Martha Stewart, who has reinvented the idea of home-making for American women and in the process turned herself into a lifestyle brand. Serious money is at stake. In the United States alone, over $260 billion is spent annually on products and services related to the home and garden.

People can only buy what they are offered, but many of us might feel that we are offered too much. Choice allows freedom of expression, but it may also reinforce a desire to blend in. Down to the last detail, according to income bracket, social mix and family background, most people are acutely aware of what their homes should look like. Mass taste is as stratified as ever.

Kitsch, of course, turns the notion of taste on its head. The devotees of kitsch revel in what others might find ugly, passé and ephemeral. At its best, this attitude can be a wonderful antidote to the feverish concerns of style as it is promoted in the marketplace. Kitsch demonstrates, very instructively, that style is always self-conscious, and it has a great deal of fun along the way. At its

worst, however, kitsch itself merely becomes another stylistic stance, or an insurance policy taken out against the dire prospect of being judged and labelled by one's possessions. As much as I enjoy the filip of wit and humour offered by these inconsequential artefacts – I have a growing collection of Mr Bibendums in various pseudo-practical forms – I cannot quite succumb.

Pierre Chareau's Maison de Verre, Paris (1927-32) imports the industrial aesthetic to the home.

There's a curious phenomenon about style, and it's something which many analysts and trendspotters have laboured long and hard over. It is the strange coincidence whereby a certain look, mood, or approach suddenly becomes the flavour of the moment and sweeps all before it. There's no word for it in English; *Zeitgeist* in German is the nearest equivalent. While there are often good reasons for the trend in retrospect, at the time, the impulse is irresistible. The sudden mania for all things Japanese at the end of the nineteenth century, the fascination for Grecian design in the late eighteenth century, the explosion of scientific imagery in designs of the 1950s can all be traced to specific discoveries and events, but their mysterious hold on the public remains to be explained. When these broad epochs of design take root, the result is a period look, which runs indelibly through all visual media, from the clothes we wear to the way we screen our windows. Knowing what's 'in the ether' adds a powerful weapon to any designer's armoury.

Given the mood of the moment, the undertow of tradition, the lure of the market and the sheer status-seeking that informs many decisions about decoration, furnishing and interior design, what should the role of the designer be?

As I have said, design can and should widen choice. Superficially, it may seem that choice on the home front is greater than ever, but on closer inspection it is evident that there are simply many variations on remarkably similar themes. As a result, good modern furniture still lacks the profile it deserves. In Britain, furniture designers working in the modern idiom have had to find employment elsewhere, joining the general exodus of design talent. There are encouraging signs, however, that the trend might be reversing. SCP, founded by Sheridan Coakley, has become a successful outlet for modern furniture design in this country, and worked to establish the reputation of designers such as Matthew Hilton and Jasper Morrison. Cassina, the flourishing Milan-based company with outlets all over the world, has helped to keep the classics of modern design in production. IKEA, with its patronage of young Swedish designers, has found room for a new line of innovative furniture – the PS range – alongside mass-market basics. Without such patronage, the spirit of design would wither and die.

Stackable Louis XX chairs (1991) by Philippe Starck are made of two sections screwed together.

Secondly, design can play an important role reworking and refreshing traditional forms and materials. Linoleum, virtually eclipsed by the arrival of vinyl flooring in the 1950s, lingered in the doldrums for nearly 20 years until the Dutch manufacturer Forbo-Kromely brought out a new and exciting range of colours and patterns. The revival of lino has reacquainted the public with a good, natural product, which is hypo-allergenic and anti-bacterial, hard-wearing, decorative and relatively cheap.

Thirdly, design can assist, inform and guide consumer choice. Furniture-buying often demands a long process of decision-making. Shops which present a unified collection or series of related furnishing themes show their customers how to assemble a look and bring diverse elements together in a successful whole. Furniture designed to be assembled at home provides instant gratification while costing less. Most people like to have some direct effect on the way their homes are furnished or decorate. Flat-pack furniture and fittings give everyone a chance to participate in some form of making and provide a first-hand appreciation of structural and material quality. In the process, products may lose some of their mystique – and you may lose your temper – but the end result is often a greater sense of personal involvement and at least some job satisfaction.

Designers must also be visionaries. True, very little is really new in design, and looking to the future sometimes means looking back, or glancing sideways. I remember once praising a modern chair to Peter Thornton of the Victoria and Albert Museum. He then patiently showed me, in reply, an eighteenth-century design of remarkable similarity.

Design should be concerned with preserving the best of the old, as well as fostering the best of the new. At the same time, it is up to designers to foster creative traffic between different spheres, to borrow and adapt ideas which first appeared as solutions in different contexts and find new life for them. We like to think of our homes as quite separate from workplaces, hotels, restaurants or even the great outdoors. Yet many furnishings, fittings and notions of arrangement we take for granted today within our own four walls were first introduced in quite different settings. Anglepoise lamps and venetian blinds migrated from the office; wicker furniture from the verandah; twinkling halogen downlights from retail outlets; kitchen planning from the ergonomic workflows of early factory floors.

The architects of the Modern Movement left little to chance, designing the shell of their buildings as well as everything they contained. The simplicity of their furnishings concentrated attention on form – for whenever you remove decoration from something, the shape attracts greater attention and so matters more. It seems to me that the true legacy of this movement is not just another 'style' to be added to the costume changes of interior decoration, but a fundamental attitude which remains absolutely relevant. Simplicity remains a valuable, not to say essential, quality in present-day life.

I remain a resolute modernist in my belief that first and foremost a home should work; it should support and facilitate the activities that take place within it and it should be designed so that the technologies of heat, power, information and so on, are properly and efficiently integrated. As technological advance continues and the pressure on the world's resources increases, this aspect of home design will only become more critical.

Getting the framework right – making sure the home functions properly – is ever-more important as space becomes a precious resource. Space is the ultimate luxury, the one thing, as they say, which you can't steal. The need for private, personal, good-quality space is increasing as the world outside grows more complex, threatening and stressful.

My own tastes are quite well defined, and I have been fortunate to have had the opportunity to convey my enthusiasms to others. If there is a common denominator in the choices to which I have been drawn it is simplicity.

Simplicity, however, should not be confused with simplistic. Shaker rooms and furniture were simple, and so, in their way, were the Gustavian interiors of eighteenth-century Sweden. Vernacular buildings all over the world are simple, from whitewashed villas to rustic farmhouses.

Simplicity does not rule out precision, craft or finesse. Think of the whisper of air when you lift the lid of a Shaker box – the audible sign of a perfect fit. Nor is comfort out of the question. I don't mean the mind-numbing comfort of the cushy three-piece suite, angled to provide the clearest view of the television. I mean the comfort of the appropriate level of lighting, the sympathetic table height, the commodious bookshelves – anything which smoothes the path through life.

Simplicity transcends fretful anxieties about status; it can be rustic or urban, rich or poor, old or new. It places human life back in the centre of the picture. If our homes should provide anything, they should provide a sense of who we are and how we got here, a sense of connection balanced by a sense of direction and progress. I believe that simplicity in design is one important way in which interiors and what they contain can make room for this essential freedom of expression.

The progressive American furniture company, Herman Miller, manufactured all of Charles and Ray Eames's designs, including the DKR chair (1951) photographed for their 1952 catalogue.

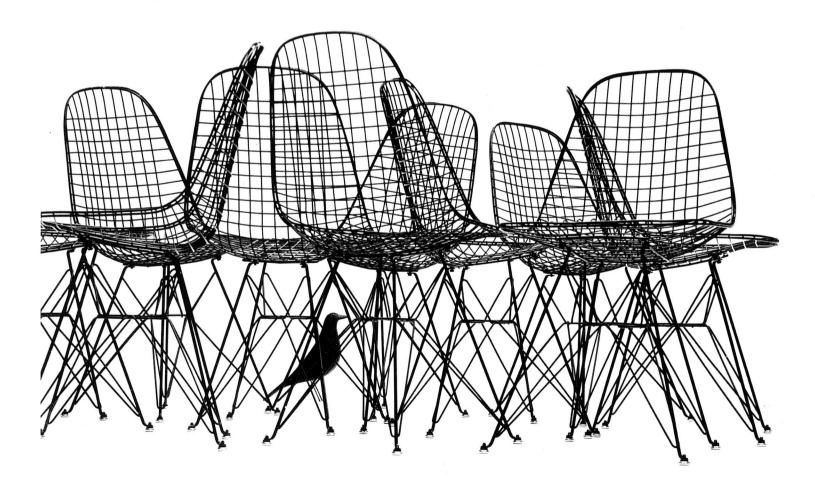

Beach hut, Belgium

Barn, Wiltshire, England

Tepee, Indian Depot Camp, Pend d'Oreille River, Washington State (late 19th century)

'... homes, as well as being made of bricks and mortar, melamine and foam rubber, are also made of ideas' Adrian Forty, *Objects of Desire*

Winnie-the-Pooh by A.A. Milne, illustrated by E.H. Shepard (1926)

A home is more than the sum of its parts. The
emotions aroused by the word go deeper than a
mere affection for a decorating style: home is
where we feel we belong, whether it is a suburban
semi, converted water tower or disused railway
carriage. These ties, for most of us, are rooted in
childhood. Play homes, such as tree-houses, distil
the notion of the home as a retreat or safe haven,
from the fictional creations in *Peter Pan*, *Winnie-
the-Pooh* or *Swiss Family Robinson*, to the real
platform of scrap planks lashed to the tree in the
back garden – or the precarious eyries of anti-road
protesters. It isn't a new instinct. There is a half-
timbered tree-house built in the grounds of
Pitchford Hall, Shropshire, which is 450 years old.
The tepee, tent, log cabin, beach hut – all homes
from home – have a lasting and profound hold on
the imagination of child and adult alike.

Tree-house, Piedmont, Italy

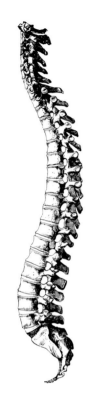

Human spine, *Gray's Anatomy*

Mieajah Burnett, Shaker staircase, Pleasant Hill, Kentucky (1839-41)

The staircase is one of the most expressive of all architectural elements. The exquisite finesse of the Shaker and Mendelsohn stairs display the human quality of design when it is rooted in nature. The sinuous curves of each stair lead the eye on and up in anticipation, and visually link one level with the next. Nothing could be further from the experience of taking a lift or escalator, mechanical inventions which contributed a great deal to the development of the high-rise building.

Helicoid shell

It is hard to beat a staircase for making a grand entrance. For many architects the design of the staircase is their opportunity to bring a sculptural element into what may otherwise be quite a hard, rectilinear space.

At Quaglino's and Mezzo, for example, the sweeping staircases provide a glamorous entrance to restaurants at the lower level.

Erich Mendelsohn and Serge Chermayeff, staircase at De La Warr Pavilion, Bexhill-on-Sea (1935-6)

Le Corbusier, double-height living-room, Unité d'Habitation, Marseilles (1947-52)

Le Corbusier, 'Modulor' Man (c. 1947)

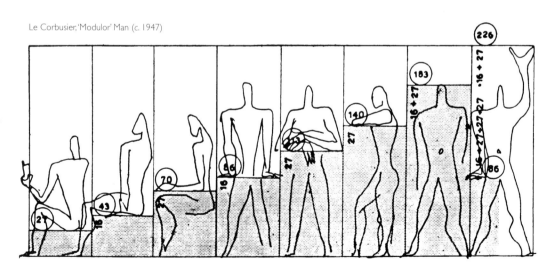

'We claim, in the name of the steamship, of the airplane, and of the motor-car, the right to health, logic, daring, harmony, perfection'

Le Corbusier

Le Corbusier, Madame Savoye's bathroom, Villa Savoye, Poissy (1929-31)

Le Corbusier, first-floor terrace, Villa Savoye, Poissy (1929-31)

Le Corbusier, exterior detail, Unité d'Habitation, Berlin (1957)

Le Corbusier – Charles Edouard Jeanneret (1887-1965) – was one of the most influential figures in design this century. Revered and despised with equal passion, his work ranged from private villas to vast urban projects, and proclaimed a new direction in building where architectural form would reflect the methods and materials of mass-production. Crucially, he believed that the plan of a building should be the generator of its design, and that houses must provide functional surroundings for everyday life. Those who associate his work with a monochromatic modernism might be surprised by the planes of colour that orchestrate space in buildings such as Villa Savoye. The living spaces at Unité d'Habitation are a far cry from the soulless cells designed by his less successful imitators. Corbusier researched classical proportional systems to devise the 'Modulor', a dimensioning standard based on the human scale, which he hoped would bring universal harmony to design.

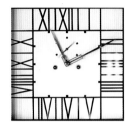

Japanese art and design have had a pervasive influence on contemporary taste. Mackintosh, like other turn-of-the-century designers, avidly studied Japanese culture. His intense awareness of light, use of screens, calm decoration and graphic purity recall the ordered spaces of the traditional Japanese interior. The Hill House table is furniture as kinetic sculpture. A shadowy grid crosses the floor as light falls on to the table from different angles at different times of day.

Charles Rennie Mackintosh, clock face (detail) and drawing-room, Hill House, Glasgow (1908)

John Pawson, Pawson House, London (1995)

Kenji Kawabata and Xavier de Castella, Kenzo House, Paris (1991)

Drawing by Lorenz, © 1972 *The New Yorker* Magazine, Inc.

The ancient Zen concept of 'thinglessness' as the ultimate richness has a particular resonance in Japan. Empty space, in a country where real estate commands some of the highest prices in the world, equates with prestige, freedom and luxury. In the West, elements of the same concept are enshrined in the modern design catchphrase 'less is more'. This notion is taken to its limit in the work of minimalist designers such as John Pawson (commissioned by Calvin Klein to design his Madison Avenue store). In Pawson's interiors, doors and windows have no frames, walls no skirting boards or mouldings, and possessions are housed in seamlessly detailed, built-in cupboards. Less empty, but still austere, the home of fashion designer Kenzo shows Japanese style in a Paris setting.

"I'm afraid, Chandler, that sometimes less is less."

'... simplicity is the end, and not the beginning'

C. F. A. Voysey

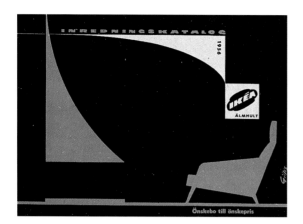

Ikea catalogue cover (1956)

Ikea catalogue cover (1955)

Ikea catalogue cover (1960)

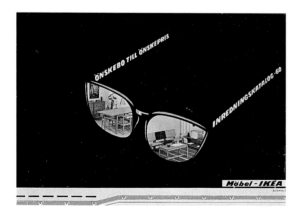

Alvar Aalto, Villa Mairea, Finland (1939)

For many people, Scandinavian design is the acceptable face of modernism. From the work of Alvar Aalto, Arne Jacobsen, Finn Juhl, Hans Wegner and Georg Jensen to the IKEA flat-pack, Scandinavia has had a huge impact on the way homes have been furnished over the past 50 years. I can remember how inspiring it all was back in the late 1950s when, like many other designers, I used to travel across to Helsinki, Stockholm or Copenhagen to see the innovative products that were just becoming available. All seemed to display a progressive spirit and a respect for craftsmanship and natural materials which made them supremely human and sensual. What was equally impressive was the social purpose implicit in such designs, and the notion that design could be sponsored – and supported – as an expression of national ideals.

Poul Hennigsen, PH-5 hanging lamp (1958)

Alvar Aalto, Villa Mairea, Finland (1939)

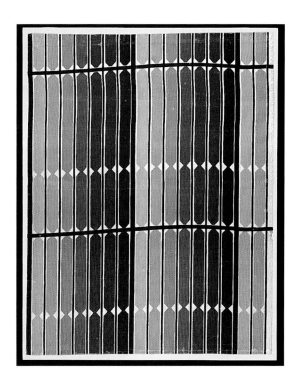

Astrid Sampe for Nordiska Kompaniet, 'Windy Way' textile design (1954)

Fallingwater House was designed in 1935, the same year as another of Wright's equally famous works, the Johnson Wax Administration Building. Designed as a guest house for the Kaufmann family, Fallingwater does not so much occupy its site as grow out of it, with its vast cantilevered, reinforced-concrete platforms sailing out over cascading water in a triumph of modern engineering. The modernity is tempered by an organic quality reminiscent of natural structures such as honeycombs and nests.

Frank Lloyd Wright, Fallingwater House, Bear Run, Pennsylvania (1935)

Frank Lloyd Wright, bedroom, Fallingwater House, Bear Run, Pennsylvania (1935)

Frank Lloyd Wright, Fallingwater House under construction (1935)

Like Mackintosh, Wright was influenced by traditional Japanese building and – like many other great designers – he concerned himself with the design of not merely the building, but all it contained. With their forthright use of materials, Wright's long, low houses are vivid expressions of the pioneer spirit.

Case Study House Number 8 is one of the earliest and best known examples of what later became called high-tech. Assembled entirely from mass-produced components of the kind normally used to build factories, the house is a landmark of the industrial aesthetic. The kit-of-parts approach is one important element; another is the willingness to import fittings designed for industrial use into the home. High-tech had a brief life as a style, but many homes today contain at least a few elements which have migrated from non-domestic sources, such as wire-mesh baskets, test-tube spice racks and photographers' lights.

FURNISHINGS AND THE INTERIOR

Charles and Ray Eames, Case Study House Number 8, Pacific Palisades, California (1949)

Charles and Ray Eames pinned by metal chair legs (1947)

Charles and Ray Eames, interior, Case Study House Number 8, Pacific Palisades (1949)

Painted alcove, India

Terracotta-coloured wall, Sicily

With the explosion of mass travel, ethnic influences in the home may be seen in something as basic as colour, or in more tangible souvenirs. Romeo Gigli's apartment displays a passionate interest in exotic artefacts, from an Amazonian hammock to Papuan shields. Hand-made and often inexpensive, such products are an antidote to what is mass-produced.

The flow of ideas is often two-way. Habitat was one of the first shops to sell Indian cotton dhurries on a large scale, and we soon began commissioning new colourways and patterns to broaden the range.

Mediterranean terrace, Mykonos, Greece

Romeo Gigli, living-room, Milan (1990)

OVER: painting walls in Rajasthan, India

Cottage, County Galway, Ireland

Little School Houses patchwork quilt, USA (late 19th century)

Farmhouse kitchen, France

The complexities of the modern world and the speed of technological change have bred a very real desire for the simple life, a yearning expressed most obviously in the form of country style. To me, much of what is popularly known as 'country' is no more than an affectation, the kind of nostalgia that results in urban drawing-rooms smothered in chintzy prints, and modern kitchen appliances lurking behind stencilled oak door fronts – no more authentically rural than Marie Antoinette playing at being a shepherdess.

Such tweeness obscures the real value of vernacular traditions, an importance which was especially acknowledged in the work of William Morris and his followers. To them, we owe our appreciation of natural materials such as scrubbed oak or terracotta tile and of the charm of plain whitewash – elements whose character have little to do with passing trends or styles.

Willy Ronis, *Le Nu Provençal* (1949)

Comfort is only a relatively recent concept in interior furnishing: for many centuries, notions of hierarchy and decorum were much more important. The challenge of fitting a chair to the human body has been made much easier in the twentieth century with the development of new materials and technical processes. Charles and Ray Eames's classic chair and ottoman – with its articulated shell of moulded plywood veneered in rosewood and lined with padded leather – is every bit as comfortable as it looks, and was manufactured, like all of the Eames's furniture designs, by the progressive American firm, Herman Miller.

The Karuselli is the most comfortable chair I know. It's wonderful to sit in when you have friends round, and it's also a very good chair to be photographed in because it relaxes you.

There's a marvellous, apocryphal story about how the chair was designed. Apparently, Yrjö Kukkapuro, its Finnish designer, was walking home rather the worse for wear after a heavy night drinking. He fell into a snow drift, and when he gathered his senses to pull himself out, he used the impression made by his body as the inspiration for the chair. It really does fit you like a glove. The seat and base are made from fibreglass-reinforced polyester; the seat swivels and is connected to the base by a steel spring and rubber dampers.

At the opposite end of the technological spectrum, the beanbag is a much more affordable expression of the principle of moulding a seat to fit the human body. No Sixties or Seventies pad was complete without a beanbag or two: seating at its most basic, where comfort is what you make it.

Charles and Ray Eames, Number 670 and Number 671, lounge chair and ottoman (1956)

Beanbags, Habitat catalogue (1973)

'I can't think how many times I've wanted to leave a dinner table after spending too long in a designer chair'

Paul Smith

Yrjö Kukkapuro, Karuselli chair (1964)

The chair has been something of an icon for twentieth-century designers. Mackintosh, Wright, Rietveld, Corbusier, Breuer, Mies, the Eameses, Jacobsen, Aalto, Saarinen, Gehry, Venturi – the list of architects who have seized the opportunity to express their theories in the design of a chair is seemingly endless. As the architect Peter Smithson once proclaimed, 'When we design a chair, we make a society and a city in miniature'.

Over a century's worth of such grand statements are on show at the Vitra Design Museum, where an example such as Harry Bertoia's Diamond chair merits its own podium, an icon at the altar of modern design. Bertoia described his work as, 'mostly made of air, like a sculpture'.

Sculpture of a different kind is evident in the famous sofa modelled on Salvador Dali's painting of Mae West's lips. Like people, chairs have arms, legs, backs and seats; they support the human body, but they also echo it, a correspondence which may explain the almost fetishistic role of the chair.

Harry Bertoia, Diamond chair (1953)

Achirivolto, Ginger chair

Marcel Breuer, B3 chair (1925) with Bauhaus student wearing mask by Oskar Schlemmer

Mae West Hot Lips sofa (1936-7)

'What a lot of things I don't need,' Socrates is said to have remarked as he passed by a market stall displaying household wares. If Socrates was so tempted in the fifth century BC, what hope is there for the modern shopper adrift in the mall?

Household goods are the everyday tools and accessories of life, our working partners in the daily routines of cooking, eating, bathing, sleeping and all the other activities that take place in the home. These ordinary objects – toothbrushes and toasters, pots and pans, handles and catches – notionally exist

in order to help us perform particular tasks, often tasks that are so mundane and universal that they demand little in the way of conscious thought. Provided the tools and accessories we require to carry out such activities do not positively frustrate us in use, one might suppose that they should blend harmoniously with the background, even drop from view. One might equally suppose that given technological progress and the general modern desire to simplify life, we might find fewer rather than more things in the average home.

household

Set of Wonderlier Tupperware bowls, designed by Earl S. Tupper (1949).

Unlike Socrates at the market stall we somehow manage to acquire a great many things we do not need. At least part of what makes moving such a traumatic experience for most people is the fact that it graphically demonstrates the terrifying extent to which possessions can gain the upper hand. We buy equipment without ever really getting round to using it; we buy gadgets that promise to save time or cut corners and never manage to read the instructions; we invest in accessories that we think we ought to have, which might come in useful one day, or which provide us with a flattering self-image. Before long, our living space has become storage space, and a large proportion of the time and effort we are supposed to be saving is spent organizing, retrieving, maintaining and generally looking after …things. And the things themselves are no longer in the background, like discreet and humble servants performing household duties, but have become objects of great significance, saying as much about us as the clothes on our backs.

This has not always been the case. For centuries, the average person in the average household owned little more than could be stowed in a chest, and a small chest at that. By the eighteenth century, as life became more settled and trade prospered, those at the upper levels of society began to acquire more worldly goods. Yet as inventories of the period show, with the exception of the richest estates, quite wealthy households owned surprisingly little.

The watershed was the Industrial Revolution. After the nineteenth century, as Penny Sparke has written, 'more people bought things instead of inheriting them, making them or doing without them'. Mass-production went hand in hand with mass consumption, and design became the means by which people were invited to choose between the variety of goods they were offered.

In the early days of industrialization, the mere fact that the average person suddenly found all manner of household goods and products financially within their reach was revolutionary in itself.

But after only a short while, sheer access to a wider range of possessions could not disguise the fact that the goods themselves were often inferior in quality to what had gone before. As mechanization replaced hand labour and craftsmanship, wider choice began to be seen as a poor compensation for the deterioration of in the quality of materials and manufacturing techniques.

The great design pioneer, Henry Cole, who laid the foundation for art and design education in Britain, was among the first to become concerned at the turn of events. Cole's aim was to restore 'art' to everyday objects and to create demand for such products by educating the public in matters of taste. He advocated technical workshops in schools, and proposed that designers should have executive status within manufacturing firms. He founded a journal of design, planned the Great Exhibition of 1851 with Prince Albert, and established the South Kensington Museum (later the Victoria and Albert) with the profits raised by the exhibition. His efforts did much to establish design as a distinct discipline, but also marked the extent of its exclusion from the world of production. He established the V&A as a museum of the decorative arts to

American housewives found Tupperware to be astonishingly versatile (1953).

guide the manufacturers of the day to the production of better designed and more aesthetically pleasing products. Its objective is clearly writ large, carved in the stone of the entrance. Sadly, the original ideals have been superseded by less focused direction, and the Museum has become a largely aimless and confusing mixture of fine arts and decorative objects, lacking objectives or purpose. It remains, however, a wonderful treasure-trove of humankind's aesthetic ambitions and aberrations.

Throughout the latter half of the nineteenth century, many strenuous attempts were made to carry on where Cole left off. Noble experiments conducted with missionary zeal attempted to square the very same circle. The Arts and Crafts Movement was one such endeavour. While its exponents had little effect on the momentum of commercialization, the movement as a whole, which focussed attention on basic country craftwork and vernacular style, managed to make some impact on the direction of mass taste. The Arts and Crafts movement marked the beginning of simple living as a concept. It was in the context of this craft-based approach that I began my own design education.

William Morris's London home, Kelmscott House, displayed his ideals in practice, one of the earliest examples of a designer, manufacturer and retailer promoting his vision through the character of his own surroundings. It attracted much contemporary comment. Bernard Shaw was surprised to see the Morris's dining table displayed unadorned – without a tablecloth – 'a concept so revolutionary it took years of domestic conflict to introduce it,' he noted. The Arts and Crafts disciples allowed their aesthetic principles to percolate through all aspects of their lives, from the reformed artistic dress they wore to the willow pattern crockery they favoured for place settings. The effect on public taste was a gradual lightening of the interior and a lessening of the turbulent density that characterized many late Victorian interiors.

Morris and his allies directed people to furnish their homes with what they knew to be 'useful' or believed to be 'beautiful'. In the realm of household goods, 'useful' might seem a fairly objective notion. After all, people could be relied upon to know what they really needed – or could they?

If you look at design in terms of its role as an interpreter of technological change, the whole notion of 'need' and 'usefulness' seems less clear cut. Did the vacuum cleaner arise out of a need to save labour in the home or did its invention help to promote the shift from labour-intensive housekeeping to servantless households? Most of the household appliances and labour-saving devices on which we now rely were actually invented and patented in some embryonic form in the nineteenth century. Yet it was not until the twentieth century that such products really made an impact on the mass market and were developed in usable, affordable forms. In the United States, where many of these machines were developed, and where the market for such goods was first established, domestic labour had always been in short supply. In Britain, where one in three young women between the ages of 15 and 20 were in service at the end of the nineteenth century, the need for labour-saving machinery was far from acute. At first, the labour saved was servants' labour, not the labour of an overburdened housewife.

In the ordinary household, the impact of design throughout the twentieth century has largely been expressed through the encroaching presence of these machines. In the beginning there seemed to be a simple equation: machines could do housework faster and more efficiently than armies of servants; machines could provide leisure for more rewarding and enjoyable pursuits.

There was another side to the story. Domestic appliances often meant that housework became more, rather than less of a chore. 'The invention of the washing-machine has meant more washing, of the vacuum cleaner more cleaning, of new fuels and cooking equipment, more courses and more elaborately cooked food,' noted Hazel Kyrk in 1933. In many early twentieth-century studies of domestic work, appliances were not found to reduce the amount of time it actually took to complete a task; instead, manufacturers in theirs sales pitches learned to stress the efficiency, professionalism and generally improved standards of work that machines could deliver.

The advent of electric light and heating had removed great quantities of dirt and dust from the home: walls and ceilings no longer discoloured with the fumes from gas jets and coal fires; sooty dust no longer settled on every surface. But bright, evenly distributed and unpolluting electric light also revealed every speck of dirt that might otherwise have gone unnoticed in a shadowy, dusty corner. New technology did not so much clean up the home as raise our expectations about how clean a home should – and now could – be.

'Labour-saving' devices can also create labour in other ways. From time to time I have appeared as a guest judge on the popular television programme, *Masterchef*, where amateur cooks compete to prepare and serve several courses of their own creation against the clock. I shall never forget one contestant who used her state-of-the-art food processor to chop half a dozen walnut halves. I gently pointed out that once she allowed for the time to set up the machine and dismantle and clean it afterwards, she would have found it far quicker to use a sharp knife.

The design of household appliances – their appearance and styling as much as their performance and function – mirrors changing attitudes to housekeeping. While servants were still the prime users of domestic appliances, little attention was paid to the way such machines looked. Early refrigerators resembled the ice-boxes they superseded; early electric cookers could barely be distinguished in terms of appearance from old closed coal ranges.

As long as such equipment was largely operated by servants, working below stairs, designs remained bulky and awkward, and preserved the traditional points of reference that linked them visually with an earlier era of technology.

All that began to change after the First World War. Few households in the United States employed any domestic help, and numbers in service were also declining in Britain and Europe. To appeal to the new consumers of appliances – the housewives in sole charge of the home – the entire concept of housekeeping was elevated to the status of a profession. The tools with which these modern women could practise domestic science and home economy were transformed into sleek models of hygiene and efficiency.

The timing of this transformation coincided with the need of manufacturers to provide greater differentiation between products. Mass-production not only allowed more of everything to be produced, it also required more types of everything to be produced, to maximize the market. Styling became a key means of creating diversity and, thus, demand for the latest 'look'.

One of the most striking examples of the impact of styling can be seen in the way the appearance of domestic appliances changed in the late 1930s. Industrial designers such as Walter Dorwin Teague, Henry Dreyfuss and Raymond Loewy applied imagery from the ultimate modern machine – the aeroplane – to the design of toasters, fridges and cookers. Superficially, of course, there is no reason why a fridge should be streamlined. A fridge is not going anywhere. Yet the imagery of speed suited a product sold on the basis of labour-saving efficiency. Its modernity flattered the housewife, who found herself in control of a highly engineered product. The gleaming white surfaces and minimal moulding were easy to keep clean; they also looked as clean and professional as a laboratory. The design expressed the manufacturing process and the way the materials could be worked; in that, at least, it was honest.

A landmark building for a household brand: Thomas Wallis Gilbert's Hoover Building, London (1934).

Naturally enough, the whole kitchen underwent drastic reappraisal during the same period. Domestic economists such as Christine Frederick analysed sequences of work, applying new time-and-motion studies, designed to speed factory production, to the performance of domestic tasks. Judicial planning could simplify household routines to models of clockwork efficiency, reducing, for example, the number of paces required to make a sponge cake from 39 to ten. The new ergonomically planned, built-in kitchens were clearly not a below-stairs backwater but the serious professional domain of the housewife-technician.

American dream kitchens of the 1920s, '30s and '40s did not become anything like reality for British women until after the Second World War, by which time another great social change was underway. Labour-saving equipment, which had compensated for the loss of servants, now permitted housewives to leave the home altogether and join the workforce. Dream kitchens became, and for many people still are, tangible signs of prosperity. Time was more precious, life increasingly informal and the kitchen found a new role in the heart of the household, no longer the sole preserve of the housewife, but the focus for daily comings and goings.

In this context, kitchen equipment and fittings began to acquire all sorts of other meanings, expressing aspirations for lifestyle and homemaking that went far beyond the simple desire for efficiency. The Aga, for example, carries a raft of cosy associations which have little to do with its origins or functions. Invented in 1922 by Dr Gustaf Dalen, a Swede, the Aga is now cultural shorthand; its name even defines a genre of fiction, the 'Aga saga'. As Deyan Sudjic has written, the Aga is 'the exact equivalent of parking a Volvo estate car outside the house, owning a Labrador, and baking your own bread. ... [It] is the earth goddess of suburbia, the last vestige of the hearth at the centre of the home.'

The dream kitchen of today takes many forms, but among the most popular is the country version, a nostalgic haven of domesticity far more common in towns than villages. Despite the considerable expense and attention to detail involved, such kitchens may see no more strenuous cooking than the setting of a microwave. Superfluous styling has made a triumphant comeback: decor panels for appliances to hide behind; bespoke cupboards and units whose mouldings and trim recall the fixtures of an Edwardian pantry; and those ghastly wheatsheaves on toasters. People who I am sure are perfectly decent and honest go about the

The 1950s' version of modernity opened this dream kitchen on to the patio outdoors.

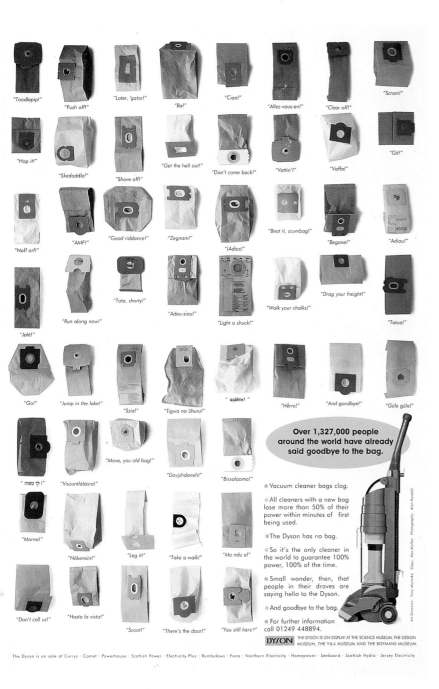

The Dyson vacuum cleaner, as its advertising makes clear, spells the end of the replacement dust bag.

way that they live in a way that is horribly dishonest. Are there really so many people terrified by the advent of the third millennium that they retreat to the ersatz formulae of some pastoral never-never land?

By the 1950s, manufacturers had discovered another means of safeguarding turnover. 'Built-in obsolescence' was a catchphrase of post-war consumerism and summarized the increasing ambivalence with which the public now regarded household machines and equipment. While a fridge, for example, offered only limited scope for stylistic variation, it could be designed for a limited life, either through its engineering or by bringing out new models with new features in a constant process of updating.

Some manufacturers strove to establish a clear identity. The German company, Braun, for example, has achieved an image of pure, functional modernity which unites the variety of electrical goods it produces, from razors to toasters. From the Braun logo, with its central rounded 'A' poking above the other characters in a clear reference to push-button technology, to the clean sophisticated lines and matt black or white finishes, design has been used to express a strong brand identity. The clarity of Braun's image owes much to 'one pair of eyes' – those of Braun's chief designer, Dieter Rams. His classically austere yet sculptural designs express his stated aim: to 'make things that recede into the background'.

By contrast, the witty, playful designs produced by the Italian company, Alessi, do anything but recede into the background. The Sapper kettle, Starck lemon squeezer and Rossi coffeepot reject the functional reticence of Braun's products and subvert traditional forms with great humour and originality. These are everyday objects that look far from mundane; in some quarters, their cachet as cult purchases has helped to put the sneer into the label 'designer'. But Alessi products are no more designed than those produced by Braun; they are merely designed or styled in a different way. I admit it might be rather exhausting to fill one's kitchen with an entire collection of these attention-seeking objects, but many display an irrepressible *joie de vivre* which I find appealing. There is nothing wrong with a product that brings a gentle smile to the user's face; in fact, it is a positive advantage.

At the end of the twentieth century, technological progress is increasingly a double-edged sword. In Britain alone, over nine million domestic appliances are discarded every year. Design could play a part in reducing this mountain of wastage. Recyclable parts and materials, slot-in technology for easy upgrading, better fastenings, fittings and finishes would extend the lifespan of appliances significantly. Whether we want this to happen – and at what cost – is another matter. We should not overlook the value that design plays in creating employment. Can we really contemplate a society in which only a small elite is in employment?

Meanwhile technology forges ahead into uncharted waters. The home is poised on the brink of another transformation, from a simple serviced shell to an interactive environment of incalculable smartness. Self-diagnosing washing machines which analyse the reasons for their own breakdown; boilers which learn your living patterns and adjust heating levels accordingly; and voice-controlled security are fact rather than fantasy. The Japanese have even devised a lavatory which reports on the state of one's health. Will the 'smart house' be too clever for its own good? Will we lose the hands-on quality of everyday life? Will we chop a few walnuts in a food-processor? Philippe Starck laments what he calls our 'vulgar' rapport with machines: 'Compare the gesture which we use today to turn on a tap … with the same action, with the same aim of getting water, of an Arab in the middle of the desert stooping and cupping his hands to raise water to his lips. We have lost all that. If we cannot rediscover the elegance of the African in the desert, we can at least rediscover the elegance of the object.'

Many of the household articles with which we share our lives are not, of course, machines. The role of design on the everyday level of pots and pans, cups and saucers, knives and forks, has less to do with technology than with presentation and selection. Previous societies expected forms to be constant and patterns to be stable. Technology has given the modern world a notion of progress and an expectation of forward movement: we constantly expect things to be improved upon. But in some areas of life, it is important that design should remind us about those things which need no improvement and should restate qualities that might otherwise be overlooked in the dash to get ahead.

No one can instinctively appreciate what is right and good about a particular design. Everyone needs to be taught how to look. The experience which had the greatest effect on the development of my taste was my first trip to France in the early 1950s.

The circumstances of my introduction to French culture were pretty favourable. My travelling companion was the incomparable Michael Wickham, whose photographer's eye missed nothing and guided me to sights I would never have noticed by myself. We were young, on holiday and travelling in some style, speeding around the country in Michael's open Lagonda. Contrary to appearances, however, we had little money. It was five years since the end of the war, and a couple of years before the end of rationing. I had never been abroad, and I had spent much of my youth in grey, bleak wartime Britain.

The colours, smells and tastes of provincial France were a shock – a very pleasant shock – to the system. What entranced me about the country – and what I still find beguiling – was the quality of everyday life that I found all around, in routier cafés, homes, shops and marketplaces. Plain white tablecloths, solid porcelain dishes, simple glass carafes, rugged glazed terracotta cooking pots and heavy cast-iron pans summed up a whole approach to living.

'Remember that cold vegetables are less harmful than ugly dishes. One affects the body, while the other affects the soul'

C.F.A. Voysey

Practical, hard-wearing, traditional and, above all, simple, these basic objects had an aesthetic quality quite unknown in Britain at the time. There was an astounding difference between the solidity of typical French kitchenware and the thin-gauge aluminium pans common in British households. In France, a cooking pot was bought with the expectation that it would last a lifetime; in Britain, pots and pans had a disposable quality. Heavy French pots provided the even, slow diffusion of heat necessary for the enhancement of aroma and flavour but you couldn't have cooked a decent dish in the average cheap, tinny English pan even if you had the finest, freshest ingredients.

It was not merely a question of utility. Glowing white porcelain, bright orange, enamelled casseroles, and salt-glazed pottery alive with handthrown splotches of colour made the perfect backdrop for the enjoyment of good food. These were simple, solid objects that begged to be used.

Of course, part of the attraction such equipment held for me was that it produced the sort of food I liked. But it was also forthright, robust and inexpensive and I can think of no better qualities for household goods. A Le Creuset casserole, for example, is the very antithesis of a kitchen gadget. It never breaks down, never promises more than it can deliver, never goes out of fashion. I am almost inclined to agree with Piers Gough, the architect, who has said that, 'the Le Creuset casserole dish is the only design icon that isn't black, white or silver. ... It looks like fire, like iron before it is cast.' Similarly, consider the wooden spoon – versatile, durable and ideal for stirring since its handle is a poor conductor of heat; or the unglazed stoneware pot which allows food to cook in its own juices, a medley of flavours permeating the pot with frequent use. If I am proud of anything in my career as a designer and retailer, it is that I have been able to share my passion for such simple, well-made products with a wider public.

Design is concerned not merely with the form and function of household objects themselves, but is integral to the process by which such products are sold and end up sharing our living space. The classic example, perhaps, is the role of design in the creation of brands. Brands now permeate every area of consumption, but it is significant that what is acknowledged to be the first British brand was also one of the humblest household products imaginable – a bar of soap.

Until W.H. Lever began marketing his new Sunlight Soap in 1885, soap was sold by shopkeepers unpackaged and often unnamed, cut from large bars supplied by the soap manufacturers. Indeed, many goods were sold in this way and what mattered to the public was not the name or image of the product, but the name above the door of the shop.

Lever's new soap, sold in the form of individually wrapped tablets, was targeted at a working-class market. The fake parchment wrapper, name, and extensive advertising and publicity campaigns which ensued created a distinctive product where none had existed before. Sunlight Soap did have intrinsic characteristics which distinguished it from its competitors, but superficially these qualities were not visible to the ordinary consumer. What was visible was the image Lever so painstakingly developed.

We are so accustomed to brands nowadays that it can be difficult to imagine life without them. As the mass market developed and branding proliferated, good retailers were no longer the decent and trusted neighbourhood purveyors of common-or-garden goods, but those shopkeepers who offered the best selection, or the new department stores, whose luxurious surroundings and attentive service brought glamour and distinction to shopping.

Retailers learned from bitter experience that their best efforts to support a brand could be undermined. It costs a great deal of money for a manufacturer to create and build a brand. Retailers

HOUSEHOLD

White on white for classic good looks.

often found themselves in the position of acting as a warehouse for manufacturers' goods, only to find the same goods being offered at a discount in an outlet without equivalent dedication to service or display. It took a while, but retailers began to realize that design could serve them, too, by creating an image that enabled the shop itself to become a brandname. By the early 1980s, high-street retailers had discovered design with a vengeance. The result has

Our skill lay in selecting products as much as designing them; as Habitat evolved, these two aspects grew closer together. With around 30 per cent of stock coming from outside sources, it was essential for our product designers to work closely with the buyers to present a coherent and unified selection of merchandise. The 'orientation' meetings where such directions were decided were among the most stimulating I have ever attended.

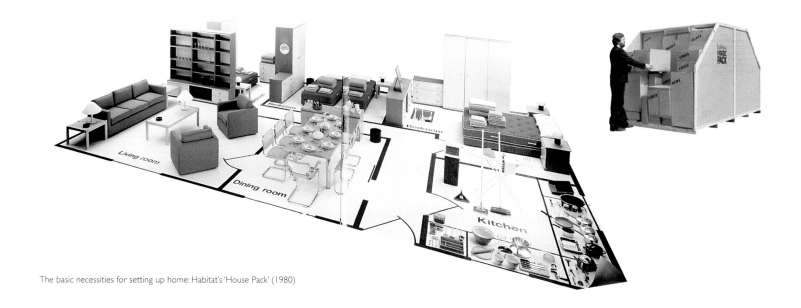

The basic necessities for setting up home: Habitat's 'House Pack' (1980)

been the emergence and dominance of the 'retail brand', where the choice of product is determined simply by the act of walking through the shop door.

When Habitat was first launched, in 1964, ordinary unbranded household items were sold alongside furniture. With the experience of French marketplaces and *quincailleries* fresh in my mind, these goods were arranged en masse, in tempting arrays that maximized the impact of colour and form.

Good selection is useless without good presentation. The energy generated by Habitat's marketplace displays broke down our customers' inhibitions about trying something unfamiliar: strange, alien products like the chicken brick. What retailers like to call 'adjacencies' were carefully considered – the grouping and display of linked items to create a bigger impression. Placing china next to glass, next to tableware, next to linen built up a stream of associations that supported and directed choice.

Packaging is another form of presentation. When Habitat merged with Mothercare, an urgent priority was to change the packaging. The old style, in dreary brown, avocado and orange, was detracting from perfectly pleasant products; the new style, in sweet-pea colours and simple stripes, was fresh and appealing. I believe packaging should be totally subservient to the product it encloses, otherwise there is built-in disappointment. But dull packaging deters people from discovering the real merits of a product.

The challenge of all retail design is to get the balance right. There are the physical parameters – the shell of the space – to consider. I believe that floors, walls and ceilings must be finished as well as possible to provide a light, warm and enveloping background that can be easily maintained. Lighting is also critical. The rash of aggressive spotlighting fashionable in many shops designed in the 1980s did little to create atmosphere. Light sources should be as diffused and invisible as possible, and spotlighting used only to focus attention where it belongs: on the products.

Within a flexible, serviceable space, displays can be moved around or grouped to create room sets and foster associations. A certain amount of stability is important: customers do not like to find everything has changed position from one visit to the next. At the same time, change brings vitality. Many shops are designed to show all their cards at once. This may promote a commendable honesty, but the result often seems lifeless. Part of what can make shopping such a pleasure is the sense of discovery. Retail design depends on the impact of seemingly small decisions. Moving a display of candles from one corner of The Conran Shop to another, for example, caused a dramatic rise in sales. Retail is always detail.

All good shops have a sense of theatre, but you can have too much of a good thing. Biba was a case in point. For many it was *the* boutique. When the company expanded in the early 1970s, it took over a department store and branched out in every conceivable direction – selling baked beans alongside boas. The effect was a hugely enjoyable theatrical experience. People flocked to see the funny, outrageous Art Deco displays ... bought very little, and stole a lot. In such flamboyant environments, it is easy to lose sight of that great retail maxim, 'the merchandise is the message'.

In the early days of consumerism, availability was enough. One early editor of the Sears Roebuck catalogue instructed that no product should be photographed to make it look better than it actually was. For customers ordering essential household goods miles from big city stores, dependability was essential. Sears sold everything under the sun; they even sold houses by mail, fully wired, plumbed and complete with two trees for the front yard.

Nowadays, choice is far from straightforward. When I wrote the first *House Book*, it grew out of the ever-expanding Habitat catalogue. The success and impact of the book arose from the fact that it was crammed with information and examples: it showed the full range of alternatives available at that time. The most recent version of the book, however, took shape with another end in view, not merely to present alternatives but to guide selection.

The Japanese chain Muji (Mujiroshi Ryohin, literally 'no-brand goods') presents exactly this type of selection: very simple, very basic merchandise in humble materials. Nothing has a brand name. Everything goes with everything else. Colours are limited, and decoration is non-existent. The careful cultivation of this non-image is, of course, an image, and it is every bit as Japanese as the latest high-tech hardware.

Design, which has done so much to create choice in the first place – in partnership with technology, branding, advertising and retail – must now help us make our choices. We have become increasingly aware of the tyranny of things. As quoted in a contemporary primer for pared-down living: 'You can't have everything. Where would you put it?'

Fireplace at Tredegar House, Cornwall (17th century)

My affection for the working parts of the house dates back a long way. The below-stairs domain of kitchen, pantry, larder, still-room and dairy has always attracted me to a far greater extent than the lavish display of wealth and status in grand state rooms. The service areas of old country houses, with their robust surfaces, scrubbed wooden table tops and neat arrays of basic equipment present a vision of orderliness and domesticity. I can't help but feel that those who worked in such surroundings must have had a better time than their masters and mistresses, trapped in all that stultifying decor upstairs – even though contemporary accounts graphically suggest otherwise. When I was first taken on tours of stately homes as a schoolchild, my preferences were fairly unusual. Nowadays, public interest in below-stairs life has increased to such an extent that organizations such as the National Trust have restored and reopened kitchens and service areas in many of their properties around the country.

Kitchen at Löfstad Castle, Sweden (rebuilt 1750)

Pestle and mortar

'Faites simple'

Elizabeth David (after Curnonsky)

Wooden spoons and forks belonging to Elizabeth David

Kenwood food processor and accessories

Electrical appliances for the home originated around the turn of the century. Since then a vast range of products has appeared, each ostensibly designed to speed up ordinary tasks. While most of us welcome the convenience of such appliances as the electric iron or toaster, how much time and effort do we actually save when we use an electric toothbrush, for example? The real need served by the household gadget may well be the need for novelty. This is not to decry the considerable advantages of such equipment as food processors, merely to observe that the benefits must be offset by factors such as the need to store, maintain, dismantle and assemble such equipment, not to mention the expertise required to make maximum use of them. Machines can't and shouldn't do everything: for most good cooks, there's no substitute for such traditional paraphenalia as wooden spoons, sharp knives, decent pots and pans   and a skilled pair of hands.

Chef at Mr Chow's Chinese restaurant pulling noodles

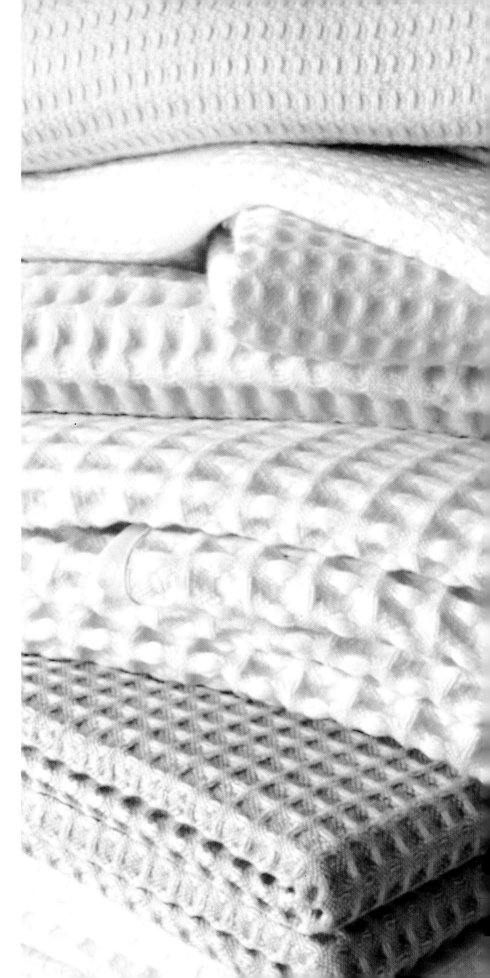

White is the colour of utility, hygiene and domesticity. The streamlined contours of a vitreous enamel refrigerator are not only easy to keep clean, the pristine finish looks pure, as uncontaminated as the food it contains. Despite the fact that such equipment could readily be manufactured in any colour, white remains the most popular: not for nothing are household appliances commonly known as white goods. With the advent of electrical light and heat, white became an acceptable and fashionable colour in areas of the home where it had previously been unknown. Mackintosh's all-white Glasgow living-room was shockingly avant-garde at the turn of the century, and must have been hideously difficult to maintain; by the 1930s, white was the height of luxury, the hallmark of fashionable society decorators such as Syrie Maugham. It can be no less luxurious today, although for a slightly different reason. White is revealing, of form as well as texture. White linen, white towels and white porcelain allow the quality of the material to speak for itself.

Waffle-weave linen

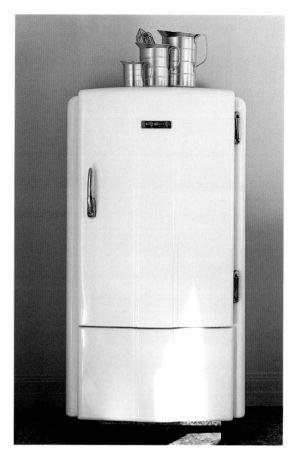

Streamlined refrigerator (1950s)

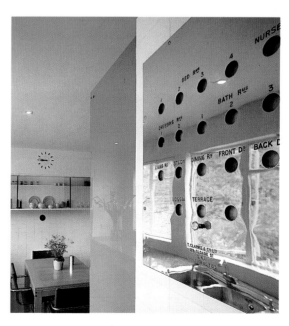

Erich Mendelsohn, kitchen at Auchett House, Hertfordshire (1920s)

Plastic toothbrushes (1986)

We live in a far more colourful world than did most of our ancestors. For many centuries, really bright clear colours were expensive and were principally found only in the homes of the rich. Nowadays, we expect all kinds of products to come in a wide range of colours. Fiestaware brings a palette of bright Pop colours to the table (Andy Warhol was a devotee). Plastic, in itself a colourless material, came into its own in the 1950s with the invention of polypropylene which could be injection moulded. The brilliant rainbow shades of everyday plastic articles, from clothes pegs to washing-up bowls, have made colour down-market and disposable. Colour may serve some practical purpose   it's useful for identifying your toothbrush in the bathroom – but mostly it's fun, renewable and uplifting.

Left: Plastic clothes pegs, Norway (1950s)

Opposite: Fiestaware crockery

HOUSEHOLD

79

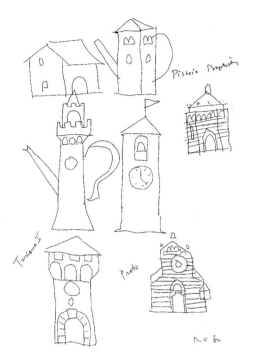

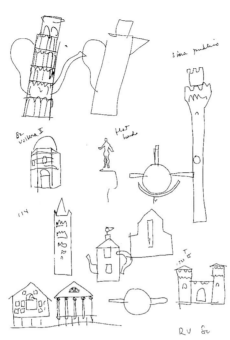

Robert Venturi, sketches for Alessi products (1980)

Riccardo Dalisi, the coffeepot as sculpture

Giovanni Alessi Anghini

The Italian company Alessi's patronage of designers and architects has resulted in a family of far-from-everyday objects which brings pure theatre to the table top. Witty and memorable designs such as the Rossi coffeepot transform the kitchen counter into a skyline of architectural forms, and provoke a new way of looking at functional objects. Alessi's use of design is one way of competing in a market dominated by large-scale manufacture of standardized goods.

'The design of a pepper pot is as important ... as the conception of a cathedral' Margaret Macdonald Mackintosh

Aldo Rossi, architectural sketch for coffeepot (1984)

Extendible shaving mirror

Articulation is one way to make furniture, household equipment and fixtures work. The need for flexibility, space-saving and adaptability is addressed equally in the extendible concertina arm of the shaving mirror or the spring-loaded folding mechanism of a sofa bed. In 1934 an English car engineer, George Carwardine, came up with the classic Anglepoise lamp, based on the anatomical workings of the human arm. Artemide's best-selling Tizio lamp is a more recent refinement, with cantilevered arms delivering a high degree of mobility, directing light wherever it is needed.

Richard Sapper for Artemide, Tizio desk lamp (1972)

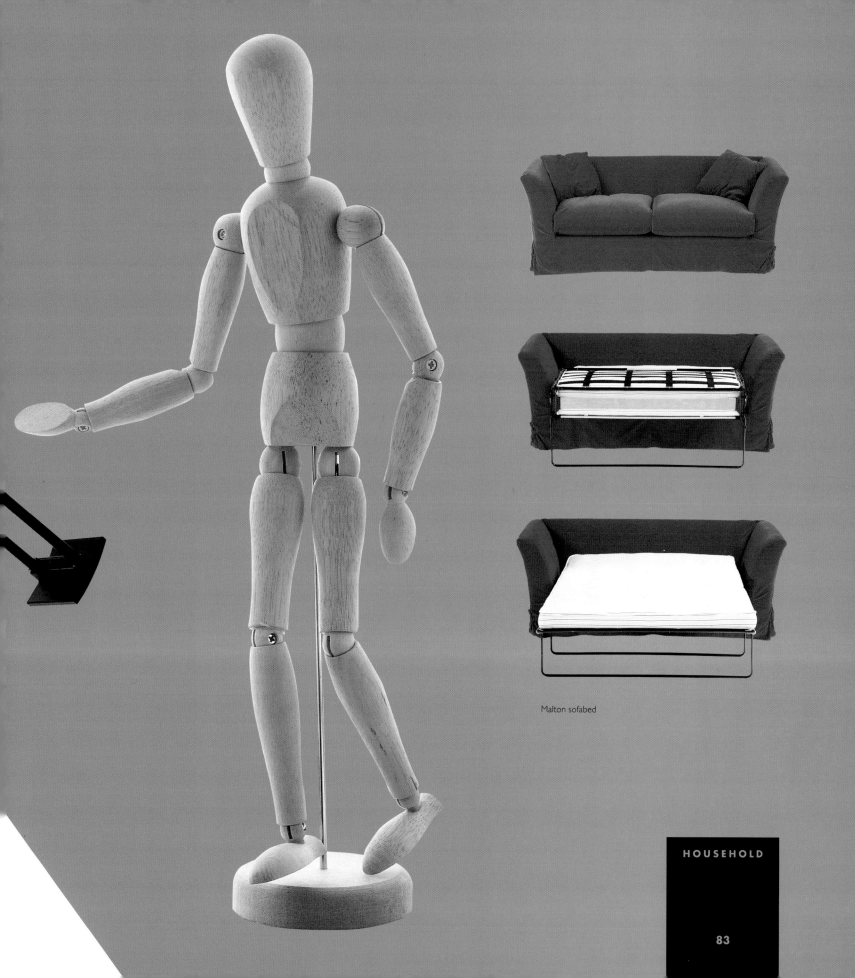

Malton sofabed

Wilhelm Wagenfeld for Tecnolumen, WD 28 door handle (1928)

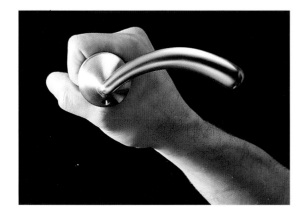

Makio Hasuike for Columbo Design, Edo door handle (1995)

Alessandro Mendini for Olivari, Aurora door handle (1994)

Studio BCF for Frascio, Soft door handle (1994)

Scissors for left-handed and right-handed users

The push-button, voice-activated or pre-set smart house is no longer the figment of a science-fiction writer's imagination. But if such advanced technology becomes the norm in the average household, will we increasingly find it hard to get a grip on reality? In countless ways, everyday tasks provide hands-on experience – catches and handles, basic utensils and tools have evolved over centuries, designed to fit the task in hand. The balance and weight of well-designed cutlery is a pleasure; the smooth operation of a latch can be extremely satisfying.

OPPOSITE: wrought-iron latch, Hancock Shaker Village, Massachusetts

Smart Design, Goodgrips paring knife

Tool storage

Michael Marriott, 'Seven Series' sardine tin collector's cabinet (1990)

Terence Conran, dressing-table (1994)

The modern home is a storehouse of belongings. Yet storage encompasses so much more than what we display on shelves and what we choose to hide from view – loose change, post, information, rubbish all threaten to overwhelm our homes, cropping up in the least expected place. From the commercial cross-over of the shop rail to the anonymity of the simple stacking box, how and where you keep possessions in order can define the way you live to a far greater extent than any decorative choice.

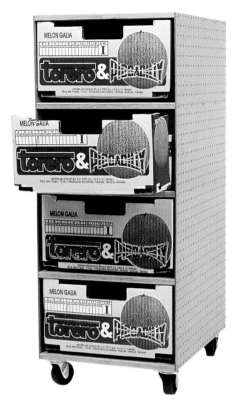

Michael Marriott, orange crate storage chest (1995)

Shop clothes rail in a domestic bathroom

Vernacular waste bin

Industrial waste bin

Noteboard

clothing

Clothing is our second skin, the face we put on for the world. Mainstream fashion is proverbially fickle, a playful means of reinvention and expressing *joie de vivre*. But ever since Chanel evoked the spirit of emancipated women with exquisite tailored suits and built an entire brand image around it, designers have sold a concept of lifestyle along with the clothes they produce. Turning this idea on its head, retailers such as Gap and Muji exploit the potential of function and simplicity to the full: genderless, classless plain clothes for modern tribes.

Clothes place people. Popular films such as *Working Girl* and *Trading Places* devote a great deal of screen-time to the comedy of dress code. When Melanie Griffiths hijacked her boss's job, she literally stepped into her shoes, and her dress. Eddie Murphy traded his trainers for brogues and his tracksuit for a Brooks Brothers suit.

Our familiarity with these subtle signals is born out of sheer exposure. It simply is not necessary to replace a toaster, car, kitchen or hi-fi every season. We do not regularly restock the contents of the linen cupboard; we make many purchases in the confident expectation that they should last, if not a lifetime, at least a decade. Clothes-buying is conducted in a different spirit and very much more frequently. Of course, some clothing is bought to last and some people only buy clothes to last. Most of us, however, buy clothes for no other reason than the fact that they are new.

If clothing touches us directly, in an immediate, physical way, fashion heightens many of the key issues of design. High art – couture – exists alongside mass market – the high street – each locked in a synergy of influence. Fashion is craft and industry, eccentric and mainstream, fickle and cyclic. It acts as a lightning conductor to the mood of the moment. Nothing dates faster, or comes around so often; and this is just what it is designed to do.

Fashion can be dismissed as just...fashion; fashion victims are scorned as the ultimate dupes of consumerism. Yet although we know we are being manipulated, most of us rather enjoy it. Fashion is, by definition, ephemeral, but it provides an irresistible way of participating in culture. Fashion provides work for designers, manufacturers and retailers, as well as many others in the complex and lengthy supply chain. Yet, for the consumer, above all else it is fun.

Fashion provides a snapshot of changing tastes and social values. There is something uncanny about the way styles of clothing mimic interior furnishing, and it is a synchronicity which has been going on a very long time. The Empire line was a silhouette for window drapery as well as Regency dresses; Victorian clothing and windows staggered under a weight of layers, trimmings, fringes and bows. In the early twentieth century, the rise and fall of

The couturier, Ungaro, surrounded by thumbnail sketches of designs and fabric swatches (1987).

hemlines tracked the graph of economic fortunes. The carefree emancipation of women in the 1920s is echoed in the boyish shifts and cropped hairstyles of the period; the exigencies of wartime are spelled out in the square shoulders and short skirts of a 1940s suit; the sexual revolution is explicit in the miniskirt.

In an industry which sells novelty, prediction is predictably big business. Forecasting agencies and exhibitions such as Premier Vision in France exist to spot trends of the future; analysts such as Dominique Peclair spend their entire time with their antennae tuned to the *Zeitgeist* trying to figure out where we are going next, in the same way as designers assemble 'mood boards' of cuttings to collect their ideas for the next look. There is commercial logic behind such analysis. Fashion depends on the textile industry, which needs decisions about colour, pattern and texture very early on in the manufacturing process, up to years ahead of the finished product arriving in the shop. Of course, it works the other way round, too. We can be persuaded into trends by manufacturers who already have a vested interest in selling them to us. But the stakes are always high; manufacturers can and do get it wrong from time to time and the effect can be disastrous.

Developments in textile technology and information-gathering have built in a degree of security. Garment dyeing, which allows clothing to be made in neutral shades and dyed to order, has decreased the time required for planning significantly. When cloth was dyed before it was made up into garments, retailers and manufacturers had to plan far in advance – and get it right. Now, with the adoption of EPOS (computerized terminals that record sales, allowing instant analysis of shopping patterns) a retailer can respond quickly to an emerging trend, and order an extra 10,000 dozen periwinkle blue shirts, for example, when the evidence shows this to be the fastest-moving colour.

The success of such retail chains as Gap owes much to their ability to react swiftly to demand. Such companies keep 747s lined up on the runways at Manila or Hong Kong, ready to jet off with the latest order. This strategy works particularly well where the basic design of clothes is classic or conservative and the main variable is colour. But even cut can be altered much more quickly these days with computer-aided design and robotic manufacturing, which also offer the potential for greater variety, since styles do not have to be made in such long runs.

At the same time, improved technology can actually work to decrease choice. Accurate analyses of trends can encourage buyers to play safe, selecting lines with a track record. With the market dominated by giants such as Marks and Spencer, what is original, new or risky can be squeezed out. Buyers for such mammoth chains wield huge powers: the dress buyer for Marks and Spencer,

for example, chooses one fifth of all dresses sold in Britain. To give some idea of the astronomical sums involved, a single bestselling item at M & S can earn the equivalent of the entire turnover of an average-sized company.

Ordinary clothes have probably never been better in terms of value for money, but quality can be achieved at the expense of flair and new designers can find it harder than ever to get a look in. We all need basics in the wardrobe, purchases which are largely made soberly, practically and conservatively. But life would be much greyer if fashion did not provide the opportunity to succumb to impulse. Diana Vreeland, the doyenne of fashion editors, once said, 'never fear the vulgar, only the boring'. The allure of the must-have item is what fashion is really all about.

Choosing clothes is one of the very first ways in which people learn to express themselves. The child who will not wear wool because it is too scratchy, or who becomes faddy about a particular colour, the teenager who dyes her hair purple and pierces her nose, and the advertising executive in head-to-toe Armani are all proclaiming something about themselves.

We take this freedom of expression for granted –and within the usual financial limits it is a freedom. But in previous centuries the scope for creating a personal image was fairly circumscribed and what clothing chiefly proclaimed was the status or caste of the individual. As far back as Ancient Egypt, there were strict codes in force. A slave or low-born person, for example, was not permitted to wear sandals.

Before the Industrial Revolution, clothing, like all products, was hand-made and there was a simple correlation between richness in dress and the wealth of the wearer. Those Elizabethan portraits of monarchs and courtiers show a confident display of finery, with doublets and bodices encrusted with seed pearls, embroidered with gold thread and fashioned so intricately that the hours of labour which had gone into their creation was made abundantly clear. Before the development of artificial dyes, bright colour was rare and expensive and only the rich could afford it. Such clothing was not comfortable or practical, but that was not its purpose. Wealthy women virtually imprisoned within their mammoth farthingales conspicuously depended upon a troop of servants to manage their daily lives.

By the end of the eighteenth century, France had established itself as the leading centre of fashion, a role which grew naturally out its pre-eminence in the field of textiles and upholstery. This supremacy was not overthrown by the coming of industrialization, and stylish late nineteenth-century women throughout Europe and the USA still instructed their dressmakers to copy the latest looks from French fashion plates. It may have been a Briton, Charles Worth, who founded the first couture house in 1857, but the House of Worth was nevertheless established in Paris, and the city remained at the vanguard of fashion for much of the century.

In the early days of couture, fashion was led by a handful of designers dressing an elite. Clothing styles in that sense trickled downwards through society, with the mass of the population adopting cheaper versions of what the rich could afford. People dressed aspirationally, and with a high degree of conformity. Paris would decree hems on the knee, and everyone would follow suit.

Conformity in matters of dress permeated all levels of society. When I began in business, City gentlemen adhered to a strict code which included that totemic symbol of Englishness, the bowler hat. As a young designer desperately seeking credit and credibility from establishment institutions, I dressed the part. I had my own bowler hat, dusted off and worn on the occasions when I visited the bank. I did not want to wear the hat, but I simply would not have been taken seriously otherwise.

When clothes bare all, there must be new ways to shock.

Coco Chanel was one of the first couturiers to broaden the scope of fashion design. Her breezy tailored suits, costume jewellery, bold accessories, and fresh modern fragrances were designed with emancipated working women in mind. The coherence of the total look was new and so was the concept of selling a lifestyle, or an image along with the clothes. In the process Chanel turned herself into one of the most instantly recognizable and most enduring brands in the fashion business.

Couture is regularly pronounced dead. It is true that the days of style dictats have gone and it is hard to imagine a modern designer creating the kind of uproar and hysteria that accompanied the launch of Christian Dior's New Look in 1948. Influences today are more often of the bottom-up rather than top-down variety. The ability to sniff the air and find style on the street is seen as the greatest proof of creativity.

In fact, there are pitfalls and misconceptions in either approach and the results can look equally ridiculous. A superbly tailored, hand-sewn article of clothing in the finest fabric simply cannot be copied successfully in the mainstream. Without the cut, the craft or the quality of cloth, the end product is bound to be cheap, and look it. Yet where style is supposed to filter up, the effect can be just as unsuccessful. Designers who quickly leapt to copy punk and produced couture versions of shredded and safety-pinned clothes (in exquisite hand-sewn detail) totally missed the point of this do-it-yourself style.

'The days of slavishly following fashion are over ... a woman knows all she needs is the right pair of trousers'
Joseph

Couture survives as an outpost of craft in an increasingly industrialized trade. There are still privileged clients who will pay for the exclusivity, cosseted service, superb fabric and sheer craftsmanship that couture houses can offer. Of these, craftsmanship and the quality of the material are probably the only ones for which it is worth paying. Clothes that are made to measure are the ultimate in individuality. Many great couturiers are first and foremost great tailors, knowing how to correct figure faults in the cut of a skirt or the set of an armhole, practised in the art of making the not-so-young shed years and the not-so-slim shed inches. The ever-pragmatic Jean Muir, whose impeccably finished clothing dressed the upmarket working woman, liked to point out that 'fashion' is a verb.

At the same time, couture survives as high art, an arena where designers constantly push back the boundaries of what wearable means. In the 1930s, Schiaparelli used her artistry to consternate and amuse, clashing shocking pinks and purples in the same outfit, or designing a hat in the form of a shoe. Artists themselves have participated in the medium. Schiaparelli commissioned Jean Cocteau and Salvador Dali to design fabrics for her clothes; Zika Ascher bought designs from Sonia Delaunay, Ben Nicholson and Henri Matisse. The work of fabric designers such as Mario Fortuny and Bernat Klein blurs the line between fashion and art.

Couture art, however, is never art merely for its own sake. Every season produces its own crop of outrageous statements on the catwalks of Paris, Milan, New York and London, clothing designed to create headlines, to photograph well and to spread the word of the designer's name. Then, in much-diluted form, versions of such designs quietly sell through the designer's diffusion lines, in the ready-to-wear collections and in the department store concessions. The most successful are quickly copied by mass-market retailers, eager for a slice of fashion's pie.

If Chanel was one of the first to realize the importance of branding in fashion design, Pierre Cardin invented the concept of licensing, applying the designer's name to a host of products only tangentially related to clothing. Every house now has its fragrance; many apply their names to both clothing and accessories not previously associated with the luxury end of the business. These are not mere sidelines, but in many instances have become hugely important commercially. Ralph Lauren started off designing and selling ties; now, however, his Home Collection brings in $500 million annually, out of a total turnover of $4.2 billion.

Versace's flamboyant designs dress the supermodels and the super-rich.

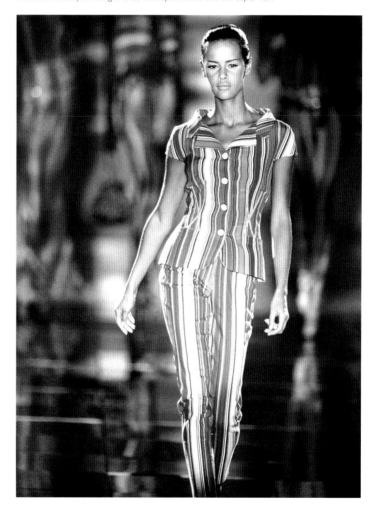

Designers in other creative fields are enlisted to produce an all-embracing image for fashion companies. High-profile architects and designers such as Nigel Coates, Eva Jiricna, Andrée Putman and John Pawson are commissioned to create exciting retail environments. When Nina Ricci launched a new line of cosmetics, the packaging was the work of celebrated designers Garouste and Bonetti, better known for their idiosyncratic furniture.

Fashion houses which diversify into furnishings sell one thing above all: the cachet of a name, label or brand. But there is a sting in the tail. Copies and forgeries of designer labels have relentlessly devalued the currency and this all-too-obvious hallmark of status has prompted those bent on exclusivity to look for other ways to express it. Labels may reassure those who are uncertain in matters of taste, but they can also force customers to ask awkward questions about real value.

Much of the pressure on couture has come from the progressive and relentless democracy of the market, a market which has increasingly found its inspirations away from court circles. Balenciaga is supposed to have abandoned couture because he believed there was no longer 'anyone' left to dress. When Clark Gable stripped off his shirt in *It Happened One Night* to reveal a bare chest, sale of men's vests across the United States plummeted overnight. Hollywood stars like Clara Bow and Greta Garbo provided the iconic faces for pre-war women and launched the modern cosmetic industry. Larger than life and ever present, cultural heroes and heroines provide a mirror for dressing up and self-invention. From the first personality models of the 1950s, through Twiggy and Jean Shrimpton, to the supermodels of today, popular images are created in the likeness of media stars rather than society beauties. Perhaps aspiration accounts for the bizarre rise in the sales of acne cream in the USA that followed the release of the action movie, *Speed*, starring Keanu Reeves.

The elegant, understated designs of Armani starred in a production of *Cosi Fan Tutte* (1995).

If the public draws inspiration from cinema and media personalities, many designers have found that by dressing the stars they can reach a wider audience than ever before. Audrey Hepburn regularly wore Givenchy on screen and off, as well as the scent, *l'Interdit*, which Givenchy created specially for her. The 40-year friendship and collaboration between actress and designer was a perfect style marriage. Nowadays, Oscar night is as much about clothes as it is about Academy Awards, with designers vying to dress nominees. Yet in some sense, everyone chooses clothes for the roles they will play. As Giorgio Armani, whose elegant fluid designs recently featured in a production of *Cosi Fan Tutte*, has remarked, 'Life is a movie and my clothes are the costumes.'

If fashion reveals social change, the development of clothing styles in the twentieth century tells us a lot about what we value. It is fair to say that clothing, for the most part, is far more comfortable today than it was a century ago. In the first instance, comfort means suitability and practicality. Women venturing out into public life in the early years of the century soon discovered that full-length skirts and constraining corsetry compromised their physical freedom. New lifestyles meant new clothing styles, new designs and new cuts. They also meant new materials. Artificial fibres, developed as an offshoot of the petrochemical industry, promised labour-saving maintenance in the form of crease-free clothes and drip-dry fabrics and were marketed heavily in the 1950s and '60s as a means of lightening the domestic load on the working woman.

Comfort also means fit. Technology has offered ways in which clothing can be made to fit the body, rather than the body being altered to fit clothing. Nylon, launched at the 1939 New York World's Fair, provided a clinging, seamless fit for stockings. Zippered fastenings allowed neat closures that followed the contours of the body. Lycra, the fibre which springs back into place after stretching, offers dependable shape, ideal for revealing modern bodies toned in the gym. The Japanese are experimenting with 'smart' fabric which 'remembers' the shape of your body. Other 'intelligent fabrics' developed in the context of aerospace or sport can change temperature as well as colour and texture.

Yet fit may not guarantee comfort. Nylon clothing fell rapidly from favour when it proved hot, static and sweaty to wear. Its recent rehabilitation was made possible by technological developments that permit the fabric to breathe. The sheer immutability of artificial fibres –the fact that clothing could be made permanently pleated, stain-resistant and easy-care – reacquainted us with the inherent beauty of those natural fabrics we had rushed to discard. Cotton, wool, linen and silk improve with use, acquiring a character and a comforting quality which is not merely physical.

More than anything, however, clothing creates image. And if people buy clothes as a way of expressing who they are and where they fit in the scheme of things, they also buy clothes in order to become someone else – or several someone elses. In the twentieth century, fashion has always greedily appropriated imagery from diverse walks of life. Everyone possesses items of clothing in their wardrobe which originated in highly specialized contexts.

The trenchcoat is one such item, on the one hand now so commonplace as to be practically invisible, on the other, replete with details and social signals that hint at its ancestry. The original design, by Thomas Burberry, addressed the need for an all-weather coat that allowed the body to breathe; when Burberry secured a contract to supply the British army in the First World War, the coat acquired its familiar military detailing of flaps, epaulettes, buckles and fastenings which provide the basis for its resonance today. Between the wars, every hero and anti-hero had a trenchcoat, a garment which did not so much keep out the rain as hint at the glorious or infamous exploits in the wearer's past. It marked him as a man of experience. Nowadays, the trenchcoat, in particular the Burberry, simply marks its wearer as British or wannabe British, a shift away from purely militaristic imagery in favour of a nostalgic sense of nationality. Ironically, and perhaps inevitably, the Burberry has now become the surest way of spotting a visitor to London trying to blend in.

Clothing and accessories which originated in the military come with their own in-built machismo. Few men today who wear fleece-lined leather jackets, carry Zippo lighters or sport aviator glasses have ever been near a cockpit, much less dropped bombs on an enemy target. In the same way, city kids wear hiking boots on the dancefloor, and tracksuits and trainers with no intention of doing anything more strenuous than lazing about.

Workwear, in particular, jeans, has offered great scope for image-making. Denim has an ancient history dating back to medieval times. Serge de Nîmes was a tough cotton twill worn by Italian and French workmen and also in use as tarpaulin. When Levi Strauss began his business in the second half of the nineteenth century, he attempted to sell a similar kind of denim canvas to the prospecting miners of the California gold rush as a tenting material. When the fabric did not prove strong enough for this application, he began selling it in the form of overalls and workpants. The rivetted seams which became a patented feature of Levi's design in 1873 were supposedly a response to the complaint that pockets tore when stuffed with ore samples. At 22 cents a pair, Levi pants were cheap, tough and durable. The brand patch introduced in 1886, which shows two horses trying to pull a pair of Levis apart, spelled out the message.

Today, more Levi 501s have been sold than any other item of clothing in the history of fashion. Jeans are ubiquitous, classless, sexless (though sometimes sexy), and ageless. According to a recent report, 80 per cent of all trousers sold in Australia are jeans; while 40 per cent of the population of Amsterdam wears jeans every day. How did a garment which began as the working wear of Californian gold prospectors become such a universal and indispensable part of the modern wardrobe?

Jeans remained purely workwear up until the early decades of this century, the practical outdoor clothing not only of miners, but also farmers and ranch-hands. But in the 1930s, America's love affair with the Wild West began in earnest. Cowboy movies introduced a bold new stereotype to the popular imagination. Every miniature John Wayne or Roy Rogers had his own cowboy outfit and a host of horseback heroes to emulate, first in the cinema and later on television, too.

If blue jeans symbolised the maverick all-American frontiersman, in the 1950s they provided the defining emblem for another kind of rugged individualist – the teenager. Wearing jeans became a proclamation of disaffection for middle-class rebels without a cause. Young people, who had previously dressed like small versions of their parents, increasingly had the spending power and the attitude to forge a conspicuous style of their own. It was only logical that in the 1960s a new generation of young people should find jeans the perfect embodiment of freedom from Establishment values and prevailing morals.

Today, jeans are big business. The image of the product is assiduously promoted through skilful advertising. The Levi's ad campaign, masterminded by John Hegarty of British agency Bartle Bogle Hegarty, plays up the cultural resonances by capturing a definitive mood. When Nick Kamen took off his Levi's in a launderette to Marvin Gaye's 'I Heard It Through The Grapevine', he became an instant star and the record became a bigger hit than it had been first time around and shot to number 1 in the charts. The ad became a kind of cultural marker in itself...and 800,000 pairs of classic 501s were sold.

The story of jeans, from specialized workwear to universal cultural reference point, could be told for many other items of clothing, if not quite so dramatically. The process by which an elitist or specific mode of dress becomes first hip or trendy and then one of the authentic wardrobe basics epitomizes the way fashion appropriates ideas from all walks of life. Fashions in footwear provide some memorable examples. Boots and shoes designed to be functional in particular contexts – such as Doc Marten's, Timberland boots and Nike trainers – have achieved a degree of universality. The late music-hall comedienne, Bea Lillie, used to close her act by performing a song in immaculate evening dress, convulsing audiences with laughter as she lifted her hem to reveal clumpy boots. Today, people would be more inclined to view this as a style in the making rather than an hilarious eccentricity.

Many fashionable crossovers began as a way of shocking other people, of rebelling or standing out from the crowd. In the end, however, conformity still wins through. We are no less inclined to blend in with the pack today than we ever were. One large Japanese fashion company decided to conduct a definitive survey of what the young were wearing in order to anticipate trends. Evidence gathered from university campuses all over the world failed to provide any sign of an emerging new trend. What they

'Only God helps the badly dressed' Spanish proverb

discovered was the boring reality that students largely dressed to look the same as other students in the same mundane combination of jeans, skirts, T-shirts and trainers.

In a neat inversion, big clothing retailers such as Gap market basic clothing as a means of expressing a confident individuality. Advertising campaigns featuring leading personalities wearing the simplest and least distinctive of clothes put across the message that wearing the same T-shirt as everyone else does not mean you have to blend in with the crowd.

In the end, however, buying a white T-shirt simply does not offer much in the way of a thrill. For most people, the appeal of fashion lies in the irresistible tug of the new. The problem is that, as the media bombard us with imagery and drain dry every source of influence in their quest for novelty, coming up with a new idea is increasingly difficult. With over 2,000 fashion writers and analysts attending the Paris shows, and immense press coverage for every tweaked detail, there is simply so much fashion about that it is harder than ever to tell what it is.

Fashion is in danger of becoming too fashionable. Designers ransack the past for inspiration, and styles which have barely left the shops are reintroduced before they have had time for a decent burial. One month women are urged to dress as if they still carried ration cards; the next month the Carnaby Street of the 1960s is sartorial memory lane. These whistle-stop tours of the recent past, and the acreage of comment and imagery which accompany them, are enough to make even the most ardent shopaholic feel jaded.

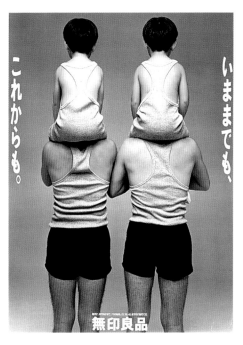

Back to the basic wardrobe: simple shapes, natural materials and neutral colours from Muji.

The 1960s, the source, yet again, of one of the latest fashion reincarnations, established Britain as a fashion leader for the first time. There was a spirit of freshness, vitality and innovation as young designers, pouring out of art schools, revolutionized every aspect of retailing. New looks left the drawing board and a few days later sold out in the boutiques. Gone, in an instant, were the orderly seasonal cycles and the traditional distinctions between day and evening wear, formal and casual. The new consumers of fashion were overwhelmingly young. A Quant miniskirt or a Biba boa was the exact equivalent of listening to the latest Stones record or buying your wok at Habitat.

The sheer energy of that time was breathtaking, yet revivals of 1960s styles only highlight the contrast between then and now. The Royal College of Art opened its fashion department in 1948,

Roger Vivier for Dior, platform sandal (1937).

and by the mid-to-late Fifties it had found its feet and, with them, an irrepressible confidence. Carnaby Street and the King's Road provided the crucible for young talent to express itself. Bursting out of the stuffy conformity of the 1950s, Britain forged a style of its own as the most creative place for all the arts. So what happened, and where did we go wrong?

In fashion design, as in other arenas, ideas are simply not enough. The infrastructure must also be in place to support innovation. Years of under-investment and high labour costs mean few factories now exist in Britain which can produce high-quality goods at a reasonable, competitive cost. Young designers in a variety of disciplines are forced to work abroad or seek foreign sponsorship. Instead of regarding design as a regenerative force, successive governments in this country have severely underfunded it. In Britain, the arts as a whole receive something like £1 billion in government grants; design a paltry £2.4 million. Sales of designer clothes are the lowest in Europe, yet the Department of Trade and Industry only supports the British Fashion Council's awards with a risible £30,000. 'The Design Factor' – a report produced in the early 1980s by financial analysts, Scrimenger Kemp Gee – gathered persuasive evidence that companies who used design intelligently consistently performed better, but such analysis is studiously ignored by the majority.

In France, by contrast, every President since De Gaulle has conspicuously supported design, as a tribute to the creativity of the country and in a spirit of progress and modernity. The French fashion industry earns £1.4 billion a year; the Italian £1.9 billion. Britain, which gave the world Savile Row and Jermyn Street, now imports 60 per cent of its suits. We, too, should be able to nurture our homegrown talent, in fashion as well as other spheres of design. We have an abundance of talent matched only by the general failure to make any use of it.

The lingering British suspicion of design may stem from a natural and ingrained philistinism that ranks the visual as low in importance. The same people who would never dream of reading a junk novel, drinking single malt from a wine glass or sullying their palate with a microwaved frozen dinner appear happy enough to stroll through life in dreary clothing and affect total indifference to their immediate surroundings at home and at work. I do not believe for a moment that design is purely about the visual, but neither do I think the visual is unimportant.

I care about what I wear, and I respond to what others wear. A suit that is well cut is comfortable, both physically and aesthetically; when the shape of clothing is right, the effect is sculptural and pleasing, and it feels good stepping in to the clothes in the morning. Accommodating the human body and all its movements and postures in cloth is a considerable challenge and one worthy of recognition and applause. My own taste in clothes is not particularly dramatic or controversial. Long ago, I knew the colours I was happy to live with … and I have been wearing a lot of blue ever since. And I have been unable to shake off my austere upbringing sufficiently readily to discard what I like, preferring good shoes that can be resoled and tolerating the odd frayed cuff on a favourite shirt rather than to subscribe to more disposable styles. But I cannot conceive of being indifferent to colours, shapes or patterns, the nap of a fabric or the way it is cut.

Inevitably, clothing is all about attraction. I cannot help but feel that those with the self-confidence and flair to dress well are worth getting to know better. This is not to say that all interesting people dress well, merely that those who do at least realize that well-designed clothes are part of the fun of living. Since fashion reflects and encapsulates so much of cultural life, I would say that a society that values the way it looks is more likely to value the role of design as a whole and to enjoy a better quality of life.

Chalkstripe suit and charcoal waistcoat by Kenzo (Fall/Winter 1993).

Indian sari

Fitting clothes to the body has often meant fitting the body to clothing, a task which may be achieved by corsetry, figure-hugging Lycra or rib-stitch jersey. Fit also entails a means of closure: the zip has superseded hooks and eyes or buttoned seams, while poppers (or Velcro) provide a practical fastening for that second skin, the babygro. But the notion of fit is turned on its head by the 2,000 year-old, one-size-fits-all sari: six yards of fabric, tucked, draped and folded.

Babygro

Mainbocher corset, Paris, photograph by Horst P. Horst (1939)

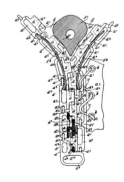

Slide fastener (early zip) patented by Whitcomb Judson (1896)

Georgia Graves swimwear by Lelong, Paris, photograph by George Hoynigen-Huene (1929)

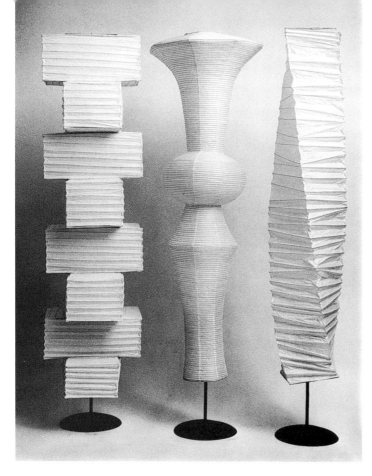

Isamu Noguchi, L10, E and J1 paper lampshades (1950s)

'I myself am for the bodily mechanical, the mathematical dance.' Painter and sculptor Oskar Schlemmer, who taught at the Bauhaus between 1920 and 1929, placed the proportions and measurements of the human body at the centre of design, deriving basic geometric forms from the swing of limbs or the angles of joints, principles embodied in the costumes of his 'comic-grotesque' Triadic Ballet. He believed that artists should be inspired by such products of new technology as artificial limbs or divers' suits to create a powerful new imagery free from reference to past styles. A similar playfulness is evident in the designs of Issey Miyake, designer of the ultimate wearable art, whose work reminds me of the springy organic shapes of Noguchi lights. Miyake uses cloth like a sculptor, bending, creasing and twisting it into strange mobile forms.

Oskar Schlemmer, costumes for the Triadic Ballet (1926)

Issey Miyake, Colourful Flying Saucer dress (Spring/Summer 1994),
photograph by Irving Penn

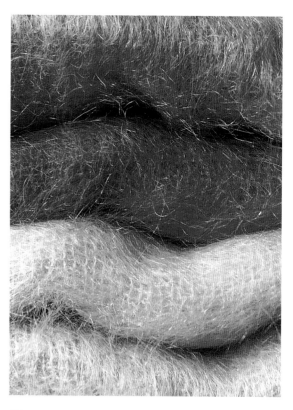

Mohair sweaters

In fashion, a high degree of discomfort is sometimes endured for the sake of style. Yet the most cherished items in the wardrobe are often those that offer comfort from the inside out, that caress the skin or follow the movements of the body (what is known in couture as 'flou'). Comfort in clothing starts from the material quality of the fabric itself. Natural fabrics improve with age, wear and washing. Denim wears into a fashionably distressed silky smoothness – and in the process offers another type of comfort, the rightness of an old favourite.

Levi Strauss & Co., 501 denim jeans

Cashmere and wool overcoat

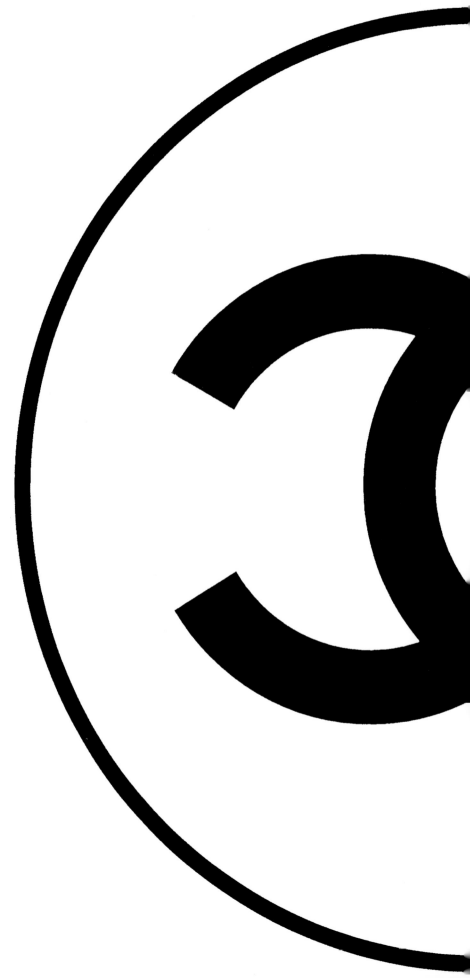

Chanel suit photographed for British *Vogue* (April 1961)

'For a woman who tried to create a revolution in the beginning, she later became the most classic person in the world'

Karl Lagerfeld on Coco Chanel

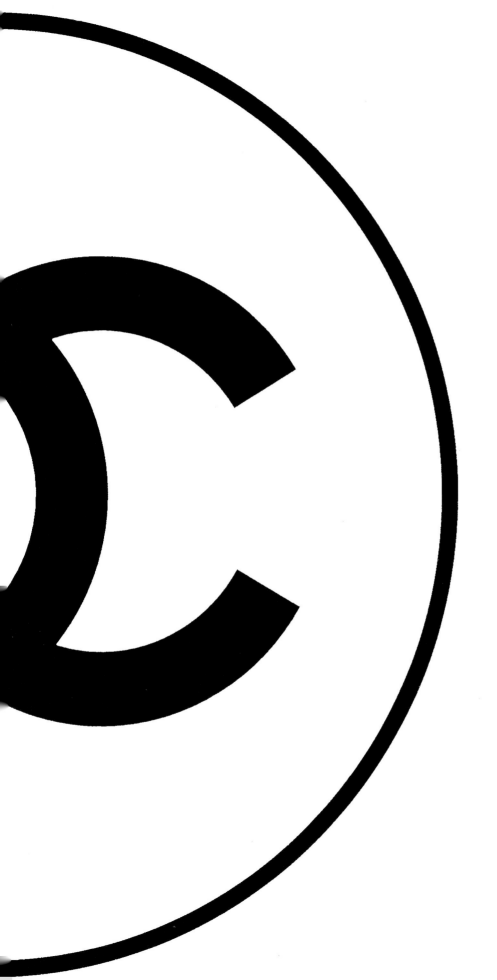

The Chanel atelier, Paris (1983)

Coco Chanel, photograph by Cecil Beaton (1956)

Espadrille shop

Ralph Lauren store, New York

Galeries Lafayette, Paris (architects:
George Chedanne and Ferdinand
Chanut, 1906-1912)

Jill Sander shop display (architects: Michael Gabellini & Associates)

Ever since the first department stores appeared in the mid-nineteenth century, leading architects and designers have been commissioned to create theatres of consumption. Retail design is now an important means of turning retailers into brand names. Nigel Coates' design for Jigsaw, the shop windows presenting a glittering stage set, addresses one kind of consumer; the traditional look of Ralph Lauren stores addresses another; while sheer luxury may be expressed by pristine pure space.

Jigsaw, Knightsbridge, London (architect: Nigel Coates, 1991)

The catwalk is the hub of a media circus which translates the theatre of high style into the glossy fashion spread. Wearability is not the point of Vivienne Westwood's platform shoes. Instead, the whole purpose is to create an irresistible buzz. A key part of this process is the fashion magazine. Fabien Baron's work for *Harper's Bazaar* is among the most original in its field, elegant, modern and innovative graphics as distinctive as the fashion they feature. Promotion of a different kind can be seen in the Benetton campaign, which builds awareness of a global brand through association with powerful universal themes and images.

Benetton advertisement, art direction by Oliviero Toscani (1991)

Vivienne Westwood, platform shoes worn by Naomi Campbell, Paris (1993)

The right shoe

This season, it's probably a finely made mule, or something fantastically delicate and strappy. Either way, a step onward from platforms... Opposite page: Camel suede wood-heel platform with woven fringe detail, about $315, by Michel Perry. Assorted eggs by Ted Muehling NYC, Madeline, and Reed Karen of Sipher Works, Inc. Photographed by Raymond Meier

'Fashion gives pleasure because it is so arbitrary, and pleasure is the one product always worth buying' Adam Gopnik, *The New Yorker*

Harper's Bazaar, 'The right shoe' fashion feature, art direction by Fabien Baron, photograph by Raymond Meier (February 1995)

Patrick Cox and shoes (1995)

Keith Haring, 'Modèle avec Personnages' Swatch watch (1986)

Cult purchases, such as Patrick Cox's Wannabe loafers, are the membership badge for those in the know. This comfortable, well-made shoe, with its classic shape, unisex appeal, and a name which satirizes the label-conscious, caused such demand that Cox's Chelsea shop employed a bouncer. If the Wannabe has made it desirable to spend more on shoes, Swatch has made it acceptable to spend less on watches. The company's success revived an ailing Swiss industry almost entirely through design. Brilliant graphics and bright, fashionable colours make cheap, disposable watches attractive and collectable. Equally collectable are artist-designed textiles, such as the scarves commissioned by Zika Ascher.

CLOTHING

112

Ben Nicholson, 'Moonlight' silk scarf for Ascher (London) Limited (1947)

Argentinian soccer fans, Buenos Aires (1990)

Every year in Britain alone, £126 million is spent on little tubes of coloured wax and oil. Lipstick is just the tip of the beauty industry, a business built on humble ingredients, a little scientific mystique and sheer allure. Ever since early screen stars such as Louise Brooks and Clara Bow gave women icons to aspire to, make-up has gradually shed its Victorian association with loose morals to become part of the working wardrobe. Like the wardrobe, fashions in make-up change with the seasons. Colours are subject to intensive market research; equally critical is the design of cosmetic packaging. What Helena Rubenstein called the 'click factor' sums up the almost indefinable sense of quality that luxurious packaging gives to what is essentially a little coloured powder or grease.

Make-up is used to confer identity – allegiance to a football team – but equally to blur gender – whether it's a kabuki actor preparing for a female role or a drag artist walking the wild side. Face or body paint has been the symbol of tribal allegiance, combat readiness, caste or mysticism; on the whole, however, it is more likely an index of fashionability as well as one of the most immediate ways of creating self-image.

CLOTHING

114

Lip Streaks, photograph by Melvin Sokolsky (1967)

Kabuki actor, Japan

glamour *n*., & *v.t.* **1**. *n.* magic, enchantment, (cast a ~ over, enchant); delusive or alluring beauty or charm; physical attractiveness (~ girl, young woman possessing this; so ~ boy); hence glamorous *a.* **2**. *v.t.* affect with glamour, bewitch, enchant.

The Concise Oxford Dictionary

Lipstick on fork, photograph by Raymond Meier for British *Vogue* (September 1995)

Paris, photograph by Helmut Newton (1978)

Vivienne Westwood, photograph by Michael Roberts (1987)

Brighton football supporters, Hove, Sussex (1911)

René Magritte, *Golconde* (1953)

Vivienne Westwood, catwalk model (1995)

'I am never happier than when I'm parodying the English'

Vivienne Westwood

Dress codes may have relaxed since the days when every British businessman wore a bowler hat and carried a tightly furled umbrella, but self-expression still tends to come second to convention when it comes to clothing. Most of us prefer to blend with the crowd.

Designers such as Vivienne Westwood put the case for individuality very forcefully. From bondage-wear to bustles, mini-crinolines to crowns, Westwood has revelled in a capacity to shock and provoke. Inspired by fine art and literature as well as historical costume, her irreverent designs transform ideas rather than merely recycle them.

CLOTHING

119

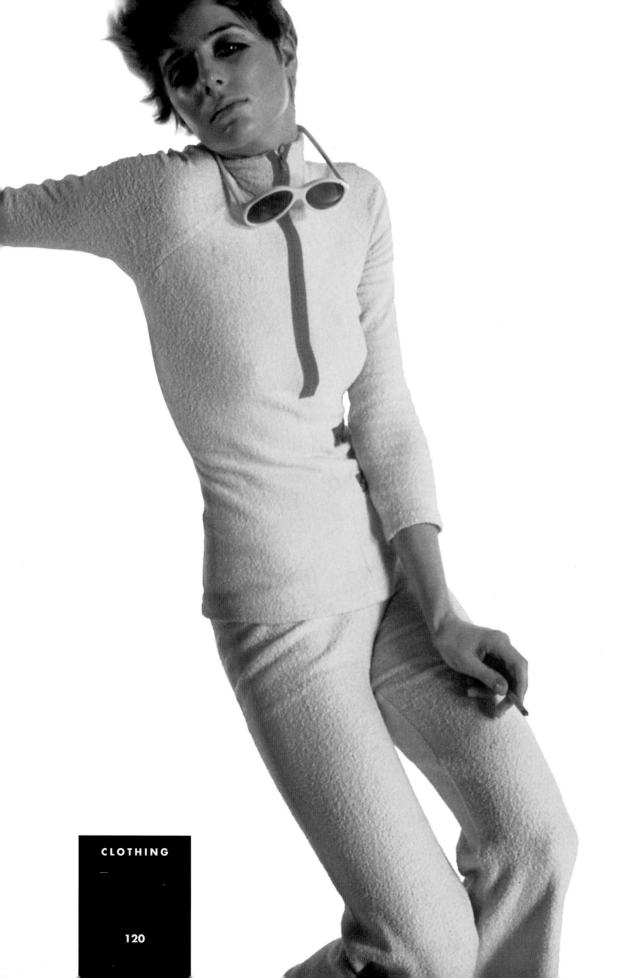

Photograph for British *Vogue*
by Lester Bookbinder (April 1967)

Voracious in the extreme, fashion is always plundering its own past for ideas and images. What goes around comes around in ever-decreasing circles, and to a remarkably similar soundtrack, as the current Sixties revival in fashion and pop music demonstrates.

Photograph for W by
Raymond Meier (July 1995)

Leather crash helmet by Holdsworthy, £2 6s. T-shirt by Ampro Sports, 11s 6d. Basketball shoes by Lonsdale Sports, £1 1s 6d.
Crash helmet by Holdsworth, £1 12s 6d. Nylon racing vest by Holdsworth, £3 10s. Boxing boots by Lonsdale Sports £2 7s 6d. Vinyl crash helmet by Holdsworth, £1 12s 6d.
Woollen leg warmers by Holdsworthy, £1 5s 9d a pair. Track shoes by Lonsdale Sports, £3 7s 6d. Crash helmet by Holdsworthy, £2 6s.
T-shirt by Ampro Sports, 10s 6d. Leather boxing boots by Lonsdale Sports, £3 10s.

Embroidered racing vests
hats all by Condor Cycle

American sportswear, photograph by Harri Peccinotti for *Nova* (August 1966)

Blast furnace workers, Nissan Seiko steel works, Japan (1987)

Lacoste logo

Sportswear has been one of the most powerful influences on mainstream fashion this century, from the universally classic Lacoste polo shirt to the covetable pair of box-fresh trainers. In the late 1940s American designer Claire McCardell pioneered the use of traditional sports fabrics in fashion; every decade sees the trend accelerating. Lycra cycling shorts, Polartec fleeces, ski parkas, leg warmers, rugby shirts, hiking boots and baseball caps are just a few in a long list of high-performance or professional clothes increasingly worn by rather more sedentary people. The same process has occurred with tough workwear, such as boiler suits and dungarees, as well as a whole range of military gear, from the trenchcoat to the flying jacket. There are many good practical reasons for the appeal of such clothing: it's practical, comfortable, and often makes excellent use of innovative materials. But the strongest attraction must be image: the prowess of the Olympic champion, the machismo of the blue-collar worker or the glamour of the combat pilot is implicit in their uniforms.

Rayban Aviator sunglasses worn by Tom Cruise in *Top Gun* (1986)

'War makes fashions'

Gertrude Stein

The design of hats and shoes share a great sculptural potential, a point once succinctly and wittily made by Schiaparelli's shoe hat. Shoes, however, must to some extent be functional, which imposes an element of constraint on form. For hats, the sky is the limit.

There's nothing new about theatrical head-dresses. Seventeenth-century court ladies displayed towering, elaborate creations perched on their wigs, such as miniature ships in full sail. Edwardian hats were broad and intricately trimmed, the complement to the hour-glass silhouette.

Until the later decades of this century, the hat was an important element of the social dress code. No respectable man or woman felt properly dressed without one. Today, weddings and grand events of the social calendar are the only occasions when this type of etiquette is even vaguely observed, but hats remain a persuasive argument in favour of the case that fashion should be fun.

Stephen Jones, a graduate of St Martin's School of Art, is renowned for his exotic creations. His early designs found favour with New Romantics; since then, the list of designers with whom he has collaborated reads like a roll-call of the world of couture. This graphic, striped hat, with its hint of Fifties glamour, expresses his view that even if a hat is grand, it should be 'clean and optimistic'.

Stephen Jones, Vertical Hold hat (1995), photograph by Gavin Bond

food

As any street trader knows, the first taste is with the eyes. The presentation of food – on grocery shelf, market stall or in a photograph – is part of the sensual enjoyment of eating itself. The eye connects very quickly to the brain, which activates the gastric juices.

What has design got to do with food? The answer is a great deal. From the label on the jar to the layout of a restaurant to the presentation of food on the plate, design plays a key role in this seemingly most direct of activities. There is nothing accidental about the buzz of pleasure in a good restaurant, the tempting array of bottles, packages and tins in a speciality food store, the voluptuous displays of fruit and vegetables in a market or the brand loyalty of supermarket shoppers.

Put to the right uses, design is an important means of broadening culinary horizons and enhancing the pleasure of shopping, cooking, eating out or eating in. Put to the wrong uses, design can allow technology to triumph over flavour and wholesomeness, can replace the warmth and conviviality of mealtimes with a packaged experience, can widen choice to the point of meaninglessness.

In its broadest sense, design has always been part of the enjoyment of food: a recipe, for instance, is a design of a sort. Even the open-air market displays plenty of design thinking. The good market trader is a natural designer, exciting appetite through the visual and olfactory appeal of the produce on sale. Superficially, the massing of colours, shapes and aromas is the sole means of persuasion – apart from price. But every clever trader has an instinctive appreciation of the power of adjacency, what to place next to what to tempt the browser.

I can think of few more pleasurable shopping experiences than a visit to a rural food market, particularly of the kind common in small towns near my house in France. The farm eggs nestling in straw-lined baskets, the hanging bunches of dried herbs, the neat handwritten signboards and the pungent scents wafting in the air invite discriminating inspection and appreciation, and promise real enjoyment to come. In such surroundings it is possible to believe one might live to eat, rather than merely eat to live.

It is all a far cry from the out-of-town supermarket, where the majority of people in industrialized areas of the world increasingly shop. In place of the bustling market square at the heart of a town, there is a giant warehouse plonked down in an ocean of asphalt, a warehouse superficially styled in some coy vernacular hand-me-down like an overgrown tithe barn or gargantuan half-timbered cottage. In place of a casual gossipy stroll among stalls, there is the visual assault of thousands of brands, graphically offensive packages and superfluous products, each vying for the

A floating market in Thailand: tempting aromas, colours and shapes make shopping a pleasure.

split-second attention of the bemused consumer. Instead of the familiar faces of stall-holders, there is the bland anonymity of the aisle, the indifference of the checkout. Lighting is even-toned and flat, temperature is controlled and smells, if there are any, are extracted away or artificially enhanced to stimulate spending.

According to a recent study, the amount of time Americans spend cooking at home has dropped from three and a half hours per day in the late 1970s to 30 minutes in the 1990s. The supermarket, that temple of convenience, would seem to be encouraging us to eat to live. This is not surprising, since the true purpose of the supermarket is not to inspire us to cook, but to inspire us to spend.

Although the supermarket made its first appearance in 1916, when Clarence Saunders opened the first 'Piggly Wiggly' in Memphis, Tennessee, it was not until after the Second World War that the supermarket boom began in earnest. Today, three quarters of Britain's food is bought in supermarkets, and it is estimated that roughly half of the purchases, both of food and household goods, made in these giant stores are not planned or intended. In a relatively short space of time, food production and consumption have altered immeasurably. Design has played a key role – sometimes beneficially, sometimes ignobly – in this modern revolution.

Supermarkets and hypermarkets are blamed for many things, from the environmental damage caused by agri-business to the moribund state of the high street. But it is important to remember the reasons why this new type of shopping evolved in the first place. The old high street of greengrocer, butcher, fishmonger and baker, the focus for so much nostalgia, had its own drawbacks and disadvantages. Service was personal; many shopkeepers greeted their customers by name, offered credit or sold goods loose in quantities as small or as large as required. But service could also be painfully slow; collecting the ingredients for a single meal could mean a visit to two or three shops and a wait in each one as the

'The fate of nations depends on the way they eat' Brillat Savarin

Designed to be different: pasta shapes display variations on a basic culinary theme.

shop assistant filled the order from stock. Quality and standards of hygiene varied widely and much fresh food was displayed unrefrigerated and uncovered. It was by no means unusual for flyblown meat to be recycled as sausages, or for goods to be short-weighed, or for rotten vegetables to slip into the string bag. Choice was often limited and when stock ran out, the customer did without.

Supermarkets offered high-street shoppers a brave new world of convenience, choice and economy. The convenience of the single weekly excursion was made possible by other conveniences – the family car which allowed a weeks' worth of groceries to be transported and the fridge or freezer which allowed it to be stored. The breadth of choice – a modern superstore stocks between 15,000 and 30,000 product lines – went hand in hand with the proliferation of brands. And the sheer scale and competitiveness of the enterprise kept prices keen.

Self-service is central to the notion of supermarket shopping. Without clerks to retrieve, weigh out or package goods, the customer meets the product head on. Supermarkets are essentially warehouses full of over-designed packages, each competing for attention. The information conveyed by packaging, both literally and symbolically, may be the only means of guiding our selection. The supermarket shelf has been called the most valuable real estate in the world; anything which fails to earn its keep is de-listed to make way for something that will. More often than not, it may be the packaging or presentation of the product which proves unsuccessful, rather than the product itself, although in many cases, it is increasingly difficult to say whether there is anything more to the product than its packaging.

Packaging is a study in itself. It has become one of the most common ways in which we consume design; naturally enough, it arouses some of the fiercest loyalties and deepest antipathies of all. The packaging of that universal food, milk, is a case in point. The traditional glass milk bottle is one of the most satisfying of all ordinary food packages and the most deeply loved. The cosy, organic shape still features in milk advertisements, evoking the secure world of doorstep deliveries. But the milk bottle has largely been superseded by plastic containers and cardboard packs; the morning milk round by the supermarket purchase. Nowadays, British milk is commonly sold in Tetrapak cardboard containers, first launched in the mid-1970s by the Swedish packaging company Tetra-Laval. From the point of view of the milk producers and distributors, box cartons are easier to pack in bulk than bottles, and require no subsequent collection and redistribution. From the point of view of the consumer, those irritating pour spouts almost never work satisfactorily and have become such a byword for domestic fury and frustration that Tetra-Laval have spent the past 13 years researching alternatives.

Packaging, of course, has many purely practical roles to fulfil. In the absence of a shop clerk or stall-holder, a package provides a ready-weighed and measured amount of a product in an easily transportable form. It protects its contents from deterioration and promises the consumer purity and freshness, as well as uniformity and predictability. It allows food to be produced, distributed and stored on a massive scale.

Occasionally the practical requirements of packaging inspire a solution which is brilliant aesthetically, too. The Ty Nânt water bottle is one such example. At an early stage of the design, it was discovered that if the bottle was dropped, it would shatter and blow up due to its gaseous contents, so a plastic film was adopted as a protective covering for the glass. Then it was realized that there was no reason why this film covering could be not be coloured and the result was the distinctive blue bottle which is wonderfully evocative of the thirst-quenching and pure qualities of the product. The company has now, no doubt for reasons of economy, turned to production of bottles in blue glass, without the protective film. Profit margins nearly always seem to rule.

Above and beyond its practical role, packaging provides a vehicle for messages, some of which are required by law, others there simply to consolidate brand image and associations. Everything from nutritional breakdowns, recipe suggestions and calorie counts to the bar code or the price is carefully positioned. These messages, however informative or reassuring to the consumer, are ultimately subservient to the one essential communication – the branding of the product. A vast amount of market research lies behind every brand name, label or image, research to determine the colours, graphics, phrases or symbols most likely to appeal to the target consumer. In many cases, these elements play on subconscious associations – white and blue with hygiene and domestic purity, for example, forward-slanting, razor-sharp graphics with energy, forcefulness and power, arcane typefaces with cosy and traditional virtues. In other cases, the success or failure of a product can hinge simply on a name. When Marks and Spencer, for example, relaunched their fresh vichysoisse soup as 'leek and potato', sales improved dramatically.

Whether we recognize them or not, the subconscious messages of packaging can be very compelling. Following the benzene scare in 1990, the Perrier bottle was redesigned in a smaller format, with the contents reduced from one litre to 75 centilitres. Some commentators suggested that the shrinking bottle was intended to suggest that 'something' had physically been removed. Sales slumped, none the less, and only slowly recovered, partly, I believe, because the generosity of a litre had been taken away.

All this is very entertaining for design theorists and commentators, but I strongly believe the basics of the store cupboard should be packaged as honestly and simply as possible. While I am occasionally beguiled by a label or tempted by a beautiful tin or jar, I find most food packaging overwhelms the product it contains and provokes an in-built sense of disappointment. One of the early commissions received by the Conran Design Group was to devise a packaging style for a range of ordinary foodstuffs produced by International Stores. Those were the days before own-branding was commonplace and our designs – which featured simple, stencilled lettering on a plain background – shone out from the rather hectically branded merchandise with which they were in competition. Utilitarian and straightforward, these designs would have lost their impact grouped together, but set alongside their rivals they looked refreshing, new and honest.

Own-branding these days generally adopts a rather different strategy. Modern supermarket brands are packaged to mimic brand leaders in a game of spot-the-difference. These subtle near-copies of logos, colours and graphics tiptoe just this side of litigation to reassure the customer that he or she is getting exactly the same product, but slightly cheaper. The furore that ensues when own-brand design strays a little too far into the domain of a well-established brand is proof of the perceived importance of image in the creation of a successful product.

There are those who believe that the days of the own-brand are numbered. But supermarkets, which house so many individual brands, still devote much energy and investment to creating a brand identity for themselves. In fact, these days, supermarkets are becoming more powerful brands than any of the products that they sell. They have realized that they can have two bites at the cherry, that 'their' brands can become the premium brands, alongside their low-price, lookalike products that 'knock off' the leading

This Prunier poster promises freshness and gastronomic pleasure.

During the early 1980s the Conran Design Group was commissioned by the Peter Dominic chain of wine merchants to review their company image. At that time the company consisted of many different outlets, with a considerable degree of entrepreneurialism at the shop level, where display staff and store managers were encouraged to contribute their own ideas on presentation and signage. Some of these displays were very good, others really awful. The intention was to improve the overall presentation without sacrificing the personal element which, when it worked, was very appealing. Accordingly, the manual took the form of a design guide, with examples of good display graphically contrasted with those which did not work. We called the guide, 'Do It Right', and the brief was to make it populist, gutsy and continental – appealing to both the duchess and her chauffeur.

Like the waxed-cardboard milk carton, packaging which cannot be accessed obviously provokes disappointment at the point of delivery. There are other ways in which packaging can let the consumer down. Many products are almost all package, or simply would not have existed without being packaged. This interface between food and technology has resulted in spurious products where nutritional content, flavour and value have been all but sacrificed in favour of convenience, image and brand. 'Convenience' or 'fast' foods sell as technology first, food a very poor second. Many require little or no intervention on the part of the consumer, beyond defrosting, reheating or serving. Some products have been designed to retain some vague element of cooking to lend authenticity to the result. On the advice of a psychologist, early cake mixes, for example, were deliberately manufactured so that one had to add an egg to the mixture to make it up, a largely symbolic gesture which retained a hint of wholesome home-baking in an otherwise wholly synthetic process.

brands they used to sell. As in any other field of business, a corporate or brand identity can have as great an impact within a company as it does on the public at large. Changing a company's identity – its logo, colours or typeface – may seem a cosmetic change, but a new 'face' can be a powerful rallying point for those working within the organization, pulling together the efforts of different disciplines or departments and generating an important sense of belonging. It can also help to clarify management structures and relationships.

Convenience foods, particularly ready meals, are big business. In Britain, we spend £300 million a year on them, £4 million alone on Marks and Spencer's Chicken Kiev. This is designed food, food which has been selected, taste-tested, manufactured, branded and marketed. It has no real antecedents, being no more authentically French or Italian or Russian than chop suey is authentically Chinese. I would say that the role of design in the creation of such products is not a cause for rejoicing – far from it. No ready meal can ever be a substitute for fresh ingredients cooked with care, passion and enthusiasm.

If the supermarket is a warehouse for packages, shopping has become an increasingly packaged experience. The trolley or shopping cart is in itself a type of package. The first trolley made its appearance in 1937, designed and manufactured by the American company Unarco. A certain amount of persuasion was necessary to encourage people to abandon their wicker or wire baskets in favour of the new mobile cart; its resemblance to a pram was said to deter men in particular from pushing it.

The post-war trolley had a capacity of about 40 litres; today's versions hold a back-breaking four and half times as much. Naturally enough, supermarkets soon found that the bigger the trolley, the more groceries they sold. Today, trolleys specifically incorporate the 'pram' element, with numerous combinations of child, toddler and baby seats integrated within the design. A new design, the Easisteer trolley by John Grantham, a former helicopter pilot, addresses the vexed problem of the trolley with a mind of its own. His design incorporates a linking mechanism which keeps both of the front wheels moving in the same direction.

The trolley is not the only means of creating movement throughout a store. The design and layout of a supermarket is devised to provide a smooth flow from entrance to checkout. It is standard practice, for example, to place fresh fruit and vegetable

How to market a world brand – with the aid of cult designer David Carson.

Supermarkets offer the customer a breadth of choice which is exhaustive – and exhausting.

displays by the main entrance. I have had numerous emotive discussions with directors of supermarket chains, trying to persuade them that such an arrangement has little to do with the logic of cooking. Most experienced cooks would find it more useful to shop for basics and staples first before selecting the seasonal or fresh items. Of course, the decision to place greengrocery at the entrance to the store is not made with the cook in mind, but reflects the way such displays function as a shop window, a 'feel-good' factor luring customers on down the aisles. Even the earliest supermarkets featured impulse items, such as confectionery, displayed near the checkout, where customers would have time to be tempted by them. The psychology of supermarket layout dictates that the premium or highest-earning site for products is on the left side of the aisle, between waist and eye level. Contrary to popular belief, supermarkets don't actually like moving merchandise around very much; the aim is to get everyone moving around the store in a predicable path, making as many purchases as possible in as little time as possible.

One might think that fresh food should be immune from such considerations. This is very far from the case; indeed, many people have never experienced really fresh food, direct from the vegetable plot. A friend of mine was so obsessed with the fugitive flavour of asparagus – a vegetable, he maintained, that lost its unique flavour more quickly than any other – that, come dinner time, he could be found racing out to the vegetable garden, with a pot of boiling water on a primus stove into which he would throw asparagus shoots newly cut from the bed. With supermarket sales largely reliant on appearance and presentation, it is small wonder that we expect tomatoes to be perfectly formed and evenly red, cucumbers to be straight, potatoes to be cleansed of any clinging soil. Needless to say, such standardized perfection is often achieved at the expense of flavour and true variety. It is far from unusual to find tomatoes marketed as 'specially grown for flavour' alongside other varieties, grown, one might ask, for what – shelf appeal? In the USA, supermarket 'butchers' in white aprons without a trace of blood package fresh meat so that it gives as few clues as possible to its animal origins – though, perhaps, given factory farming methods, this is not so surprising after all.

Convenience in the context of fresh food means year-round availability, an eternal supermarket summertime. It would be difficult indeed to guess the time of year from a supermarket's stock of food alone. Seasonality is more likely to be conveyed in holiday promotions and ancillary goods, such as charcoal for barbecues and Christmas decorations, than in the type of food available. Technology has a way of bringing us full circle. Computerization has the potential to revolutionize food shopping once more; in some areas of the United States, it is far from uncommon for the weekly provisions to be ordered up on the home computer terminal and delivered to the door. If such a system were to catch on, the implications for the role of design in food would be tremendous.

FOOD

The supermarket would be reduced to a genuine warehouse; the 'virtual' supermarket heavily dependant on visual presentation flickering across the screen. The consumer would gain push-button convenience, roads would become less congested, but the result would be an even greater distancing from the tangible qualities of food itself. How many young adults even know how to determine the ripeness of a melon? Supermarkets are already using their 'club cards' to build huge databases of customer spending habits; with such information at their disposal our diets could become even more predictable and standardized by age group, family profile and income bracket. As a consequence, life – and especially our diet – would become much, much duller.

In such a context, it is easy to imagine the renaissance of the high-street shop and the speciality food store, perhaps not for the bulk of household necessities, but certainly for the purchase of fresh, seasonal food. Food shopping should be an enjoyable and sensual extension of cooking and eating. The sensory deprivation of virtual shopping may well send us back to the corner grocery with its human contact, evocative smells and good things to eat.

A great deal of design thinking in the supermarket is devoted to making food shopping more convenient and hence cost-effective and profitable – convenient, that is, for the food manufacturer, distributor and retailer. Research undertaken in the USA has rigorously analysed shopping phenomena: tinned soup sells more if it is shelved out of alphabetical order; own-brand products sell best when placed immediately to the left of the brand leader; the optimum shelf position is 15 degrees below eye-level; by slowing background music from 108 beats per minute to 60, sales increase by 38.2 per cent (and the customers' blink rate slows from 32 blinks a minute to just 14); if the layout encourages you to turn the trolley one way, your eye looks the other way, to what is called the 'strong side'. Nothing is accidental.

Supermarkets also promise choice. In some cases, the choice may be no more than half a dozen differently labelled tins with more or less the same baked beans inside. But, unquestionably, what has changed immeasurably over the years is our willingness to try new and different foods. Recipes and ingredients that would have been considered utterly exotic a decade or two ago now feature in many home cooks' repertoires and store cupboards.

The expansion of culinary horizons is directly related to another late twentieth-century phenomenon, mass travel. People who began holidaying abroad after the war brought back memories of new tastes along with their souvenirs and snapshots. Great pioneers such as the food writer, Elizabeth David, introduced Mediterranean flavours to a generation which had recently endured rationing. Our horizons have expanded to such an extent that we now expect lemongrass, galangal and miso to be stocked by supermarkets which would have been hard pressed to shift fresh garlic 30 years ago. The role of design in this context has to do with another kind of presentation. We may wish to recreate that green Thai curry or bouillabaisse, but we need someone to show us how to do it. Many cookbooks today function more as another form of armchair travel. The presentation of food in luscious colour photography allows us to have our cake without eating it or even making it.

With cookbook sales often tied in to television programmes, the effect of media presentation has been to provide new cooking ideas in the context of fail-safe recipes that anyone can follow. As such, the appetite for novelty in food has transformed eating into a form of self-labelling, just like home furnishings and fashion.

Restaurant design can have a tremendous impact on our attitudes to food, on our tastes and the way we cook at home. The best, and I don't mean necessarily the most expensive, are true theatres of food, offering sensual enjoyment. The worst have the opposite effect, dulling the senses with a packaged or themed experience.

I remember visiting one particular restaurant in Barcelona which generated precisely this feeling of delight. There was a food shop at the front of the premises, a kitchen at the back and a long corridor with tables on either side in between. There was much scurrying back and forth, as fresh ingredients were taken from the shop to be prepared and cooked in the kitchen; it all added up to an atmosphere of care and quality, with a bit of performance thrown in.

Another memorable experience was eating at the Moti Mahal in New Delhi. Unlike the tandoori in the local high street, with its red flocked wallpaper, this open-air restaurant possessed a stunning elemental quality: scrubbed tables, big galvanized tubs filled with ice to chill drinks and squares of canvas looped up overhead to keep air circulating. It was very simple, very effective, and provided excellent food in a generous, basic fashion.

Designing a restaurant is just about the most interesting job there is, and certainly the most demanding and most challenging. Restaurant design encompasses practically every design discipline: product, ergonomics, servicing, use of materials, image and atmosphere, graphics and computerization. A restaurant is a unique combination of manufacturing and retailing, and the high degree of risk only adds to the excitement and sense of adventure.

As with any other space, the first job of the designer is to get the basics right. The challenges in this area alone are immense. Integrating all the services – water, heating, cooling, ventilation, deliveries, refuse disposal, fire exits – so that the most ergonomic, and profitable, use is made of the space demands an exceptional level of technical skill. The designer must take into account work sequences, environmental control, health regulations, maintenance, safety and a host of other necessary practicalities. With custom-built equipment ordered from manufacturers all over the world, there are few, if any, margins for error and mistakes can be costly. When the huge 'piano' (or stove) at Quaglino's was fired for the first time, it expanded by a couple of inches and knocked down a wall.

Ever since I worked as a washer-up and vegetable boy in a Paris restaurant, I have been fascinated by restaurant life. In a good restaurant, the buzz of a roomful of people enjoying themselves is mirrored by the near-balletic teamwork behind the scenes. It is the role of the designer to facilitate both sides of the equation: the welcoming, convivial, even theatrical atmosphere of eating out and the minor miracle of preparing and cooking different dishes for scores of people under great pressure, in a short time and in relatively extreme conditions.

I have been involved in many restaurants over the years, starting with the Soup Kitchens back in the 1950s. In my experience, the design of a restaurant should complement the food it serves. Even before the practicalities begin to be sketched out, it is important to get a sense of the mood you wish to convey. The process of dragging half-remembered impressions out of the memory, sketching, meditating on the quality of light and space a particular site has to offer eventually begins to crystallize into specific notions of colour, form and material. My tastes tend towards the simple, but simplicity alone is not enough. A successful restaurant has a sense of theatre, even if it does not ascend to operatic heights.

The restaurant kitchen has had an increasing impact on the way we cook and eat at home.

'There is no such thing as a pretty good omelette' French proverb

One important distinction must be made. Creating atmosphere through good design is nothing like the same as 'theming' a restaurant. Remorselessly themed or branded restaurants, which spell out their message in ersatz decor, jokey menus, gimmicky staff uniforms and the food itself, are as dismal as a punchline repeated too often. I would never consider opening a restaurant where the food wasn't the single most important element; in fact, I would like to do a restaurant where there was next to no design or decoration at all. The immediacy of the 'cook and serve' approach, the approach you find in a Greek taverna, an Italian trattoria or a Japanese noodle bar, should lie at the heart of every restaurant experience.

This approach inevitably leads to a re-evaluation of the restaurant kitchen. Like M.F.K. Fisher, I believe that good food cannot come from a bad kitchen. If you replace the cramped inferno behind the scenes with a well-designed working space, you gain the opportunity to integrate the kitchen more closely with the front of house. Specifically, this allows kitchen activity to be visible, a strategy we have taken to the limit in the design of Mezzo, with its double-height glass wall dividing the kitchen areas from the two eating levels. When people can see chefs preparing the food they are going to eat, the experience of eating out becomes more natural and less contrived. The sheer energy of a kitchen in full swing whets the appetite and contributes to the theatrical buzz. This is not mere showmanship, but testimony to the fact that good cooking and fresh ingredients are what it is all about. Involving the chefs in the 'life' of the restaurant allows them to interact with the customers, and the customers to interact with them, encouraging mutual respect. Is this design? Of course it is. Good design is all about thinking how people can better enjoy their work, their leisure and their lives, and about facilitating that enjoyment.

The sense of a common purpose can be gained by designing the restaurant so there is a fresh food counter at the entrance, for example. At the Butlers Wharf 'Gastrodrome' I extended this idea beyond the restaurants to encompass bars, grills, a wine merchant, and specialist shops.

The best, most relaxing and convivial restaurants remind us that eating is one of the greatest pleasures of life. I suppose my ideal would be a restaurant sited in the countryside, within sight of the sea. There would be seafood landed daily, crayfish and trout from a freshwater stream, wild mushrooms gathered in the woods, milk and cheese from cows at a local pasturage, lamb from the green hills and a vegetable garden to supply the tables. In such surroundings, you would indeed live to eat.

FOOD

Picasso with Bread Fingers, photograph by Robert Doisneau (1952).

Frank Gehry, Rebecca's Restaurant, San Francisco

Successful restaurants share an atmosphere and air of expectation. The Oyster Bar at Grand Central Station suggests grandeur and simplicity at the same time. Basic lunch counters under a richly detailed, vaulted ceiling are the setting for some of the best seafood in the city. Frank Gehry's extravagant design for Rebecca's restaurant on the West Coast shows that eating out should be fun.

Chartier in Paris (overleaf) has been serving basic fare to working people since the 1900s. Appetites are whetted by the bustling atmosphere – a sense of anticipation derived from the sheer scale and vitality of the place as much as the traditional fittings and decor. The large Parisian brasseries were very much in my mind when designing Mezzo in Soho, with its 750 covers.

FOOD

Warren & Wetmore Architects, Oyster Bar, Grand Central Station,
New York (1903-13)

Chartier, Paris (1896)

C.D. Partnership, Mezzo, London (1995)

Braised chicken and sausages in tomatoes, served with flat noodles

Sushi, Japan

Barbecued bananas, Australia

Restaurant place setting, Japan

According to the nineteenth-century French epicure, Brillat Savarin, 'The discovery of a new dish does more for the state of human happiness than the discovery of a new star.' Yet that new dish has to look appealing if we are to be tempted to try it. The highly stylized arrangement of food on a plate seems to come quite naturally to the Japanese, a formal presentation which expresses the style of cooking and the rituals of eating. In the West, however, treating food as art is often a means of displaying status, as evident in those towering Victorian creations in aspic: food to impress the neighbours. More recently, *cuisine minceur* saw bite-sized morsels artfully arranged in a puddle of raspberry coulis. For me, food is most appetizing when it is put on the plate in a simple way, without pretending to be something it is not.

FOOD

143

À La Mère De Famille, Paris (19th century)

Le Petit Parisien, photograph by Willy Ronis (1952)

Open-air market, France

Dean & DeLuca, New York

The epitome of the speciality food shop, À la Mère de Famille presents a tempting array of produce to draw in customers. The shop itself is a beautifully designed package, with bands of gilt lettering encircling the windows. Daily shopping had its drudgeries, but the price the supermarket shopper pays for convenience is the loss of the very real pleasure of selecting fresh produce from a market stall, which, like the morning outing to the baker's for a warm loaf of crusty bread, is fast disappearing, even in France. Real variety is still on offer in shops like New York's Dean & DeLuca or Balducci's, where the senses are assailed by the mingling aromas of fresh bread, cheese and good coffee the minute you walk through the door.

Packaging, with its carefully considered graphics, logos, colours and shapes, has become the first step in consumption. It shapes our experience of many products, but never more critically than in the case of food. The friendly milk bottle, now largely superseded by plastic 'jugs' or cardboard packs, is the focus for much nostalgia and still features in milk advertising for precisely that reason. The egg box is another packaging form which inspires affection, at least partly because it works well. Eggs obviously require protection and there is little wastefulness in a container that recycles so easily as a child's model or paint tray – I remember how well egg boxes worked as insulation on the walls of the particularly damp basement flat in whichI had my work-shop in the 1950s. But perhaps the ultimate twentieth-century package is the supermarket trolley, the package on wheels where we stack all the other packages we pluck from the shelves.

In a very different tradition, the packaging of even the humblest Japanese products betrays the cultural value placed on presentation, an art which in the West is often overriden by more commercial considerations.

Cardboard egg box

Traditional packaging for eggs, Japan

Supermarket trolleys

Glass milk bottles, Britain (1930s)

OVER: packaging for noodles, Japan

FOOD

147

Fish and chips, photograph by Kevin Summers (1995)

Fish Dishes, photograph by Tessa Traeger (1983)

Food photography is the gastronomic equivalent of armchair travel. In books and magazine features, the function of much food photography has been to give hestitant cooks at home an idea of what the finished dish is supposed to look like, even if the shot has been achieved with the kind of photographic trick that substitutes mashed potato for ice cream.

Plateau de fruits de mer, photograph by Ken Kirkwood (1992)

These images go a step further, addressing an audience which is increasingly sophisticated both in culinary and visual terms. Tessa Traeger's classic work for *Vogue* recalls the paintings of Arcimboldo, creating tableaux from the colours and shapes of the ingredients, while Kevin Summers' photographs directly convey the texture and aroma of cooking. I particularly enjoy Robert Freson's work, timeless still-life compositions which would inspire anyone to cook. One of the most visually exciting of all meals, a *plateau de fruits de mer* would inspire anyone to eat.

Ingredients for *Quenelles de brochet á la lyonnaise*, photograph by Robert Freson (1983)

Packaging liquids: mineral water, balsamic vinegar, vodka, Japanese soup stock, orange oil, herb-infused olive oil, Chinese plum sauce, Japanese saki, herb vinegar, gin, balsamic vinegar, flavoured olive oil

Coke is simply the best-known brand in the world. The second most recognizable word world-wide (after 'OK'), Coca-Cola is not an average success story. World-wide annual sales are worth over £12 billion, a figure which surpasses the gross domestic product of many developing countries. Apollo astronauts, returning from the moon, were greeted by a sign in Times Square: 'Welcome back to earth, home of Coca-Cola.'

The invention of an Atlanta pharmacist in 1886, this soft fizzy drink has a legendary 'secret ingredient', supposedly known only to three people, who never travel on the same aeroplane.

Authenticity – the 'Real Thing' – is one weapon in the commercial war with imitators. Brand image is another. The famous logo – white, flowing Spencerian script on a bright red background – is fiercely protected.

REFRESHER COURSES AVAILABLE IN ANY LANGUAGE.

Even the most reviled food has cultural associations that evoke fond memories or carry potential humour. The wit of Moschino's almost-edible handbag is a reminder not to take serious pleasures quite so seriously.

'We all need a splash of bad taste'

Diana Vreeland

Model and fry-up, photograph by Ellen von Unwerth (1995)

Moschino chocolate handbag (1996)

Photo Gianpaolo Barbieri   Art. Moschino

Travel in the twentieth century is the ultimate expression of modernity. Few air travellers expect to travel in surroundings reminiscent of a nineteenth-century gentleman's club. While such trappings may convey a reassuring sense of tradition and nostalgia in a high-street clothing shop, for example, they are anything but reassuring for passengers thousands of feet off the ground. Modernity, which seems to be so threatening in other contexts, is welcomed in the area of transport as proof of technological advance, speed, efficiency and, above all, safety.

Transport is at the leading edge of design. It is an enormously competitive field with a high profile and attracts huge investment, which in turn attracts the best designers eager to share the glamour. Compared to house design, for example, car design is the subject of far more research and experimentation. At the same time, the public, quick to dismiss the efforts of designers in other fields, tends to hold the Issigonises or Innocentis of this world in rather more esteem – who do you know who has not dreamt of driving a Ferrari?

transport

Commemorative Space Shuttle stamp (1995).

Intense creativity in the field of design has inspired a number of cross-fertilizations. Concern over his son's comfort as he rode his tricycle led John Dunlop in 1888 to adapt an idea which had first appeared 40 years earlier – the pneumatic tyre. (In its original incarnation, as the brainchild of Robert Thomson, it comprised a canvas skin with leather treads over a rubber tube.) Seven years later, Edouard Michelin fitted rubber pneumatic tyres to a Peugeot competing in the Paris to Bordeaux Motor Race and a key element of modern mass travel slotted into place.

One of the best known cross-overs, perhaps, is the development of the Maclaren buggy, the first lightweight collapsible pushchair. Owen Maclaren was retired, and a grandfather, when he came up with the idea – it was the effort required to manoeuvre his grandchild's heavy, conventional pushchair which convinced him of the need for a better design. Maclaren had been a test pilot and an aeronautical designer with specific involvement in the design of the undercarriage of the Spitfire. Applying his knowledge of one kind of light, folding, load-bearing mechanism to another context, he came up with the design of the first buggy (patented in 1965), whose tubular aluminium structure was robust enough to carry a toddler but could collapse into a neat umbrella shape.

A more recent example of such creative crossings over can be seen in the design of new turnstiles for New York City Transit. Cubic Corporation, a Californian firm, applied technology similar to that found in modern weapons systems to enable subway tokens to be quickly and accurately verified by means of crosshairs, giving commuters a speedier progress through the turnstiles.

Travel has provided some of the most powerful metaphors in twentieth-century design; speed is the essence of contemporary life. Yet early cars did not look fast; the 'horseless carriage' preserved the coachbuilt appearance of horse-drawn carriages, which is not surprising since they were made and assembled by hand by

The Rover safety bicycle (1885): bicycles' tubular frames directly influenced the modern furniture designs of architects such as Corbusier and Breuer.

the same craftsmen who made carriages. Even when Henry Ford set out to produce a cheap car for the masses and the days of the coachbuilt car were numbered, the resulting simplicity of the Model-T did not suggest either speed or power. The car was still a functional machine, not yet an object of desire.

At the dawn of the motor age, in the days when the approach of a motorcar was signalled by a man walking in front waving a red flag, a speed of 30 miles per hour was the height of reckless abandon, beyond the wildest dreams of any Mr Toad. The very first British car journey, in July 1895, was made in a French Panhard et Lavassor, which took eight hours to cover a distance of 56 miles. The first speeding ticket in London was issued to a driver travelling in his car at two miles per hour. By the early 1920s, with the building of the Italian Autostrada – the first fast multi-lane roads – the lure of speed began to take hold. Designers searched for a new aesthetic to express the liberating power of the car.

That aesthetic was streamlining. The streamline or flow of air over a body had been studied for some time, but the development of aircraft provided new impetus to apply the research. The taut lines of a fish swimming through water, the profile of a bird's wing, and the tapering curves of a teardrop were all naturally stream-lined forms which suggested to early car designers a combination of smoothness of movement, powerful forward direction and dynamism. And by providing a potent visual link between ground transport and air flight, streamlining helped to create a unified image of modern transport.

Streamlining took a long while to infiltrate mass production. Scientific research eventually established that the teardrop was not the most aerodynamic shape after all, but in the meantime, its impact on car design was tremendous. For the first time, designers considered the car as a whole object. The image of streamlining, which could suggest speed and power even when the car was standing still, depended on uninterrupted smooth lines and the suppression of features such as wing mirrors, bumpers and door handles. Streamlining brought a curiously tactile quality to an inanimate steel machine and, with it, a sense of character. The car not only had a body; with oval inset headlamps and shallow curving bumper, it also had a face.

Some of the most satisfying of all car designs – those classics we hold in such affectionate regard – are the fruit of this streamlining period. The Volkswagen Beetle, designed by Dr Ferdinand Porsche, owes much to the Tatra 87, a pioneering Czech design of 1936, as well as to the teardrop car of Paul Jarey, who worked on the design of the Zeppelin.

Frank Costin, who established the look of Formula One racing cars in the 1950s, was originally trained at the De Havilland Aircraft Company and had a passionate interest in airflow and aerodynamics. His tapering, curvaceous, dramatic designs such as the Lotus Elite and 1957 Vanhall summarize the glamour of motor racing in its heyday. Costin was dedicated to practical experiment. An anecdote related by Stephen Bayley in Costin's recent obituary recalls how he was once seen strapped to the side of a Lotus as it sped around the track – the best means, he believed, of inspecting the effect of airflow on wool he had glued around the wheel arches.

Nowadays, the design of Formula One cars reflects the need to keep the car from lifting at increasingly incredible speeds – and the result is a far less beautiful object. But those early post-war racing cars still define the classic sportscar profile, a shape enshrined in the E-type Jaguar and Porsche 911. Driving such a car is rather like driving a Brancusi sculpture – only slightly cheaper.

Another classic of the road owes its origins to technology and engineering borrowed from the aircraft industry. The Vespa (or 'Wasp'), Piaggio's bestselling scooter, was designed in 1946 by Italian engineers and designers formerly employed making planes.

Simple to operate and easy to handle, the Vespa's streamlined shape gave it a visual coherence that was instantly recognizable and that contributed to its immense popularity.

Streamlining also proved irresistible to industrial designers of the 1940s such as Raymond Loewy and Walter Dorwin Teague. They did not invent the concept, but they applied it far beyond the sphere of travel to such mundane domestic or commercial machines as refrigerators, pencil sharpeners and cash registers. Superficially, of course, there is no reason why such essentially static objects need to be styled in this way, but speed had ceased merely to imply the rate of movement from place to place and had come to express the entire concept of technological progress.

The arrival of streamlining coincided with the point when styling in general began to be appreciated as a means for manufacturers to maximize their markets. In the beginning of mass car production, it was enough to produce a cheap, reliable model (T or otherwise) and sell it to those who had never dreamed of owning a car before. But the 'any colour as long as it is black' mentality, to quote Henry Ford's famous saying, could not survive long once car ownership became widely established.

In order to sell more cars to more people, or more cars to the same people over and over again, it was necessary to offer stylistic choice – colour, shape, specification, performance – in short, to invest the car with a whole host of social meanings and values through style. From the basic Model-T, the car of everyman, we now have a multiplicity of brands, models and marques: sportscars, family saloons, hatchbacks, runarounds, off-road vehicles, people movers – each with its target market. An essential element in the design of a new model has become deciding for whom the car is designed. There is nothing wrong about taking such factors into account; indeed, they are essential if a car, or any other object or piece of equipment, is to function efficiently.

However, 'giving the public what they want or say they want' may be neither entirely desirable nor particularly straightforward. Consumer research, like polls of voters' intentions, can be misleading. The most thoroughly researched car of all time, Ford's Edsel, launched in 1959, was designed on the basis of incredibly detailed information about customer preferences. The company anticipated a guaranteed success; instead the Edsel was an historic flop.

The car, arguably the most dominant factor in the shaping of modern culture, is today the ultimate design object, expressing every nuance of status and aspiration. Junior executives on their way up the corporate ladder know to the last detail the exact specification of the car to which their rank should entitle them.

One of the most upwardly mobile of all recent car designs was the Mark 1 Golf GTi – or 'Guaranteed Theft Item' as it has been colloquially termed in some circles. The quintessential 'hot hatch', with its phenomenal acceleration, won a cult following on the street as the first cheap high-performance car – 'the next best thing to Michelle Pfeiffer,' in the words of one reviewer. The identification of a car with sex, potency and career aspiration is not new; but the GTi was the first relatively inexpensive small car to fall squarely into this bracket.

Of course, status can be signified by attributes other than speed. I once had a rather depressing conversation with a director of BMW. While I have every appreciation for the sheer quality of the marque, I had noticed that the console of one of the top-range models featured a particularly nasty bit of plastic-covered wood trim. Why, I wondered, spoil a perfectly honest piece of engineering with this trivial, ersatz – and, frankly, offensive – detailing? The director replied that the customers wanted and expected it; in other words, the trim, in its feeble attempt to recall the old walnut or mahogany fascia of pre-war motorcars, was somehow essential as a symbol of rank and authority.

'Ugliness does not sell' Raymond Loewy

Raymond Loewy's streamlined Pennsylvania Railroad locomotives (1936) had a radical simplicty.

Quality has an important place in car design, but I believe it must be real quality, not a simulation of it. When the Conran Design Group was commissioned to design the interior of the 'Discovery' Range Rover the elegance of the solution arose from a basic understanding of the materials involved and the way they could be worked to create a unified image of quality. This, to my mind, is far more valuable and satisfying than the type of 'creeping featurism' which clutters up the fascia with gadgets offering the kind of information that you do not really need to know, and that can be dangerously confusing to the driver.

I think a bashed-up Citroën 2CV is a wonderfully quirky and desirable object. Articulated like an insect and designed to take knocks and bumps, the 2CV is an appealing 'anti-hero' of the road. Unfortunately, the same qualities which give it character also prove unacceptably risky for modern motorists, who expect a much higher margin of safety from their vehicles. After all, it was originally designed for the French farming community, who have a refreshingly carefree view of life.

I believe that over-specification is a spurious means of adding value. But it is easy to see why car manufacturers and designers concentrate on such features, not to mention catchy names, jazzy colours, hectic graphics and go-faster stripes: the scope for real innovation and diversity would seem to be narrowing all the time. It is a common complaint today that all cars look alike, in the middle range at least. The predictability of mass-market cars reflects, to some extent, the real successes of research and design in identifying the safest, most aerodynamic, fuel-efficient and cost-effective solution to mass-production.

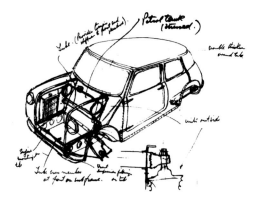

The Morris Mini Minor (1959) by Alec Issigonis revolutionized car design.

Ford, for example, used to make cars for a specific country, such as the British Anglia; then the company made them for a particular continent. Now, with different parts made in different places around the world and assembled somewhere else, 'national' identity has become something of a fiction. Yet, despite global marketing and production, what one might still call national characteristics seem to linger in car design, supported, in many cases, by advertising imagery. Car design has been a means of expressing national pride and sentiment throughout the century. Indeed, in the post-war period, the car offered one of the most conspicuous ways in which design could be used to forge a new national identity for the defeated powers of Germany, Italy and (later) Japan, a means to economic reconstruction.

The most extreme example of the car as a national symbol, of course, is the KdF-Wagen, otherwise better known as the Beetle. Nothing could be further from the Beetle's lovable contemporary image than its origins, under the auspices of Hitler, as the *Kampf durch Freude Wagen*, or 'Strength Through Joy Car'. Designed in the late 1930s by Dr Porsche as a car for the people (it was basically conceived as a motorbike on four wheels), the project found favour with the leaders of the Third Reich who were keen to provide the German population with the type of mass mobility offered by the Model-T Ford.

The American press provided the Beetle with its familiar nickname in 1938, but the interruption of the war years and the subsequent reconstruction of the German economy meant that it was not until the mid-1950s that the Beetle first appeared on the American market. When it did, its association with an inglorious period of German history was forgotten and a brilliant campaign by Doyle Dane Bernbach helped to win the car a cult following as the antidote to the tail-finned gas-guzzlers that every American family aspired to own. Using black-and-white photography, wry catchlines and editorial copy which emphasized the Beetle's quiet virtues, the campaign was revolutionary for its understatement and effectiveness. In the film, *Sleeper*, Woody Allen, awakening far into the future, comes across an old Beetle which starts first time – a joke which plays on the common theme of the advertising.

With approximately 22 million Beetles sold, the car has become a universal cultural reference point. Yet while its origins remain fairly obscure for the majority, the Beetle has also done much to reinforce the image of German motor car manufacture as efficient, reliable and functional. Immediately after the war, Volkswagen was offered to the British company, Rootes; having been rejected by Lord Rootes, it was the British decision to allow the Wolfsburg plant to reopen that proved pivotal in the revival of Volkswagen in particular and German car manufacturing in general. Sadly, the sale of Rover to BMW in 1994 marked the end of mass car production by a British-owned company. We now assemble cars for the Japanese, Americans and countless Europeans, though we remain world-leaders ... in the production of traffic cones.

The Beetle has humour. Wit and character are also evident in the Renault Twingo, the S-Cargo van or the Nissan Micra, something of a departure for Japanese car manufacturers who have tended to have a reputation for producing slick products with more of a computer-generated feel than a true spirit of innovation.

'Design makes us think about problems and solve them with our own ideas' Michael, aged 10

Despite an often lukewarm critical reception, the phenomenal success of Japan in transport design cannot be ignored. Part of the Japanese miracle has been their nurturing of small-parts firms, and their recognition that such links in the manufacturing chain have made the Hondas and Toyotas what they are today. Another aspect of their success has been the Japanese devotion to research, to the extent that a Japanese survey of the American market identified the importance of the intangibles such as the satisfying clunk of a closing door or the classy aroma of leather upholstery.

Renault's Fiftie concept car reflects a renewed interest in traditional styling.

One hundred years after the first car took to the road, designers are now beginning to return to motoring's glorious past for inspiration. While it has been a fruitful, creative wellspring in other cultural forms, from interior design to fashion, the past has never been much of a reference point in travel. As we have seen, modernism is intrinsic to car design and to the whole field of transport in general. We accept the absolute logic of form always following function, and while the results have often been beautiful, even sublime, technological progress – newer as in better – has been the selling point of each succeeding model. Now, however, we take certain standards of efficiency, road-worthiness, safety and reliability for granted. Style alone is increasingly seen as what differentiates one car from the next. It is not surprising, in this context, that the car's rich cultural and aesthetic heritage should begin to be plundered, sometimes successfully, sometimes not.

Rover's decision to return to the classic design of the Rover grille as a means of consolidating the Rover identity is one of the more sensitive examples of reclaiming tradition in car design. The Mazda MX-5 has enjoyed considerable popularity. But to my eye, at least, Japanese streamlining just misses it, and lacks the confident tautness of a Porsche, for example. The new Concept 1 from Volkswagen, due to be launched in 1997, is a deliberate attempt to revisit the success of the Beetle, driven out of European and North American production by safety and pollution legislation. Such

The crash-test dummy plays a key design role.

designs prey on our fond memories of the cars we once drove or in which we once rode, and address the growing market of classic car enthusiasts, who may or may not warm to the fact that the engine of the Concept 1 is no longer air-cooled and lives at the front.

Where modernism, even futurism, still retains a stronghold is in the field of aviation. It is no accident, surely, that some of the most confident, exuberantly modern buildings are airports, and it is curious how much we welcome such innovative and expressive designs in this context while dismissing and scorning them in others. A classic example is Eero Saarinen's TWA terminal at Kennedy airport, a building which embodies the spirit of flight.

I think it is a fantastic design. Approaching the building, you feel as if you are already beginning the process of flying, as if you only had to fasten your seatbelt at the departure desk and the whole terminal would take off into the air.

Stansted Airport, to the northeast of London, designed by Norman Foster, is another such inspiring place. Here, by contrast to many places where masses of people gather, natural light is treated as a positive element, as the soul or spirit of the building, or a reminder of the sky into which they will shortly be jetting off. Stansted manages to express the excitement of travel, an emotion which can be easily quashed in the tedium of queuing and delay. Yet it is also calm and soothing, a pristine, perfectly engineered space to calm the nerves of the most phobic of air passengers.

A similar experience – of rising excitement matched with control and order – is offered by Nicholas Grimshaw's Eurostar terminus at Waterloo. The station is the point of departure and arrival for passengers undertaking a very different journey, not through the skies, but under the English Channel. The sinuous glazed roof of the station, echoed in the articulated silvery fish on the concourse, add drama, theatre and wit to an undersea crossing.

These are good examples of how to handle passengers in transit. Unfortunately, those in charge of mass travel are not always inspired to commission such masterpieces of design. Airports are increasingly viewed as opportunities to indulge in a little spending; a flight is a journey with a shopping trip at each end. Duty-free shops take precedence over adequate provision of seating areas. The commercialization of airport space means that no matter how innovative the building design, the interior has come to resemble a frenetic shopping mall, with such a confusion of shop signage and logos that it is difficult to locate the way to the plane. The purity of Stansted owes much to the fact that this airport is not a popular point of departure; if it were, it would also be filled with shops.

Renzo Piano's Kansai Airport (1994) is a synthesis of nature and technology.

I have had a practical involvement with airport interiors myself, and I know how difficult it can be to reconcile deeply held design principles with practical necessities and the requirements and budgets of the client. Air travel, no matter how commonplace it has become for the majority of the population, is still stressful. It is necessary for the designer to reassure passengers, to inform them clearly and direct them efficiently, to prevent accidents and to create a rational traffic flow. At the same time, the sheer volume of people passing through means that materials used must either be of the variety that age sympathetically or so tough they will resist the roughest wear and tear.

In 1967, which was still the early days of mass air travel, my design group was commissioned to come up with a scheme for fitting out the interior of Heathrow Terminal 1. The client, British Airports Authority, had some disagreements with the architects of the building and eventually rejected their designs for the interior spaces. We were then given the task of designing a modern space within the framework of some unsympathetic detailing, such as heavy teak handrails, which we could not replace. In the end, our solution managed to overcome the rusticated detailing through the boldness of its approach – all curves, chrome and sculptural plastic. Everything had rounded edges, facilitated by our use of fibreglass, laminate and rubber – sympathetically space-age, we thought, and agreeably modern.

This particular job is one of those of which I am personally most proud. The almost industrial quality of materials and design was tempered by the curves and soft edges, a practical decision, since square edges are more readily knocked and damaged, and an aesthetic one, since sharp edges look forbidding and sharp, damaged edges look tacky very quickly. Admittedly, our vision of modernity, had it survived, would look pretty dated by now – but not as dated as what is has been replaced by.

Our task, some years later, at Gatwick's North Terminal, was rather different. Here we had the opportunity to work closely with the building's architects, YRM, from the very beginning. Over the seven-year course of the project, we approached the design of the interior with close reference to the design of the terminal as a whole, so that everything appears to share the same 'handwriting' – what, at the time, was called 'seamless design'.

We endeavoured in the design of the internal layout to create a smooth, logical flow of traffic that would require little additional signage. In large public spaces the temptation is always to fall back on complex signage systems to direct people here and there. I believe that signage can never be a substitute for solving interior design problems; if a space is functionally designed, next to no signs ought to be needed at all. Unfortunately, our taste for simplicity and order in this context was eventually undermined by commercial considerations. By the time the terminal was cluttered up with a variety of different shops, each emblazoned with its own graphics, there was a need for more directional signs simply so that passengers could find their way past the shops to the planes.

The difficulty, or perhaps I should say the challenge, of working with clients arises when designers finds themselves pushed into directions they do not want to go. In the case of North Terminal, BAA was adamant that the floor should be carpeted in a heavily patterned design. My own instinct and preference would have been hard flooring, which works so beautifully at Stansted, but in the end we were forced to bow to the economic argument put forward by the client that carpet is easier (and hence cheaper) to clean than hard surfaces, and to the research they had commissioned which stated that their customers preferred softer, cosier environments. I personally find the concept that heavy pattern is preferable to plain surfaces because it does not show dirt offensive; in my view, floors should always be clean and seen to be clean. However, we were obliged to come up with a heavily patterned carpet and we managed to produce a lively, colourful design which looked neither muddy nor depressing – though I cannot say I was proud of it.

The aspect of our work at Gatwick which pleases me most was the design of two sculptures. BAA had stipulated that they wanted some kind of 'feature', a visual statement to give the terminal a sense of identity. Our idea, for which we argued long and hard, was for each sculpture to consist of a simple polished steel cone with water gently playing down its sides. The dynamism of the steel shape, with its aeronautical echoes, combined with the soothing sound of the water, seems to me to be perfectly symbolic of the atmosphere we were trying to create and of the tension between excited anticipation and calm, confident efficiency that all airports should provide.

More recently we have been asked to act as consultants to Japan Air Lines, who wanted a European perspective on Japanese style. One of the first aspects we considered was how to improve the quality of life for the passenger. Some while ago, I flew in an Aeroflot jet. In first class there were tapestry-covered club seats, pilasters up the walls and windows screened with velvet curtains tied back with silken ropes. As soon as we were airborne, a very large air hostess set down a bottle of vodka and a generous bowl of caviar in front of each one of us strapped in our seats. The entire effect was incredibly charming, if mildly disconcerting. In an attempt to create the sense of luxury and privilege that might appeal to Western travellers, the Soviet airline had adopted the incongruous, bygone aesthetic of an upper-class Victorian lounge.

Our expectations of air travel have been revised down extremely rapidly since then, to the point where most people dread the discomfort and inconvenience of flying rather than look forward to a special experience. One of our suggestions to JAL for restoring an element of quality and service included the use of ceramic, steel, bamboo, glass and wood for eating utensils and containers. Another was to adopt a neutral background for all the fixed parts of the interior to act as a foil for coloured headrest covers, cushions, napkins, blankets, staff uniforms and aprons. We recommended that the colour of these items should be changed seasonally to counter the depressing uniformity of modern air travel. The serenity and simplicity of traditional Japanese style

could be conveyed very elegantly with the use of classic Japanese flower arrangements, clear graphics and accessories such as eye shields and slippers, all beautifully designed and made.

Design at this level is always about infinitesimal detail, a sum of parts that add up to more than the whole. No detail is too small. The designers working on the new Boeing 777 spent much effort ensuring that when the lid of the lavatory fell down it did so, not with a bang but a whisper. The small device which slowed the lid so that it did not hit the seat was part of the attempt to create a sense of quality and comfort.

JAL were looking for a way to convey a specifically Japanese quality; national identity or 'flying the flag' is a feature of much design in the field of travel. One has only to look at the heraldic flourish on the tailfin of a BA jet for an obvious example – although it was put there by an American designer, Walter Landor. Ironically, this desire to express national difference comes at a time when the world is shrinking rapidly and travellers may arrive halfway across the globe to find that there is no 'there' there.

It is very difficult to imagine – especially when marooned in an airport lounge waiting for a delayed flight to be called or stuck nose-to-tail in an endless jam – that there was ever a need to promote the concept of travel at all. It is even harder to appreciate how the car, in its infancy, was seen as a way of restoring the romance of travel. Early motoring enthusiasts put up with considerable discomfort to journey to all the out-of-the-way places inaccessible by rail. Today, we are acutely aware that our personal freedom to go where and when we want has been achieved at a cost. Pollution, the carving up of the countryside to accommodate more roads, the pressure on natural resources and the human cost of road accidents are the dark side of car culture. London air is now dirtier due to car exhaust than it was in 1952 before the clean-air legislation.

TRANSPORT

Few people view the car as an unqualified blessing, but hardly anyone is prepared to give it up. The attractions of car ownership in the first place – speed and independence – are no longer the main issues. Most cars today are capable of speeds well in excess of human reaction times, but the opportunities to drive this fast are fairly constrained, by traffic as much as legislation. With much city traffic moving no faster, and often slower, than it did a century ago, speed and independence are severely curtailed. What most people do value, however, and what they would find very hard to give up, is the convenience of the car.

Is the future of mass travel a design problem? Perhaps. It is certainly conceivable that the solution to the current crisis affecting the whole area of transportation could be design-led. Throughout the post-war period, design has become increasingly based around consumption rather than production, and in the process has created a language for communicating values.

Design, in every field, has been seen as a way of participating in culture as well as a means of determining it. When the oil crisis of 1974 began to bite, and the classic American 'dream machine' – half a block long and with petrol consumption to match – seemed almost unpatriotic, designers found a role creating cars that were smaller and more energy-efficient, but still attractive. These persistent late twentieth-century conflicts – between the simple life and technological sophistication, between the drive for expansion and innovation and the necessity for conservation and renewal – offer plenty of scope for designers, both creatively and analytically. At the same time, we all need to reassess how and when we choose to travel – a properly funded rail network could and should tempt both passengers and freight to take the train, freeing our roads of congestion at the same time as alleviating air pollution. By devising alternative forms of transport – such as the electric car – which are not only practicable but desirable, designers again may help to move us all forward.

Getting nowhere fast in John Salt's *'58 Ford without a Hood* (1973): the future of mass transport offers new challenges to designers.

In the golden age of motoring, the idea of travel for pleasure was promoted most effectively not by car manufacturers but by companies such as Michelin and Shell, whose sales of tyres and petroleum depended on increasing the frequency of journeys. 'The art of motoring has just been born; it will develop with each year; and the tyre will develop with it, since the tyre is the essential organ without which the car cannot travel,' proclaimed the first Michelin guide to France in 1900. The motto 'Nunc est Bibendum' ('Now is the time to drink', which referred to the tyres' ability to 'drink' glass, nails and flint without puncturing), the jovial mascot Mr Bibendum and the Michelin guides listing restaurants, hotels and sights were all part of a carefully considered process of image-making with the purpose of associating the company name with the idea of having a good time.

In Shell's classic British advertising campaign of the mid-1930s, artists such as Graham Sutherland, McKnight Kauffer and Abram Games were commissioned to produce what is now considered to be some of the finest poster art of the century; the Shell guides featured contributions from writers such as John Betjeman. The message stressed confidence and reliability, while the eminence of the contributors suggested integrity and excellence.

Michelin, Mr Bibendum mosaic

Michelin, selection of Red and Green Guides (1900-)

THE RYE MARSHES

PAUL NASH

Paul Nash, *Rye Marshes* poster for Shell (1932)

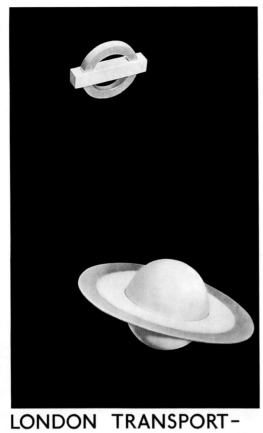

LONDON TRANSPORT–

Man Ray, poster for London Underground (1939)

H.C. Beck, original sketch for the 'Diagram' (c. 1931)

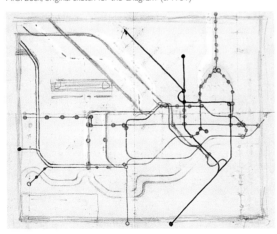

H.C. Beck, Quad Royale 'Diagram' for London Underground (1949)

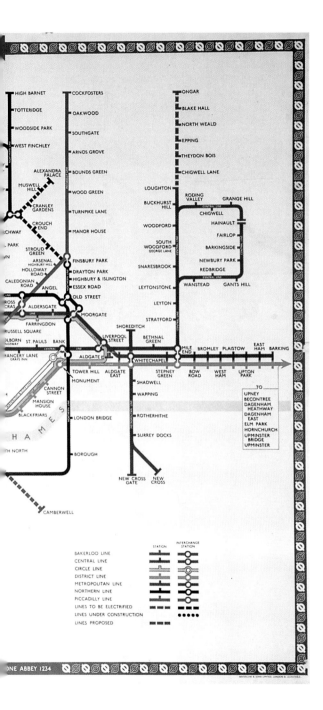

When London bus, tram, rail and underground services were integrated in the early 1930s, London Transport's chief executive, Frank Pick, initiated one of the most successful exercises in corporate identity. Previously, as commercial manager of London's Underground, Pick had commissioned the typographer Edward Johnston to create a new sans-serif typeface, still used today. Throughout the 1930s Pick also commissioned the architect Charles Holden to design or redesign tube stations. Strong geometric forms, large windows, reflective materials and dramatic lighting transformed stations into new focal points of public life in the city. At the same time, the involvement of artists in poster design had a great influence on popular taste. One of the most enduring of all innovations was the 'Diagram': the redesigned tube map presented routes as simple colour-coded lines, a schematic rather than geographically accurate plan that is a model of clarity and user-friendliness.

Charles Holden,
Boston Manor station (1935)

A B C D E F G H I J K L M N O P Q R S T U V W X Y Z 1 2 3 4 5 6 7 8 9 0

Edward Johnston, Johnston type lettering for London Underground (1916)

Rush-hour traffic, California   Airstream trailer (1936)

The lure of the open road – the personal freedom to go where you like when you want – has shaped our expectations of travel in the twentieth century, even if a day out in the country means half a day stuck in a motorway jam trying to get there. The Citroën Dyane, a rather less basic version of the 2CV, addressed the need for a simple family car. The Vespa was the epitome of chic mobility in the 1950s and early '60s. As a young designer, I owned a Vespa and even used it to deliver furniture, which I strapped to the back. But its shortcomings as a long-distance vehicle were made clear one freezing January night when I set off to visit my parents and was forced to turn back barely halfway, so cold I could no longer steer. Comfort, style and freedom come together in one of the most beautiful of all twentieth-century designs, the Airstream trailer.

Corradino d'Ascanio, Piaggio Vespa (1946), ridden by Antony Perkins

Pierre Boulanger, Citroën Dyane (photograph, 1967)

Van Peterghen and Laurent Drevost, Primagaz catamaran (1989)

'As the car devoured the street and leapt

forth on the high road through the open

country, he was only conscious that he was

Toad once more, Toad at his best and highest,

Toad the terror, the traffic-queller, the lord

of the lone trail...'

Kenneth Grahame, *The Wind in the Willows*

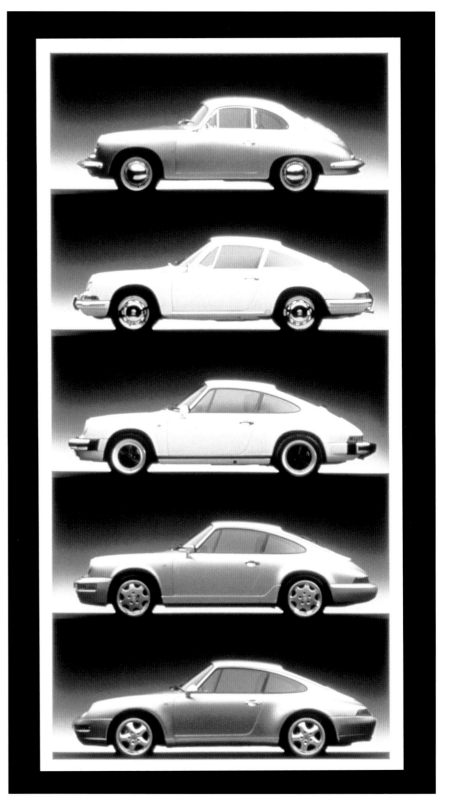

Ferdinand-Alexander Porsche, Porsche Type 911, Marks 1-5, (1964-94)

Eero Saarinen, TWA Terminal, Kennedy Airport, New York (1962)

Harley Earl, Cadillac Coupe de Ville (1959; model shown, 1962)

Speed is intoxicating. The study of aerodynamics has given a shape to speed; the contour of car bodies follows the lines of airflow in the wind tunnel. Like the catamaran with its shallow draught, the long, low profile of a fast car is designed for least resistance in the medium through which it travels. But design can also make things look faster. The rocket fins of Cadillac took styling into the supersonic age just as Saarinen's TWA terminal expresses the power of flight.

TRANSPORT

Santiago Calatrava, Puente del Alamillo, Seville, Spain (1992)

Opposite: Nicholas Grimshaw and Partners (engineering by YRM/Antony Hunt Associates), Eurostar terminal, Waterloo station, London (1994)

The impact of engineering on structures related to transport dates back to the great Victorian train sheds and suspension bridges. The Channel Tunnel terminal at Waterloo is a sublime modern example of this tradition, with its 400 metre-long glass roof snaking through south London. This beautiful and expressive structure was devised with the aid of computer analysis, enabling parts to be standardized; a system of flexible neoprene gaskets allows overlapping panes to move with differences in temperature and pressure.

Swiss-based Spanish architect and engineer Santiago Calatrava is renowned for bridges such as Puente del Alamillo, built for the Seville world's fair in 1992. The huge concrete pillar, encased in steel, supports 13 pairs of cables holding up the bridge deck. The organic quality of the vaulted steel-ribbed roof at Santiago's station in Lyon reflects the designer's interest in natural forms: he is said to keep a dog's skeleton in his office.

Santiago Calatrava, train station, Lyon, France (1994)

TRANSPORT

179

Concorde cockpit (1976)

Alfa Romeo dashboard

Being in control implies receiving the appropriate levels of information. Despite the fact that the data required by an airline pilot or the helmsman of an ocean-going yacht is of rather greater complexity than that required by the average motorist, car manufacturers clutter up fascias with a host of dials, displays and gauges. I remain unconvinced that the outside air temperature is a critical piece of information for ordinary drivers. The classic car dashboard is a more worthwhile reference.

Luca Brenta, Wally Gator yacht (1994)

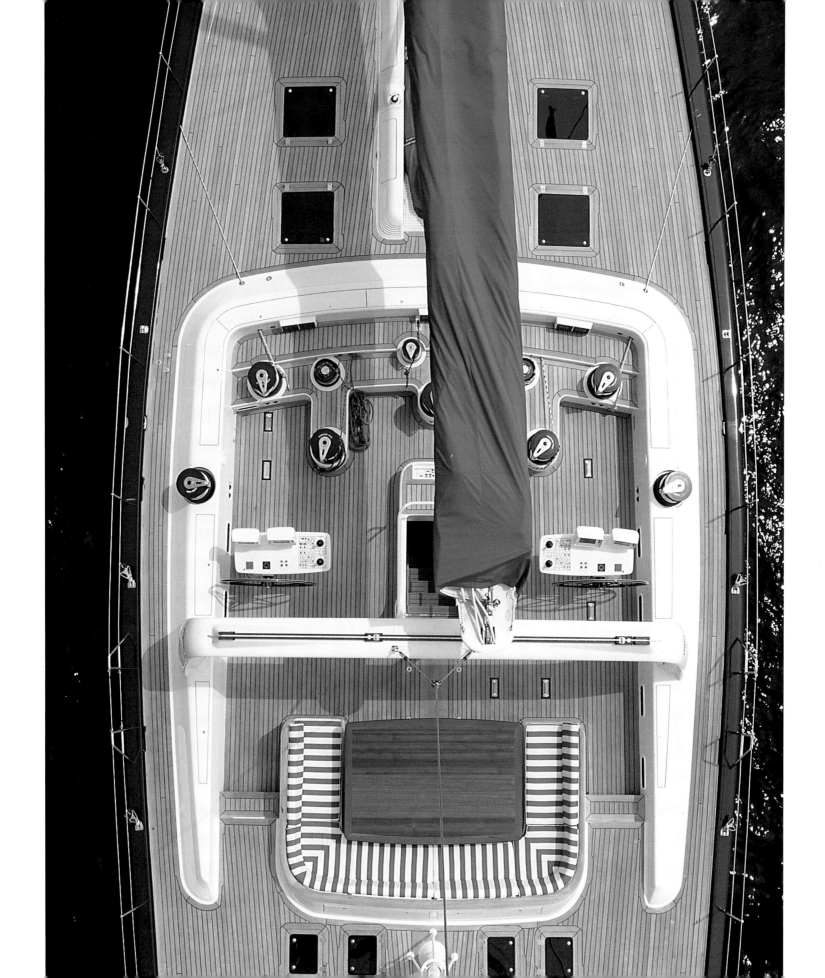

'Don't Walk', Japan

Wildlife warnings, Australia

Routemaster bus, London

'Walk', Japan

'Turn right', Europe   'No Entry' Europe

Motorway direction, Britain

Traffic lights on 'Stop', San Francisco

Taxi on call, New York

Signage is a critical field of design, especially where misleading instructions can have serious consequences for drivers travelling at speed. The design of road signs relies on common perceptions: red means STOP the world over. The format for British motorway signs was devised by Jock Kinnier and Margaret Calvert in 1963: the lettering size indicates the class of the road, and the size of the signs are proportionate to content, with the largest lettering on motorway signs, which are read at distance. Irrelevant detail – slashes in fractions – is omitted for clarity.

Marc Sadler, 'Bap' back protector (1993)

Lord Rootes' myopic judgement on the car which would go on to sell more than any other ignored the source of its lasting appeal. Christened the Beetle almost as soon as it first appeared, the anthropomorphic qualities of this enduringly popular car gave it a personality which overcame any technical drawbacks. Beetle owners loved, customized and named their cars, as if they were family pets. Designers ignore charm and gentle humour at their peril. Marc Sadler's design for a motorcyclist's protector is a strikingly similar-looking carapace.

'The average car-buyer will see no attraction in it. It is too ugly and too loud'

Lord Rootes, of Rootes Cars, on the Beetle

There's nothing reticent or self-effacing about Grand Central Terminal, a people's palace if ever there was one. Built between 1903 and 1913, the station straddles Park Avenue, the façade adorned with a huge clock and sculpture group, the interior equally grand, with a 125-foot vaulted ceiling painted with the constellations of the zodiac and lit by enormous arched windows. The heroic scale of the station makes it a remarkable point of arrival or departure, imparting a sense of drama and occasion to even the most mundane commuter journey – a monument to an age when travel was still exciting and often pleasurable.

Warren & Wetmore Architects, interior detail, Grand Central Station, New York (1903-1913)

Few find daily commuting much to sing about, but measures can be taken to improve the experience. Eduardo Paolozzi's mosaic murals at Tottenham Court Road underground station in London are part of a programme to put a fresh face on long-neglected stations, giving each some kind of visual theme related to its immediate locality – here, the mosaic draws on the image of electronic circuitry, Tottenham Court Road being the centre of London's electronics retailing.

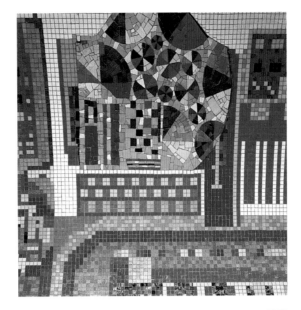

Eduardo Paolozzi, mosaic at Tottenham Court Road station, London (1983)

Warren & Wetmore Architects, exterior detail, Grand Central Station, New York (1903-1913)

IN
VISTAVISION
MOTION PICTURE · HIGH FIDELITY

Paramount Pictures

PARAMOUNT *presents*   **CARY GRANT** and **GRACE KELLY**
IN ALFRED HITCHCOCK'S   **"TO CATCH A THIEF"**
with JESSIE ROYCE LANDIS · JOHN WILLIAMS
Directed by ALFRED HITCHCOCK   Screenplay by JOHN MICHAEL HAYES   Colour by TECHNICOLOR
Based on the novel by DAVID DODGE

Cert 'A'

Sunbeam car featured in *To Catch a Thief* (1954)

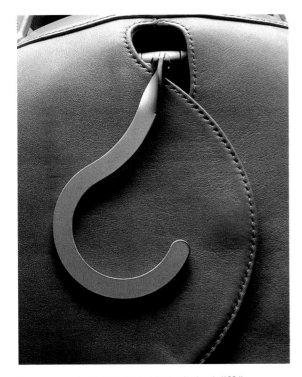

Ross Lovegrove for Connolly Limited, leather backpack (1994)

With the advent of mass tourism and car owner-ship, travel has inevitably lost its sense of glamour and luxury. Even the 'jet set' seems a quaint concept today. Half a century ago foreign travel was rare, expensive, lengthy and sometimes risky, which gave journeys a rather momentous quality. Nowadays boarding an aeroplane is no more exciting than catching the No. 38 bus. Luxury in travel is now less about the quality of the experience than the quality of the accessories that go with it. Ross Lovegrove's designs for Connolly, the leather goods manufacturer which makes bespoke car interiors and upholstery, have a wonderfully tactile and evocative appeal, a good example of an established company using design to tap new markets.

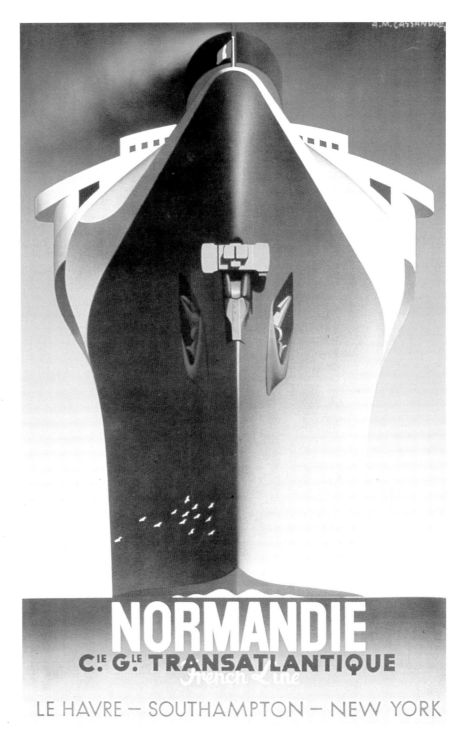

Cassandre poster, Normandie ship

Just Imagine (1930)

When we dream of the future, what does it look like? Modernity is expressed, in fact and fantasy, by modes of transport. Ever since Jules Verne and H.G. Wells were writing, we have found it difficult to imagine the future without imagining how we will move from place to place.

The dewy-eyed lovers in the 1930 musical sci-fi film, *Just Imagine*, could be swooning over the side of a Packard, rather than Hollywood's fanciful version of what we would all be driving, or flying, in the future; the future, in this case, being 1930's take on the 1980s. It is not merely the lovers' pose which looks dated, but the optimistic faith in progress and modernity implicit in the gleaming towers. *Bladerunner*, directed by Ridley Scott, offers a far darker view of what the future may hold.

None the less, the futuristic city in the film finds a strong echo in the flyovers, tunnels and high-speed train lines that form the transport arteries of many major modern cities. Tokyo's high-speed bullet train takes commuters to the heart of one of the densest of all urban environments.

Japan Railways, bullet train

At the Boilerhouse, the forerunner of the Design Museum located within the basement of the Victoria and Albert Museum, we once put on an exhibition devoted to hand tools. One of the most intriguing aspects of that particular show was the way in which it demonstrated how difficult it is to find an ugly working tool. Ordinary implements such as hammers, planes and wrenches, which have been designed to fit the hand and fulfil the function required of them with little or no thought of styling, have a natural beauty of their own.

Hand tools and practical utensils of various kinds seem to provide the perfect example of form following function, a design purity, if you like. Tempered with use, handles shaped by the grasp of those who employed them, the form of such tools displays the clarity of design when it is solely concerned with problem solving. Yet the apparent 'rightness' of the claw hammer, for example, can be somewhat misleading. What would happen if we reanalysed the process of hammering and discovered that the hammer was improvable after all?

By and large, designers do not concern themselves with reinventing the hammer, because most people are satisfied with it exactly the way it is. The hammer, which has evolved over many centuries, fulfils its function adequately enough to have survived relatively unaltered. The impetus for change and improvement comes when there is an obvious problem with the way something functions, or when a new material or manufacturing technique is invented which causes someone to reassess the traditional material or method of use.

work

Function would seem to be a straightforward issue, and in the context of design related to work, an especially pertinent one. Yet many of the designs and inventions in this field which have shaped the course of our century have not precisely or solely arisen out of need, but have come about through the relentless adapting, improving and applying of processes that characterise human activity. Once something new becomes available, we often learn to need or want it, or find new needs it can satisfy.

Hand tools express a direct link between a person, the work they do and the material they do it with. This intimate connection is part of what we find so appealing about these designs and may be part of the reason we are not very keen to tamper with them. Before industrialization, a tool was often made by the craftsman who would use it, for the particular job it had to perform. A tool was itself a trade secret.

Almost as soon as industrialization became established, nostalgia for handcrafted work began to take hold. The standardization of components, separation of skills and predictability of products demanded by industrial processes and mass markets ruled out any individual interpretation of material or expression of artisanship within the realm of manufacturing.

The Arts and Crafts Movement and successive groups in Europe, such as the Wiener Werkstätte, sought to restore 'art' to ordinary things by re-establishing craft skills as a basis for production. While the work of Morris, Moser and Hoffmann has been enormously influential in the shaping of contemporary taste, as commercial enterprises such designers and groups were largely unsuccessful within the terms they set themselves. Lovingly handcrafted work could simply not be made in sufficient quantities to bring the price of such manufacture within the reach of ordinary people, a bitter fact which Morris acknowledged in his complaint that he spent his life 'ministering to the swinish luxury of the rich'.

Much of what the Bauhaus produced was also rooted in craftwork, but unlike the Arts and Crafts followers, the leading lights of the emerging Modern Movement did not reject the machine as a means of production. Forward looking rather than nostalgic, modernist designers looked to new materials to forge a machine art of pure form that would be available to everyone. Their vision, however, was not shared by manufacturers. When Le Corbusier approached Peugeot with a proposal to make furniture from the tubular steel used in their bicycle manufacturing, he was turned down flat. The designs were later produced in a limited edition by the (then) more progressive firm of Thonet.

Morris did not believe that a well-designed object or beautiful artefact could arise from an industrial process which separated the role of the designer or artist from the role of the maker or producer. The designers of the Bauhaus, approaching the question from a different angle, sought to ensure that machine processes gave rise to products which expressed their own honest, functional beauty. Each was addressing, in different ways, the dilemmas posed by mass production.

Mass production had entered a new dimension in 1913 when Ford introduced the moving assembly line, a concept which revolutionized the entire nature of work. Previously, drawing on the research conducted by efficiency experts, he realized that if car parts were simplified and standardized and assembly broken down into small repetitive tasks, there would be no need for skilled craftsmen and cars could be produced very much faster. But neither standardization nor applying the principles of time and motion studies was enough to achieve the production levels that Ford desired.

In a factory converted to a moving assembly line, conveyors delivered parts to the appropriate places on the line and workers had to keep up with the speed at which the line was moving. The factory in effect became a machine which operated the worker, as the tool had never before worked the hand. This was a revolution, and the result was a phenomenal increase in production – the time taken to produce a Model-T dropped from 14 hours before 1913 to 95 minutes by 1914. By 1925, it was just 20 seconds. The success of this method soon led to the assembly line being adopted in many other spheres of production – but with little regard for the quality of working life.

The mechanization of manufacture meant that products could be made cheaply and in great numbers, but also predictably. Standardization and the logic of efficiency soon meant there was little to choose between something manufactured by one firm and the equivalent something made by another. Before long, the designer found a new role in industry, as a stylist, in the creation of brand or corporate identity and as an interpreter of technology.

Industrial design was first used as a form of marketing in America in the early 1930s. One of the undisputed leaders of the field was Raymond Loewy. French by birth, Loewy began his career as a fashion illustrator in New York in the 1920s, but soon became engaged in trying to convince manufacturers that the appearance of their products mattered. Loewy found most consumer goods of the time worthy enough functionally, but sorely lacking in imagination. Where attempts had been made to attract customers to a product by the way it looked, it was through applied decoration rather than the form of the object itself.

The assembly line turned men and women into cogs in the machinery of mass production.

Loewy was a showman and a considerable self-publicist. One of the first products to receive the Loewy overhaul was the Gestetner duplicating machine in 1929. Loewy simplified and humanized the appearance of this cumbersome piece of office equipment by concealing elements of its mechanism and encasing the machinery in wood rather than metal. In the process, he did not alter the way

Frank Lloyd Wright's administrative building for Johnson Wax (1936-9).

the machine functioned as a copier, but he gave it a look of greater efficiency and hence made it more saleable. Essentially he did what many industrial designers have done since: he put as much as he could into a package and styled it.

Many of Loewy's transformations did, however, show that styling can be more than skin deep and that an industrial designer need not be dismissed as someone who is solely concerned with the superficial or cynical manipulation of markets through appearance alone. Stylistic changes to the outward appearance can result in products which are easier to manufacture, cheaper to produce and more pleasurable to use.

'There is no curve so beautiful as a rising sales graph' Raymond Loewy

Manufacturers gradually saw the benefit of industrial design as a means of distinguishing their products from those of their competitors. As mentioned in the chapter on transport, this strategy was adopted wholeheartedly after the Second World War by the defeated powers of Italy, Germany and, later, Japan, as a means of creating not only an identity for individual firms competing in the international market, but as a way of promoting a national identity around which economic reconstruction could focus.

The need for these shattered economies to rebuild from scratch provided an opportunity for design to be more closely allied with manufacturing than it had ever been before. The strategy of creating a 'family of objects' which shared a common aesthetic was adopted by companies such as Braun, Sony, Olivetti, Cassina, Kartell and Artemide, and quickly established them as world leaders in contemporary design.

Olivetti epitomizes Italian industrial design. The full integration of design within the manufacturing process and company ethic is expressed in a recent Olivetti corporate brochure:

'Design is not just a methodology for the industrial age ... it also creates a sort of "continuum" between private and working lives, and provides a focus for reconciling man to technology. It is thus a valuable source of inspiration and an important means of expressing intellectual and artistic values. ... This philosophy deeply influences all the activities of the company and is particularly evident in its products, architecture and graphic design. Olivetti believes that technological progress must be linked with society's intellectual development, and so has always drawn on the most original designers and thinkers.'

Those original designers and thinkers include the best-known names in Italian design: Marcello Nizzoli, Ettore Sottsass, Vico Magistretti, Gae Aulenti and Mario Bellini, among others. From the outset design was never hived off into a separate department,

but infiltrated every area of the company's activity. The Lexicon 80 typewriter, designed in 1948 by Nizzoli was the first of a series of classic designs he produced for the company; its success helped to consolidate Olivetti's image as a design leader, while its sculptural quality earned it a place in the permanent design collection at the Museum of Modern Art in New York.

West German companies adopted a similar approach to the role of design within industry. But unlike Italy's more organic and artistically inspired aesthetic, the German version of a national design identity combined Bauhaus principles with rigorous technical efficiency in a more stylized or formal design language. This approach is typified by the the electrical goods produced by Braun and AEG or the cars manufactured by BMW (whose logo incorporates Bavarian colours) and Mercedes-Benz.

In both Germany and Italy – and for Scandinavian companies such as Orrefors, Bang & Olufsen and Marimekko – design was selling products. At the same time what was being sold was 'design' itself, design as excellence, quality and thoughtfulness. In their expression of functional efficiency, what such products offered the consumer was a reinforced image of professionalism in the workplace. Although many of the products emanating from Europe were more highly priced than their American equivalents, design had not yet acquired the connotations of spurious luxury which went along with the perception of 'designer' goods in the 1980s.

American companies in the 1950s used design in a rather different way. This was the era when the entire notion of corporate identity began to take off, and firms looked to outside design consultancies to devise ways of supporting a brand name or company image that would maintain their competitive edge.

Nothing looks more wasteful to the public at large then spending huge amounts of money on a change of livery, logo or masthead. It is true that there is often a tendency for designers to over-intellectualize the subject, but the costs involved in changing or updating a company's image compare very favourably to installing new computer equipment, for example. A new corporate identity can have a tremendous impact on the way the company functions in the marketplace as well as from within.

If the rewards of a successful corporate image are high, so is the price of failure. The cost of getting it wrong is the weakening of important ties of loyalty, both outside the company and within it. Inappropriate or inept changes of identity are all too conspicuous and can not only make the company in question look foolish but give the whole process of image-making a bad name. Nor will a superficial graphic gloss give long-term credibility to a company with a poor range of goods to sell – sows' ears cannot become silk purses however brilliant the packaging. As in other areas, corporate identity and image-making is a design process which cannot be conceived in isolation.

The first-ever fully fledged corporate identity is generally acknowledged to be that which Peter Behrens devised for the German electrical giant AEG (Allgemeine Elektrizitäts Gesellschaft). From 1907 onwards, Behrens and his team (which included Walter Gropius and Mies van der Rohe) tackled not only the company's logotype and presentation material but also its product design and factory buildings, replacing the firm's outmoded nineteenth-century image with one of vigorous modernity, a powerful expression of AEG's dominant position in the field of electrical engineering.

By the 1950s, with the arrival of mass consumption, corporate identity was responsible for establishing national and international brands, and became an important means of distinguishing between rival producers of similar products – sometimes, it could be argued, the only means. The successful design image of Olivetti inspired IBM to hire Eliot Noyes, who is generally acknowledged to be the pioneer of corporate identity in the United States. Noyes had been the director of industrial design at MOMA; under his direction, IBM's design policies were reshaped. Noyes commissioned Paul Rand to tackle the graphics and hired leading modernist architects to design new company buildings. He himself focussed on product design, applying the rationalist Bauhaus principles to which he adhered to the form of office equipment such as typewriters and dictating machines.

Corporate identity has evolved into a highly sophisticated form of graphic and conceptual presentation. The basic idea of using a memorable visual device as a badge of membership, allegiance or identification is, of course, hardly new. Just look at the intricate visual language of heraldry; of crosses, stars, crescents and other religious imagery; of crests, flags, coats of arms, and school ties – on every level and at every age symbols have been used to identify the bearer as a member of a particular group.

Yet despite the indisputable power of such symbols, the public often display a remarkably poor visual memory. Who would find it easy to reproduce the ICI logo? Or recall what a fluttering bird stands for? A symbol or logo which incorporates the name of the company or brand is often more effective in the long run at keeping the public's attention. Coco-Cola's flowing mock-copperplate logotype, adjusted imperceptibly over the years, is a case in point. Closer to home, the Habitat logo was a sympathetic marrying of the company name and the Baskerville typeface, the lower case style an important signal of informality and fashionability at the time of its inception.

Companies generally alter their identities in order to signify change. For those with an established, successful image, fine tuning may be all that is required to demonstrate that they remain in touch: the evolution of the Shell 'shell' is one such example of a logo fractionally adjusted over the decades.

Paul Rand's logo – a strong and enduring identity for the giant IBM corporation.

New companies seeking to make their mark or those in need of radical update will require a more significant level of change than a company which has worked hard to build a successful image over the years. Surprisingly, many companies find it hard to articulate what their philosophy actually is and the designer's role is to act almost like a company psychologist and tease out common purposes and ideals. Here, the fact that the designer is brought in to advise the company, rather than hired as a permanent member of the team, can be very useful.

In 1958, the Conran Design Group was responsible for one of the first thorough-going corporate identity programmes in Britain, for the wine company Harvey's of Bristol. We spent a considerable time analysing the company – determining the qualities for which it was recognized by its customers and which could be built upon, and the general direction in which it wanted to go. For Harvey's we devised one of the first corporate identity manuals in Britain, which gave clear examples of how the identity worked and how it could be applied. Instructions for printing, sign-writing, details of colour, type and placement ensured that the identity remained consistent after the initial changeover. The success of the programme led to work for other major firms over the succeeding decades, as the importance of a well-thought-through corporate identity became recognized as good business practice.

Much of the preliminary investigative work centres on how the change of identity will be implemented – and how quickly. This is not merely a question of public relations – the public launch of the new image, for example – but also involves an analysis of how the new identity will affect basic structures and practices within the company itself. During the course of discovering how many signs, labels, van liveries, uniforms, letterheads, forms, and cards will need to be changed, opportunities may well present themselves for rationalization. Reviewing the number of different sizes of letter

The severely functional design of this 1960s New York office expresses the corporate ethic.

paper (which can proliferate in large companies with many departments), or redesigning a form can save time and money, increase efficiency and help to project a coherent image to the public. In this way, a new identity can be a powerful rallying point for those working within the organization, pulling together the efforts of different disciplines or departments and generating an important sense of belonging. For a corporate identity to have some meaning (and any success), its relevance must permeate through the whole company, from the Chairman to the newest recruit.

Sometimes, however, what is required is a major jolt. The new identity for British Home Stores was a case in point. When Habitat/Mothercare joined with them, we decided that a new image was required to alter the public's perception, an important forerunner of change in a process of modernization which would

Office at Night by Edward Hopper (1940) captures the desperate tedium of the office routine.

take longer to accomplish in other areas. The makeover was planned to happen literally overnight. The new 'BhS' identity, which preserved the initials of the old name, hinted that the best qualities would be conserved even if change was radical. For maximum impact the new identity was put into effect all over the country during the course of a single weekend. Naturally such a dramatic change made high organizational demands, from planning permissions for new shop fronts and signs to producing stickers to remind telephonists to answer with the new name.

How individuals relate to the work they do, where they work and what they work with are just as much design issues as what is produced, how it functions and what it looks like. An important role of the designer should be to think about work in its broadest context,

to dream of how the world might be, yet few are prepared or equipped to deal with this level of analysis. Many furniture designers, for example, fail to concern themselves with what an office or workplace should look like, or how its organization could affect the pattern of working lives.

In the area of work, technology has acquired a momentum of its own which has brought about a remorseless distancing of people from the work they produce. The loss of physicality has been inexorable, from hand tool to machine, from assembly line to computer terminal.

I am no Luddite or technophobe, but I do recognize a need to compensate for this missing human dimension. To me, the processes of writing and drawing are very important and these are not activities I would particularly wish to carry out on a computer. Making marks with a pen on paper is a fundamental pleasure but it is also thought-provoking and exploratory. By contrast, a computer programme, no matter how sophisticated, seems to eliminate quirkiness and to restrict the free flow of ideas. It does not readily permit error or even personality, and, in design, it is human error that often opens up a new avenue.

Computers facilitate many processes, but their facility may come at the expense of deeper understanding. Designing and detailing a staircase, for example, is a tricky piece of architectural thinking. With CAD (computer-aided design), an architect can knock out a staircase axonometric in a fraction of the time it would take to make a model, but I believe a model may offer a better appreciation of the design factors involved, a physicality that can only be simulated on the screen, not directly experienced.

Of course, I am expressing no more than the common concerns of anyone confronting the impact of new technology on established working practices and habits. Technology has a tendency to inspire fear and distrust and the speed of technological change today means that many people find themselves in a state of mild anxiety as the working tools of their lives are constantly updated, refined, revolutionized or made obsolete. Many of these anxieties are simply based in ignorance or the carrying over of old models of thinking. The lady in James Thurber's story who fretted about unplugged power sockets 'leaking' electricity everywhere, imagined, presumably, that electrical flow was something like the flow of water through a pipe.

'User-friendly' is a marketing catchphrase which sums up our increasingly uneasy relationship with machines. The somewhat patronizing implication seems to be that technology can indeed outsmart us – or dominate and work us – and that we need some low-tech route into this sophisticated realm. All machines and all forms of technology, I believe, should be user-friendly. If they are not, they are both badly designed and badly conceived. We should feel comfortable with everything we use, and we shouldn't be afraid of abandoning the computer for pencil and paper at times.

The Filofax is a good case in point. You can easily store all the information you need – and a lot you don't – on a small notebook computer, but the Filofax is so much more personal. It feels good in the hand, it smells nice, it ages alongside you, and it evokes memories and carries tear-stained messages, occasional doodles, all manner of mementoes and souvenirs. A Filofax becomes attached to its owner in an intensely personal way.

I remember finding a mould-covered Filofax in a ditch near my house in France. To my amazement, its contents were written in English and, through phoning some of the numbers in the back, I eventually managed to track down the woman it belonged to. She was so grateful when I called to tell her that I'd found her Filofax you would think I was returning her long lost child to her. Somehow, I doubt that the return of an electronic personal organizer would rouse the same level of emotions.

Henry Dreyfuss, the Bell '300' telephone (1937)

For adaptive creatures, human beings are remarkably resistant to change. Henry Dreyfuss, the industrial designer responsible for the classic Bell telephone design of 1933, had an absorbing interest in so-called 'human engineering'. He believed that innovations must preserve a 'survival form', a conspicuous link to a previous age of technology which will permit people to accept and accommodate new ideas. The Apple Macintosh – with its graphic use of familiar symbols, from the watch to the 'trash-can' icon, and the cosy anthropomorphic mouse – can be seen as a similar attempt to lead hesitant and worried users gently over a new technological chasm.

Computer keyboards still retain the QWERTY format originally devised in 1872. The three Americans who came up with the idea and sold it to Remington had established that this particular arrangement of letters was least likely to cause typewriter keys to clash. There's no reason to worry about this any more, nor has there been for some time. Research has also identified that QWERTY is not the most comfortable or ergonomic arrangement for typists, since a number of letters which are frequently used, including A, fall on the margin of the keyboard where they must be operated by the weakest fingers (not that strong fingers are required to operate an electronic keyboard). But the sheer familiarity of QWERTY, which has survived the transition from manual to electric to electronic keyboards, makes it reassuring, and overrides its functional deficiencies.

Design or technological improvements are often spurred by the failure of something to function as it should, or they may arise out of a designer anticipating a need which had not previously existed. Yet these projected scenarios often turn out very differently from what was expected. The paperless office which was supposed to accompany the advent of computerization provokes a wry smile today. The ease of printing documents and the perfectability of each alternative means that more, not less, paper gets consumed.

The fear or expectation that one form of technology will supplant another is not always justified. The death of the book, widely predicted with each multimedia innovation, has not come to pass. The ability of different forms of technology to coexist and cross-fertilize is not necessarily an indication that a few diehards are clinging to outmoded technologies, but that different levels of technology serve different purposes. Paper copies of computer-generated work are lighter and more transportable than laptops and offer a different, more physical kind of interaction.

The role of design, as more becomes technically possible, is to sift through such issues and remind us of the real quality of life. The typeface, for example, can theoretically be exploded by computer programming, which enables letterforms to be produced randomly and anarchically throughout a text. Avant-garde graphic designers such as David Carson, best-known for his work on the American music magazine, *Ray Gun*, overturn all the rules of print design, deconstructing grids and formats in favour of a wild mix of type styles, sizes and placement. The results may be highly entertaining visually, but the words are sometimes unreadable. Carson defends his work by maintaining that pages of boring grey type don't inspire people to read, whereas type that looks exciting can arouse interest in its content. I would argue that designers should be able to arouse visual interest without sacrificing readability, since this must be the prime function of type.

The design and furnishing of working environments and the tools and accessories associated with the world of work are not solely defined by their efficiency or functionalism. They have a broader cultural meaning as well, and many objects and materials once exclusively residing in industrial or commercial contexts have seeped into other areas of our lives.

Many designers, myself included, find Victorian warehouses, factories and stations infinitely more appealing than the ornate, cluttered interior decoration and domestic architecture of the era. Gutsy, raw, and robustly engineered, these forthright buildings express the energy and entrepreneurialism of the age.

The Victorians maintained a sharp separation of home and work. When the head of the household crossed the threshold of his home at the end of the working day, he entered a cosy, encompassing domain stuffed with curios and swathed with fabric and trimmings that obliterated any outward sign of function – an environment as different as possible from the workplace. The Victorian home was not an efficient place to live or maintain, but it was not meant to be. It served instead as a refuge from work and a place to display the status symbols and luxuries that wages could buy.

As we have seen in the Household chapter, the kitchen was the first area of the home to see elements borrowed from the working environment applied in a domestic setting. Ergonomic planning, industrially designed machinery, neatly integrated fittings upgraded a humble service room into a model of efficiency, with the housewife as workforce and factory manager rolled into one.

Gradually the migrants have multiplied, materials and approaches as much as products. At the same time, office design has seen a certain softening, with the rigid lines which formerly expressed a hard-nosed commitment to professionalism beginning to give way to more flexible and friendlier working spaces that attempt to bridge the gap between home and office.

There is a certain time lag inherent in the cross-over. High-tech, which introduced industrial components, materials and fittings to the home, arose at a time when old-style manufacturing was on the wane and large commercial buildings in the heart of the city – from warehouses to machine shops – were newly redundant. Perhaps our willingness to welcome such hard-edged elements as studded rubber flooring and steel system shelving into the home reflected a nostalgia for a disappearing era of production.

Glamour and status, as well as nostalgia, infect our choice of work accessories. Most of us would feel rather foolish strolling around wearing a hard hat if we had no business on a building site, but it is somehow more acceptable to pack your papers into a metal photographer's case even if your photographic expertise only extends to the taking of holiday snapshots. The cult objects of the desktop, from Filofax to Rolodex, are ways in which we enhance our image of professionalism, proclaim our status and show that we take work seriously.

The desk chair is also charged with meaning. A big, comfortable expensive chair is a power seat, as much a token of managerial privilege as the key to the executive washroom. Herman Miller's 'Aeron' chair (1994), designed by Bill Stumpf and Don Chadwick, challenges these long-held notions of an office hierarchy. With modern workforces far more mixed in terms of gender and ethnic origin, the need for office equipment to suit a diversity of users has become more acute. Accordingly, the 'Aeron' comes in three sizes – small, medium and large – to accommodate different human builds. It also incorporates a special tilt-and-twist mechanism which enables the chair to move with the body in a series of smooth adjustments. The three models are distinguished only by size; they are marketed at the same price and share the same specifications. The ergonomic advantages of the chair design provide an obvious improvement in the quality of working life, yet initially the manufacturers have found that the mid-range size is most often specified. Companies have found it difficult to abandon standardization in favour of individual comfort and practicality. For managers, it may be harder still to choose a chair which accommodates their physical frame rather than proclaims their status. Sadly, despite its innovation, I find the chair rather ugly.

The ultimate power office, as conceived by Hollywood in Tim Burton's *Batman* (1989).

A lot of office design is steeped in perceived notions of what is acceptable or what supports the status quo. When Lord Gowrie was Minister of the Arts he commissioned our design group to revamp his offices. The scheme caused a furore, chiefly because it departed from the expected view of ministerial style. Instead of a clubby Westminster office, stuffed with antique desks and leather chairs, we opted for a cool, elegant, modern design which actually cost far less to realize. Never the less, it was seen by his colleagues as an extravagance, inappropriate for the sober corridors of power.

'Things are in the saddle,
And ride mankind' Ralph Waldo Emerson

Messages about status are equally apparent in the design of those home offices which perpetuate the aesthetic of the office workstation when there is no longer any real reason to do so. As home-working becomes more commonplace, the need to reassure oneself and others that proper work can be accomplished at home will become less acute and we may relax more into our surroundings, allowing the line between home and work to blur a little more.

It is inevitable that, with the coming of the Internet, the trend to work at home will increase. The growth of information technology is already having profound effects on working patterns; on the individual level, such changes will focus attention more sharply on the quality of the built environment. The implications go far beyond the four walls of the home office and out into the city itself.

If work is no longer tied to the workplace – office block, factory, out-of-town industrial park – opportunities arise to redefine urban space. Many of the problems faced by towns and cities are the legacy of previous working patterns. The dormitory village, the commuter town, the featureless suburb as much as the urban slum are the products of a rigid compartmentalization of working life and social life. The effect has been to knock the heart out of many cities, at the same time creating satellite communities with no sense of vitality. Towns such as Milton Keynes, originally modelled on Los Angeles, are based on the premise that private transport removes the necessity to live near one's place of work, or indeed near shops and leisure facilities. Yet the places most people enjoy the most, and those which often prove most successful at adapting to change, are areas of 'mixed use' – where housing is supported by shops, workplaces, schools, parks, restaurants, cafés and other public meeting places bound together in a tight, bustling network.

As our dependency on technology increases, there will be an even greater need for such interface. At the same time, by removing the distinction between home and work, technology offers an opportunity for more community-based life. The ultimate challenge for design in the area of work may be in the field of urban planning – to help integrate social and working life once more.

How and where we work are key issues, but whether we will be able to work at all is the huge question now facing us. Human beings have always worked, but the job, in the sense of organized work at a designated workplace, only came about with the advent of the industrial revolution. Two hundred years, however, is long enough to become accustomed to the security of employment and the predictability of the working routine. All this is now under threat, as computerized systems of information retrieval and factory automation gobble up jobs in every sector of the economy. Only one in three people currently employed in Britain now works a nine-to-five, Monday-to-Friday week, while it is estimated that 90 out of the 124 million American jobs are of the kind most likely to disappear as a result of digitalization. Machines began by operating their workers; now they are replacing them. Many people are going to have a lot of free time on their hands in future.

People want to work; they need integrated lives which allow physical and mental exchanges. This remains as true today as it was when the Arts and Crafts pioneers searched for ways to restore the dignity of work. John Ruskin, who had an enormous influence on succeeding generation of designers, wrote in *The Stones of Venice*: 'The workman has not done his duty, and is not working on safe principles, unless he so far honours the materials in which he is working as to set himself to bring out their beauty, and to recommend and exalt ... their peculiar qualities.' I would hope that in a post-industrial world, where basic needs are met with little human intervention, small workshops and factories, where products can be designed and made with individual care and attention, would spring up and flourish. If that optimistic scenario came to pass, we would see design at the heart of the working process once more.

Modern commercial offices, with their modular system furniture, tough surfaces and finishes and rectilinear layouts, are designed to be practical and economical. But those relentlessly hard edges and sharp angles – neatly satirized in the *New Yorker* cartoon – also serve to project an image of business-like efficiency and cost-effectiveness by rigorously excluding any reminder of domestic life. An altogether different corporate ethic is expressed in the design of such innovative workspaces as the Imagination building in London, where the central atrium and connecting walkways give the entire enterprise a sense of openness, light and vitality. Appropriately enough, the building is the headquarters of a creative design agency.

To my mind, people work better in attractive surroundings where order and organization are not achieved at the expense of mind-numbing uniformity. The engagingly pod-like Clipper CS-1 workstation, designed by Douglas Ball, addresses the need to create private enclosures for concentrated work within open-plan office floors. Whilst I don't think people would want to spend days on end shut up in the workstation, the natural materials (plywood and canvas) and organic cockpit shape domesticate the technology, creating a refuge or thinking space. It's all a far cry from the desk of the past, with its towering mountains of files and paperwork.

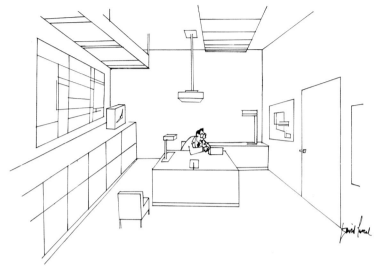

"Miss Jenkins, would you please bring a round object into my office?"

Drawing by David Pascal; © 1980 *The New Yorker* Magazine Inc.

Ron Heron, Imagination Building, London (1988)

My study in London – where I like to work

Douglas Ball, Clipper CS-1 workstation (1993)

Government office, Paris
(1940s)

Charles Rennie Mackintosh, staircase, Glasgow School of Art (1897-9)

Charles Rennie Mackintosh, alcove seat, Glasgow School of Art (1907-9)

'Do all your work as if you have a thousand years to live or might die tomorrow'

Sister Ann Lee, founder of the Shakers

The Glasgow School of Art, the masterwork of Charles Rennie Mackintosh, still serves the purpose for which it was designed a century ago. The brief specified a 'plain building', the site was awkward, narrow and sloping, and the budget severely restricted, but Mackintosh triumphantly overcame these limitations to create a robust, functional building imbued with artistry and richness: a working environment that expresses the spirit of creativity. An attention to detail runs throughout the building, from the Director's office to the school corridors.

Charles Rennie Mackintsoh, Director's office, Glasgow School of Art (phase one, 1897-9)

WORK

Charles Rennie Mackintosh, 'hen run', Glasgow School of Art (phase two, 1907-9)

206

'Technology is the knack of so ordering the world that we don't have to experience it'

Max Frisch

Robotized car factory, Japan

Knoll factory, Pennsylvania: polishing one of the Breuer Collection chairs

Hand-finishing a hunter's knife, cutlery factory, France

Dieter Rams and Dietrich Lubs, Braun Control ET44 calculator (1978)

For many people, the physical dimension of work has shrunk to the point of contact between fingertips and keyboard. The shallow concave shape of keys, the familiar QWERTY format, and the incline of the keyboard itself are ways in which comfort and ease of operation are maintained. The Microsoft Natural Keyboard goes a step further: the fluid contour prevents repetitive stress injury by forcing the user to sit properly, with squared shoulders. The ergonomic design cost £10 million in research development.

Both the Braun calculator and the Olivetti portable typewriter are examples of office machines transformed into objects of desire. The Braun calculator is shaped like a pocket; the clarity and simplicity of the keypad make it a pleasure to use. The typewriter, the first with an integral case, marries bold colour with sculptural form.

Ettore Sottsass, Olivetti Valentine typewriter (1970)

Microsoft Natural Keyboard (1995)

'I have just taken delivery of my electric typewriter, and I am in love with my electric typewriter. Indeed, I may marry my electric typewriter' Noel Coward

Girl with abacus (1955), photograph by J.P. Charbonnier

Apple Computer Inc., logo

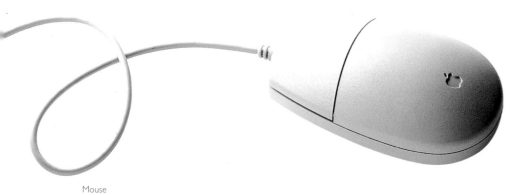

Mouse

Development of Apple Computers: Apple 1 (1976)

Wooden prototype model for Apple 3 (1978)

The first Apple Macintosh (1984)

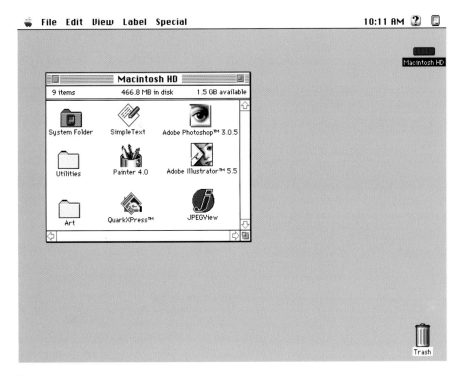

Desktop

Trash icon (empty)   Trash icon (full)   Calculator

Apple Computer offices, Cupertino Campus, Silicon Valley, California

The Apple Macintosh, the computer that set industry standards for a decade, was revolutionary for its 'graphical user interface' which allowed the operator simply to point and click on icons using a 'mouse'. Designed by a team of engineers (average age 21) headed by Steve Jobs, Apple's co-founder, the seal on the Macintosh's success was the subsequent development of postscript technology, which enabled exactly what was on the screen to be printed, a breakthrough that heralded the birth of desk-top publishing. Since Apple designed and manufactured both the hardware and software, there was a seamless quality to the operating system, a sense of elegance and user-friendliness.

Fire station, Dallas, Texas

Quaglino's restaurant kitchen, London

'Designing is not the abstract power exercised by a genius. It is simply the arranging how work shall be done'

W.R. Lethaby

Heinz typing pool, Pittsburgh, Pennsylvania

Charles and Ray Eames, Executive soft-pad chair

Rolodex

Mont Blanc fountain pen

No thrusting executive would be without the latest mobile phone, but many desk-top icons date back to a much earlier era: the Filofax is 75 years old. Other cult accessories migrate across the professions. Non-lawyers write on yellow legal pads, non-photographers pack their papers in Halliburton cases.

WORK

216

Filofax

Anglepoise lamp

Halliburton case

Legal note-pad

Nokia mobile (cellular) phone

Cafetiere and 'designer' sandwiches

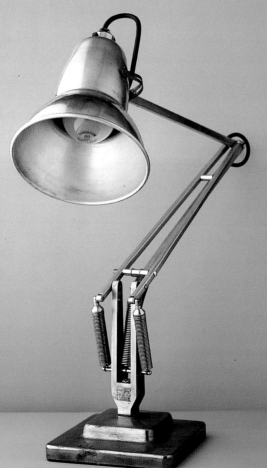

The Lloyds Building in the City of London is a welcome antidote to the typical, bland commercial building. Exposing the service parts on the outside of the building provides a flexible interior space housing a ten-storey insurance market. External servicing allows maintenance to be carried out without disruption. At the same time, this controversial design projects an evocative image of work – the office as a powerhouse. The Lloyds Building evokes the functional quality of other working buildings. Grain silos, hydro-electric dams, windmills and brick kilns all have a strong appeal for many designers.

Richard Rogers Architects, Lloyds Building, City of London (1986)

Grain silo, Montana

The quality of life is a fundamental consideration in every area of human activity; in the context of what we do with our free time our expectations are even more acute. Free time, after all, is supposed to be 'quality' time, that part of our lives not framed by duties and responsibilities, but given over to enjoyment and self-fulfilment.

There can be no doubt that the way people amuse and entertain themselves has changed out of all recognition since the beginning of the century. It is only a hundred years since the birth of cinema, yet in the succeeding

free

decades we have seen the advent of a
seemingly endless list of innovations. But
audio-visual technology increasingly defines
leisure activity in terms of the equipment
and products with which it is carried out.

Free time itself, in the sense of predictable
chunks of time at weekends and after
working hours, is a relatively modern idea.
At the dawn of the machine age, as labour-
saving equipment in the home and the office
provided ordinary people with more leisure
time, manufacturers were quick to supply
products to capitalize on this new need.

time

Hollywood movies have exported American culture around the world.

I suppose most people would define free time as the opportunity to escape from the rat race or the daily grind, the chance to indulge in activities which are instructive, amusing or simply pleasant: time for its own sake. Increasingly, however, free time is anything but free. For many people, spending time equals spending money. The relentless commercialization of every leisure pursuit is expressed in the ultimate modern pastime – shopping. Nor is free time precisely free in terms of the personal expression of individuality. From the package holiday to the blockbuster film, we are offered choices which lead to conformity rather than true variety of experience, while new technology threatens to blur the line between simulation and reality.

Getting away from it all, it seems, increasingly means finding that everyone has come out to join you; either that, or it entails escaping into the hermetic world of a machine. Surely, then, there must be room for improvement. The question is, should designers be expected to put the genie back into the bottle? While I do not suppose that design alone could ever restructure our social lives, there are certainly good and bad ways in which design can be employed in this area, as in any other. The best of these, to my mind, place the individual and his or her social life back in the centre of the picture.

Our changing leisure patterns are social issues as much as they are issues concerning technology and design. Yet Penny Sparke, the design historian, points out that asking which comes first – social change or design change – is always a 'chicken and egg' question. It is impossible for designers to live in a vacuum, divorced from social trends and customs, or ignorant of the changing environment in their field of work. I would argue that it is also irresponsible for designers to ignore the wider impact of their work.

The advent of electronics has seen monumental changes in the way we live and in the products with which surround ourselves. In home entertainment, no less than the workplace, we engage with a host of black boxes that act as intermediaries and interpreters of the world. In the context of free time, the fear of technology and what it can do is often the fear of being left behind as the pace of change accelerates. It is estimated, for example, that the power of silicon chips is doubling every 18 months, an exponential growth in technological potential.

In the past, products were developed within a tradition of craftsmanship. They were physically made. Even if you lacked the relevant skills, it was still possible to understand the process by which something was created. With each technological generation,

The French House, London, has changed little since the days it was a haunt of the Free French.

the tendency has been to understand a little less. As chips replace working parts we have entered an era where very few people understand how the majority of products they use actually operate. That irresistible impulse to bash the television on the top when the picture goes wrong betrays the fact that, deep down, we still expect machinery to be mechanical, to have moving parts that can jam.

In the face of all this technical sophistication, the temptation is to plead ignorance. Instead, we should demand that designers work on our behalf to create products that really work for people. This means that designers, instead of simply styling the black boxes which house the smart parts, must understand both what is technically possible and what is humanly desirable.

Technological sophistication, of course, is a selling point. When a radically new product is launched, the challenge for manufacturers is to overcome our innate resistance by presenting the functions of the machine as irresistible and revolutionary. In other words, they target an initial market of trendsetting enthusiasts – a group market-researchers call 'innovators' – who will be flattered by the power and complexity of the product rather than intimidated by it. Only once an innovation becomes a standard is much thought given to the ordinary users and what they require.

The Japanese electronics industry, which has dominated the market for home technology, has been heavily influenced by the 'black box' aesthetic of German designers such as Dieter Rams. To this fine-tuned, rational style Japanese designers have added their own twist, the deliberate expression of complex functions that adds a professional allure to their products. The proliferation of dials, knobs, buttons and digital displays is a design strategy intended to convince consumers that they are at the cutting edge of technology, and that they also have the expertise to exploit it.

Few people, however, really want much more from their video recorder, for example, than simple playback and recording functions. None the less, they are offered a bewildering range of features which express what the machine can do rather than address what users actually want it to do. I believe that for a video recorder or any other piece of equipment to be well designed it should present some hierarchy of functions so that the essential operations can be distinguished at a glance from those which are peripheral. This approach is evident in the recent VCR designed by Priestman Associates for Hitachi, where the controls used most frequently are prominently grouped on the right of the console, while more esoteric functions are controlled by hidden buttons. The role of design in this context should always be to simplify and organize technology in a human way.

The third stage in the evolution of an advanced piece of technological equipment arises when it achieves such a degree of acceptance that it is possible to play around with its form and appearance. Colour is often the first introduction, subverting the classic metallic or black image of professionalism and efficiency. Then come the wilder flights of fancy which give us products like Daniel Weil's 1981 see-through radio, its components housed in a transparent plastic envelope, or Philippe Starck's deconstructed 'Jim Nature' television, encased in a tactile shell of recycled wood chips. Such playful and original expressions of design verve and flair must be preferred over the type of cynical fakery which disguises televisions as Sheraton cabinets.

On the other hand, design in the service of commercialism often results in pure stylistic manipulation. Sony, which has been called the 'single most important company in Japanese history', has a great track record of innovation, dating back to their inspired application of the transistor, an American invention, to the radio in 1954. The Walkman, designed in 1979, represented another such conceptual leap, revolutionizing the way we listen to music by exploiting the potential of advanced electronics to increase personal freedom and mobility. Now, more than 15 years later, and with more than 130 million units sold, Walkmans come in a wide and increasing range of different models – distinguished chiefly by their colours, graphics, materials and trimmings – to infiltrate every possible market niche.

Style – or styling – sells. When Norman Bel Geddes was commissioned by Philco to redesign their radios in 1931-2 the result was a 50 per cent increase in sales. Early radiograms resembled pieces of furniture. The work of designers such as Bel Geddes and Wells Coates, the originator of the classic, round Bakelite Ekco radio, helped to make radios more popular by giving the products they worked on a unique visual identity.

It seems to me that aesthetic pleasure is very closely related to memory. An intelligently designed, state-of-the-art music system which delivers excellent sound quality and is easy to operate is pleasing by virtue of its efficiency. But the speed at which such equipment is superseded by the latest advance does not inspire attachment. The value that some people are prepared to place on a sense of continuity is demonstrated by the growing market for revivalist design, even within the highly sophisticated field of home entertainment.

The Roberts radio, for example, a classic British product which was a familiar sight in many kitchens of the 1950s and '60s, has recently been successfully reintroduced to cater for those who find that tradition in design can outweigh the enticements of technical performance. Just as the act of pouring a drink from a Pernod bottle is like pouring a memory of French café life, revivalist forms encapsulate and evoke particular times and places. Perhaps there is also an unspoken acknowledgement that there is a point beyond which technical progress becomes irrelevant. Our senses, after all, are not capable of infinite discrimination.

My parents were reasonably well-off, yet they went abroad only once: for their honeymoon. My children have been everywhere in the world. In many countries, tourism is now an entrenched part of economic life; in some countries, tourism is almost the sole industry. What has been called the 'cultural arm of globalization', tourism is the way in which many of us choose to spend our free time.

Philippe Starck, Jim Nature television (1993).

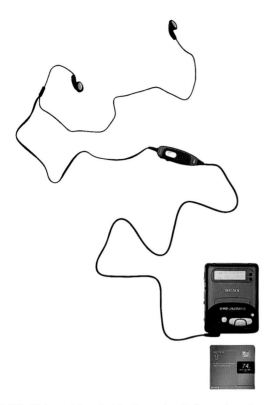

Sony's Mini-Disc Walkman delivers the latest in sound quality for people on the move.

But while travel is supposed to broaden the mind, tourism serves to shrink the world and narrow the difference between one culture and another. The package holiday in the chain hotel is only the most extreme example of the way in which national identities can be eroded and experience made predictable.

Design can be used to collude in this process or as a means of resisting it. Where design is seen as an agent for recreating national identity – rather than a means of preserving an image of the past in aspic – it provides a jolt of the unexpected which keeps culture alive. Compare, for example, the audacity of I.M. Pei's pyramid in the heart of the Louvre with the cosy world of the National Trust, with its tasteful tea towels, pot-pourri and hand-labelled pots of jam. Mitterand's legacy – the new Paris monuments – proclaims faith in public life and the future, a faith which also serves to enhance what has gone before. In this country, our failure even to attempt to produce anything like a coherent vision of modernity, coupled with the tendency to transform every historical site into an upmarket theme park, speaks of stagnation and faint-heartedness. Conserving the best of the old is a worthy and necessary ambition, but it cannot be achieved by ignoring the new or avoiding the future.

Spain, in recent years, provides another example of a culture expressing its distinct characteristics through a progressive use of design. The centre of this flowering has been Barcelona, which, as capital of Catalonia, has had a strong historic, political and cultural identity of its own. The city has a rich past, evident in its lively old quarters, seafront and in the work of its great, idiosyncratic architect, Antonio Gaudi. It also has a tradition of progressive planning, dating from the grid format worked out for the nineteenth-century expansion of the city.

Since the 1980s, Barcelona has been the focus of a remarkable design boom, culminating in the revitalization of the city for its hosting of the 1992 Olympic Games. The architecture and furniture designs of Oscar Tusquets, whose metal mesh bench features in many of the city's public spaces, and the explosion of new bars by designers such as Alfredo Arribas, Andre Ricard, Eduardo Samso and Javier Mariscal (also responsible for the Olympic mascot) have made the city a mecca for design enthusiasts all over the world. All this has not happened in isolation, but is part of a positive strategy supported by official authorities, notably the mayor, Pasqual Maragall. The Olympic village, for example, was not sited out of town but integrated in the run-down waterfront area, and the entire scheme was seen as an opportunity to revive the district and restore the city's historic connection with the sea.

Barcelona demonstrates the invigorating power of design and how local flavour can be enhanced without resorting to parochialism. On a smaller scale, C.D. Partnership is currently engaged in revitalizing the waterfront at Leith in Scotland. Our Ocean Terminal will provide a point of arrival and departure for sea passengers, as well as providing shops, cafés, bars and restaurants, a hotel, gym, cinemas and a host of leisure activities. We have also been working on two major hotel projects in Vienna and London. In both of these cases, the challenge has been to avoid the obvious but to express elements of each city's life and culture that will provide the hotels with a sense of character and destination.

In the case of the Viennese hotel, we wanted to avoid the temptation of making it look Hoffmanesque. The design process, accordingly, has entailed distilling elements of Viennese life in an original interpretation – the cosy bar accessed directly from the street, the mingling of influences in a Central European location. A copy or pastiche of 'Austrian style' would have represented one more devaluation of a cultural currency; the imposition of an unthinking, international format would have undermined any real reason for choosing this location over any other.

If hotels provide an introduction for visitors to a country's identity, the design and presentation of museums and their collections highlight many other cultural and national issues. Many museums owe their origins to the passionate obsessions or acquisitiveness of single individuals; they then grew to assume a wider role as repositories for national heritage, learning and culture. Now they have assumed an almost religious function as gathering places where the public can commune with the past.

Museums, once run largely by and for a peer group of academics, are now major tourist attractions for home visitors as well as those from abroad. This shift of focus has not been without its controversies, many of which have centred on the role of design in making collections more accessible and museums more attractive places to spend time. The conflict between the two functions of serving the needs of scholarship and attracting the general public has only been heightened by the state's withdrawal from the financing of cultural life. The hard economic facts are that for museums and cultural landmarks to survive, they must be financially viable, which in turn means increased dependency on such commercial enterprises as cafés and shops.

I see absolutely no reason why museums and other cultural sites should not be designed in such a way as to make them more pleasant to visit, with decent cafés and restaurants offering good food, coherent signage, and well-presented collections. I have always liked the idea of a museum layout which combines a general path the public can follow to see the 'hits' of a collection with more contemplative backwaters for serious academic study – similar to the brief for a grand plan which the Victoria and Albert Museum gave to the architect Michael Hopkins.

Something of this approach is evident in the new Glass Gallery at the V&A, where the space is split into two levels. The mezzanine floor is filled with display shelves packed with glass, while the ground floor is a more spacious area where cases highlight spectacular examples supported by more considered captioning. The mezzanine, co-designed by glass artist Danny Lane and the gallery's architect, Penny Richards, features Lane's glass balustrade, a dramatic and evocative design that heightens the pleasure of viewing the collection. Intelligent planning has ensured that 80 per cent of the collection is on view, with background information supplied on computer terminals and touch-screen videos. Instead of rows of badly lit Victorian mahogany cases, the displays have a sparkling transparency which convey the excitement of the material. The result is both a simpler, more coherent place to study glass and a wonderful place to visit.

What really makes purists uneasy, however, is not so much the role of design in the museum display and presentation, but its association with retailing, as manifested by the museum shop. There was once a V&A advertising slogan which exhorted the

'One half of the world cannot understand the

public to visit 'a really ace caff with quite a nice museum attached'. Nowadays, 'caff' would have to read 'shop', and there are those who would fail to see the joke. There is no getting away from the fact that many visits are made to country houses, museums and other cultural sites with the chief purpose of shopping, nor that such enterprises depend on the revenue from their shops to keep going.

The impulse to collect a souvenir, as tangible evidence of an experience or visit, is hardly new, of course. All those visitors to stately homes, filing past the crimson ropes, crane their necks to view the souvenirs long-dead aristocrats had once crated back from their Grand Tours. However, the quality of the 'heritage' or souvenir shop, its design and the design of the products it stocks, can make the difference between dismal prepackaged commercialization and the opportunity to acquire something of more lasting interest and value than a leatherette bookmark stamped with the name of a castle, stately home or other landmark.

Shops within museums and cultural centres have grown increasingly sophisticated, employing the strategies of successful high-street retailers to theme their merchandise and reinforce the identity of the whole 'product', the destination itself. Where design has been used to paint a fresh new face on a tired institution or to add gloss to products which are little more than trinkets, the results are bound to provoke cynicism and dismay. Yet there are examples of shops, such as the one at MOMA in New York, which could stand in their own right, outside the framework of the organization they promote, offering excellent ranges of educational, inspirational and desirable goods that do not so much peddle a theme as extend understanding and appreciation of an area of cultural life. Commercial art has probably done more to shape cultural and social development in the late twentieth century than fine art. Given this, it is not surprising that people are drawn to shops every bit as strongly as they are drawn to museum collections. After all, design in all its forms touches the lives of everybody in society, while fine art is, sadly, prohibitively expensive.

As a designer who is also a retailer, but more especially as the founder of the Design Museum, these issues are understandably close to my heart. The Design Museum grew out of the Conran Foundation, which I established in 1980 with the primary aim of educating industrialists, designers and students, as well as the general public, about the importance of industrial design as a means of bettering the quality of everyday life. Our first site was a small area in the old boiler rooms of the V&A . We called it the Boilerhouse, a name which recalled the fact that the V&A, in its original incarnation, was fondly known as the 'Brompton Boilers'.

During the five years we spent at this site, 26 provocative exhibitions covered a wide range of design-related subjects, from in-depth profiles of companies such as Coca-Cola and Sony to the problems of designing for the elderly; from a lighthearted survey of the shopping bag as image-maker to a detailed analysis of the design process of the Ford Sierra.

The Boilerhouse lived up to its name and our objectives, stirring up opinion, providing insight into the role of design within mass production, and pulling in the crowds. At times more people visited this tiny 4,000 square foot space than the remaining thirteen acres of the V&A.

In 1989, the Design Museum moved to its permanent home at Butlers Wharf near Tower Bridge. Housed in a 1940s warehouse building, which was stripped down to its structure and rebuilt, the museum includes exhibition spaces, a permanent collection of twentieth-century design artefacts, a library and lecture theatre, a shop, and, of course, an 'ace caff' – the Blue Print Café, which looks out over the Thames from the first-floor. Major international exhibitions have drawn a consistently high attendance, while our

pleasures of the other' Jane Austen, *Emma*

educational programme brings in busloads of schoolchildren who make very active use of the museum's resources when they come. Success, however, has been qualified by a constant struggle to make ends meet. The increasing need to find corporate sponsorship to cover the shortfall caused by lack of state funding is the cold reality faced by many museums and institutions in Britain today, a situation that is becoming ever-more crucial as more and more lottery-funded projects come on-stream.

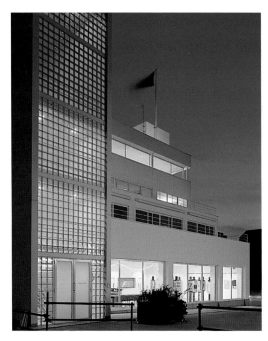

The Design Museum, London (1989) expounds the role of design.

One of the early Design Museum exhibitions looked at the exciting ways in which new materials and design ideas are employed in the highly competitive field of sports equipment. Design has a particularly immediate impact on sporting performance; there are many instances where redesigned equipment has directly led to a competitor's success. The uninhibited nature of design in this field, coupled with the high degree of innovation in material technology, has had a huge influence on other design areas.

I find most accessories and equipment associated with sport to be as aesthetically pleasing as tools, largely because such articles are driven primarily by function. Today, however, everything – from Grand Prix cars to tennis rackets – is so emblazoned with logos that the eye is constantly distracted, and the beauty of the original form is completely obscured. The hidden persuaders are not so hidden any more.

The branding of leisure activities has reached such a peak that there is danger of overload. Branding essentially works on a subliminal level: we note the reference, clock the association and file it away without realizing it. Today, however, branding is so ubiquitous it has become self-defeating.

Branding is just one aspect of the rampant commercialization of leisure and is symptomatic of the way in which the worlds of art, marketing, mass media, graphics, product design and fashion have increasingly converged. The term 'admass' was coined for post-war American society, where sales were fuelled by appetites whetted in cinema, television, newspapers and magazines. The use of design as a marketing tool, rather than as part of a production process, has arisen from the simple fact that mass production necessarily demands mass consumption.

In the affluent Western societies of the post-war period, manufacturing expanded at a phenomenal rate – a growth of 100 per cent in the ten years between 1958 and 1968. This was matched by an equivalent growth in mass communications. In 1951, 1.5 million Americans owned a television; by 1960 this figure was 85 million. Advertising and the mass media gave products a visibility and desirability they had never had before. At the same time, the

  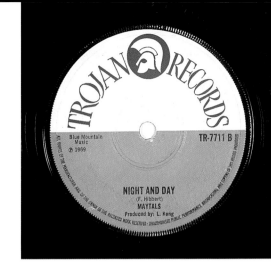

Superseded by technology, the record label has gone the way of the album cover, once the vehicle for new graphic styles, now collectors' items.

spending power of a new market sector – young people with a disposable income of their own for the first time – became a serious force to be reckoned with.

Out of this potent mix came pop culture. A logical development of the 'admass' society, pop made the medium the message. Fifties' mass style was a confident modern aesthetic expressed in images derived from science as well as modern art. By the 1960s, all the barriers were down. The rapid turnover of styles promoted by mass media, as well as the blurring of distinctions between one aspect of culture and the next, gave design a new role – the task of satisfying the frenzy for novelty.

Today we are unsurprised when an advertisement for a bank targets first-time customers using graphics borrowed from the rave scene. Or when Microsoft pays the Rolling Stones £8 million for the use of one of their songs to launch new software. Or when Saatchi and Saatchi wrap an island in the manner of Christo to promote British Airways. We are so accustomed to layers of irony and cross-reference that it is hard to tell where one product ends and another begins.

Endorsement and merchandising confuse the issue further. A recent ad for British Telecom featured the British pop musician, Dave Stewart, and looked like a pop video – which, of course, it was, in addition to a BT promotion. The Fifties dance track chosen for a Guinness ad became a hit record and inspired a new cult.

While ads borrow from films (and are often directed by the same people), films often serve as ads. In the 1950s, American movies reaching a Europe ravaged by war sold the the whole consumer lifestyle. Later, James Bond sold Aston Martins, just as *Disclosure* sells information technology and Uma Thurman in *Pulp Fiction* created an international shortage of a particular shade of dark nail varnish. The most blatant examples are product placements – those familiar brand names casually framed in closeup.

Off-screen, merchandising rules. The costume designers working on *Batman Forever*, for example, had to come up with their concepts early enough to allow sufficient time for the manufacturers to put their T-shirts, key rings, pencil cases and plastic bat models into production – merchandise which earned three times more than the film took at the box office. We might be forgiven for thinking that now the tail often wags the dog.

The toy market is dominated by this type of merchandising, where the T-shirt of the film-of-the-book crops up again as the plastic figure on the Saturday morning cartoon show. Supported by saturation advertising, such hypes have a short, but extremely profitable life, introducing children to the giddy world of the cult purchase. Children reared on a diet of television images are perfectly poised to be snared by a bold logo, able to distinguish the brand they want across a crowded toy shop, just as pre-schoolers learn to 'read' potato crisp flavours from the colour of the packet.

Merchandising, and the design work that supports it, cynically exploits the gap between what children want and what parents want them to want. In other areas of the toy market, the designer's role can be more beneficial. In the field of 'educational toys', design equals the appliance of a different kind of science – the science of behavioural and conceptual development. Toys that teach toddlers and young children to sort shapes, push buttons and stack cups are often the product of intensive research and many have the genuine simplicity and functional rightness of any other tool or instrument.

Some of the best examples are system or constructional toys, such as Meccano, K'nex and the classic Lego. Lego, which means 'play well' in Danish, was founded in the 1930s by Ole Kirk Christiansen, a carpenter. Up until the end of the Second World War, the firm produced a range of robust, handcrafted wooden toys. It

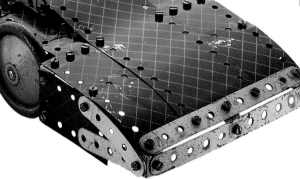

Meccano model of Malcolm Campbell's record-breaking Bluebird car.

was Christiansen's son, Gotfred, who came up with the idea for a 'system of play' based on simple interconnecting bricks. Since then, of course, the product line has expanded and diversified, with the introduction of wheels, motors, lights and figures. Like Meccano, Lego is now more often sold in the form of kits to make a specific model rather than in open-ended component sets, yet another example of the potential for creativity and individuality being stifled. The success of this essentially simple system owes much to its roots in the craft tradition, yet I sometimes wonder if we are raising a generation that can expertly follow the pack and copy the latest 'look', but has no experience of thinking creatively.

Given the bombardment of media imagery, much of which is exhorting us to buy, it is small wonder that most people's idea of a good thing to do with their spare time is to go shopping. The shopping mall as a destination makes irresistible sense when so many destinations include shops.

It would be somewhat hypocritical, not to say self-defeating, if I argued there were better ways to spend one's time. Although I would not advocate shopping to the exclusion of all other leisure activities, I enjoy shopping, and I go to considerable lengths to ensure that other people enjoy shopping in my shops. Never the less, I believe there is a definite line which should not be crossed if people are to remain at the centre of their own experience. This line marks the difference between the theme pub and an atmospheric bar, between the sealed mall and a delightfully idiosyncratic shop, between the precinct

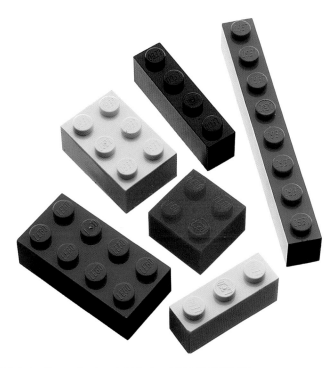

Well-designed toys such as Lego build the foundations of creative play.

and a bustling town square – between virtual reality and reality itself. In the former, almost nothing is open to chance; in the latter, the unexpected and the spontaneous enrich our lives.

Providing scope for fantasy and escape should be just as important for designers as keeping a grip on real experience. Each year, the Design Museum invites someone under 35 with a background in design to select products to add to the Conran Foundation Collection. Each person is given a budget and must select only items that are currently in mass production and which they would like to own themselves. The 1995 Collection, selected by the design writer, Alice Rawsthorn, includes flatware designed in 1957 for Jensen by Arne Jacobsen. As the display caption reads, this cutlery was chosen by Stanley Kubrick for use in his 1968 film

2001:A Space Odyssey, the only props he considered futuristic enough not to be specially commissioned. It is a fitting repayment from the 'real world' of design to the 'reel world', if you like. What Orson Welles called 'this ribbon of dreams', the cinema has provided some of the most memorable images, and our experience of the twentieth century has been fundamentally shaped by it. From Fritz Lang's *Metropolis* to Nick Parks' Wallace and Grommit films, animators, simulators, costume-, set-, special effects- and production-designers have played captivating tricks with reality that transport us to other worlds. That the snowbound dacha in *Dr Zhivago* was a Spanish set plastered in marble dust, candlewax and Epsom salts, or that *Jurassic Park*'s dinosaurs were computer generated simply shows that the level of technology matters less than the magic of the effect.

Converging media can lead to cynical manipulation and increasing opportunities for marketing, or they can provide a fruitful source where ideas cross-fertilize in an endless and delightful fund of inspiration. It all depends on what you do with them. The days in which different cultural activities resided in watertight compartments are gone. Designers should remind us about what is human about our pleasures while giving us room for the type of free expression and play in which we can all engage. However much we enjoy the fantasy creations and escapist pleasures that new technology makes possible, they provide only a temporary refuge from the real world and the problems it presents us. Improving the quality of life for everybody – in the real world as well as the virtual one – is the designer's most important task.

'The broader one's understanding of the human experience, the better designs we will have'

Steve Jobs, founder of Apple Computers

Gustave Eiffel, Eiffel Tower, Paris (1889), photograph by André Kertész (1929)

Cities need to thrill. The Eiffel Tower attracted fierce criticism when it was built, but has outlasted its critics and become the enduring symbol of Paris. I believe the Millennium Wheel could provide a similar rallying point for London. The proposed design, 500 feet in diameter, will offer stunning views of the panorama of city life. Over half the energy required to turn the Wheel will be generated by the tidal power of the Thames.

David Marks and Julia Barfield with Ove Arup & Partners, proposal for Millennium Wheel, London (1995)

'Simple pleasures are the last refuge of the complex'

Oscar Wilde

Heidenheim Public Baths, Germany (1906)

Skating rink, Rockefeller Center, New York (1931-40)

Medicinal Baths, Gellert Hotel, Budapest, Hungary (1918)

Christo and Jeanne-Claude, Wrapped Reichstag, Berlin (1971-1995), © Christo 1995; photograph by Wolfgang Volz

Frank Lloyd Wright, Guggenheim Museum, New York (1959), photograph by Ezra Stoller

Museums and galleries are cathedrals of the modern world. Frank Lloyd Wright's design for the Guggenheim Museum takes the form of a spiralling pathway: the experience of looking at art defines the structure. The work of Christo and Jeanne-Claude provokes a new way of experiencing public monuments and landscapes. Art and event are merged in a way that challenges preconceptions. The deceptively simple strategy of 'wrapping' or packaging a building expresses a sense of monumentality and attention is directed at the elemental qualities of form.

FREE TIME

236

Herzog and de Meuron, Goetz Gallery, Munich (1991-2)

The invention of photography has had a tremendous impact not only on the way we view the world, but also on the way we experience it. Today, with the world's great cultural sites crowded with coachloads of tourists trying not to get into each other's pictures, photography might even be said to stand in for experience.

Picture-taking was an expensive and technically demanding process until George Eastman brought out the first camera targeted at the mass market in 1888. From the beginning, the Eastman Kodak Company spent a fortune on advertising; its first slogan – 'You press the button, we do the rest' – reflected the fact that, in the early days, both the camera and the exposed film had to be sent back to the company for processing and reloading. By 1900 when Eastman brought out his box Brownie, the Model-T of photography, the age of amateur photography had well and truly arrived. The photographic market today is dominated by the Japanese. The Olympus mju: (renamed the Stylus in the USA) provides both technical sophistication and ease of use in a remarkably compact and well-integrated design. The lens barrier conceals the flash and viewfinder as well, and the camera is small and light enough to slip into a pocket.

Martin Parr, tourists at the Acropolis, Athens

Eastman Kodak, 'You press the button... It does the rest' (1946)

You press the .

"Getting the picture" with Kodak Ve
Film is as carefree a pastime as anybc
wish...Eastman Kodak Co., Rocheste

A CHRISTMAS GREETING CARD with
"snapshot of the year" is the persona
you alone can send. See your Koda

Only Eastman m

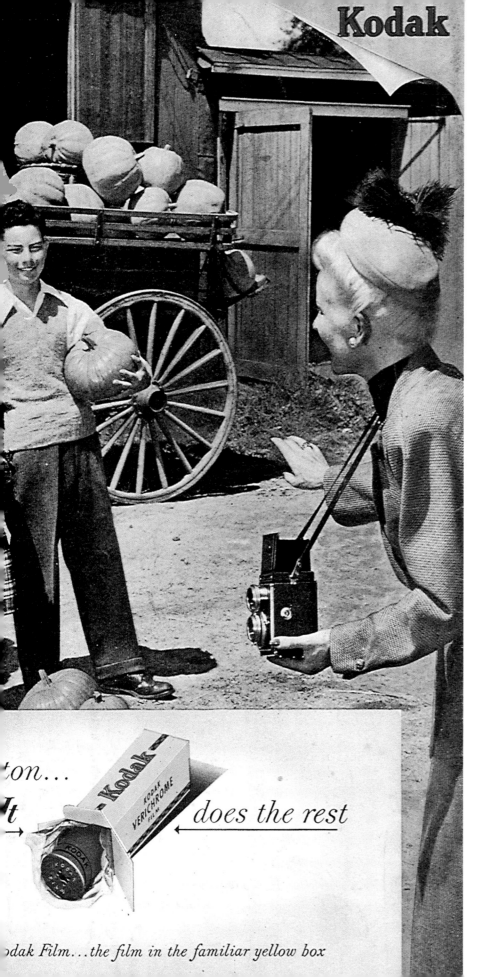

Kodak

...Kodak Film...the film in the familiar yellow box

does the rest

Olympus Mju:1 compact camera

The Dark Room photography shop, Beverley Hills, California

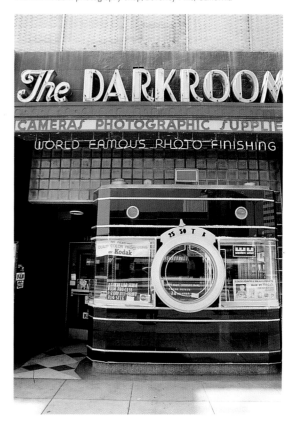

Football

Tennis ball

Nothing about these balls is accidental: the football is just as designed as the stadium or the team strip. The hard dimpled shell of the golf ball conceals a tightly packed inner core of wound rubber, making a responsive ball that can be struck hard to fly over the fairway or putted gently to roll across a green: its characteristics define the game.

Basketball

Cricket ball

Squash ball

Softball

Golf ball

Rugby ball

From football to opera, design plays a key role in enhancing our enjoyment of events. Looking like a giant spaceship, Renzo Piano's Bari stadium seats 60,000 under Teflon-covered roofing: the radial design, with 26 axes, provides a safe, easy flow of traffic. Landscaped areas around the car parks help temper the climate in the stadium.

Renzo Piano, Bari Stadium, Italy (1987)

Sports stadium, Paris

In an opera house, sight and sound are critical for audience and performers alike. Michael Hopkins and Partners' new Opera House at Glyndebourne resembles a beautifully crafted musical instrument, which is exactly what it is. The absence of decoration and the warmth of materials give the space intimacy as well as a resonance and clarity.

Michael Hopkins and Partners, Glyndebourne Opera House, Sussex (1995)

FREE TIME

Adolf Loos, Café Metropol, Vienna

Turrett Collaborative Architects, News Bar, New York (1992)

DRY**201**

Ben Kelly, Dry Bar and beer mat, Manchester, England (1989)

Club flyer for Cream, Ibiza (1995)

FREE TIME

The French café, New York coffee shop or Viennese coffee house may serve very similar fare, but they each have a distinctive flavour, an essence of city life that is the very opposite of a themed experience. Design can play a key role in creating such evocative surroundings; equally, design can be used to confer a strong sense of identity, making a place a rallying point for those in the know.

Deux Magots, Paris

News-stand, New York (1935)

Allen Lane founded Penguin Books 60 years ago with the democratic aim of making great literature available to everyone at a price they could afford. From the beginning, Penguins had a coherent identity – a friendly logo which was also graphically strong, a uniform pocket format and colour-coded jackets and spines (orange for fiction, green for crime, blue for science, history and art). This graphic style spelled out the quality and consistency of the list – and all for sixpence.

With the improvement in colour photography and reproduction processes after the war, the market for printed media grew at a incredible rate. Every leisure pursuit now has its own special-interest magazine and the public are bombarded with images in glossy magazines and colour supplements, while new media, from television to CD-ROM, create a vastly different frame of reference. This is the context in which graphic designers such as David Carson operate. Carson sets out to meet the competition head on, subverting formal rules of print design. The spread from *Cyclops*, a book about the photographer Albert Watson, who is blind in one eye, displays his highly subjective approach.

cycl   ops

watson
a Y b e CLOPS
cyclops

albert wats n

Introduction by James Truman, Editorial Director of Condé
Nast Publications. Essay by Jeff Koons, Artist.

BROODINGLY POWERFUL, intensely emotional, seductively erotic, and
always dramatic, this collection of truly extraordinary images, published here
in book form for the first time, bears witness to the quarter-century-long
career of one of our greatest photographers—Albert Watson. Though blind in
one eye since birth, Albert Watson is the invisible force behind many of the
most iconic images of our age and is best known for his unique and hugely
successful work in advertising and fashion. His client list reads like a Who's
Who in the fashion and beauty industry: Chanel, Christian Dior, L'Oréal,
Revlon, The Gap, and Levi's among many others. Watson is also highly sought
after as a portraitist by celebrities the world over: Mick Jagger, Jack
Nicholson, Gore Vidal, Alfred Hitchcock, Jeff Koons, and the Royal Family
to name a few. Yet despite Watson's prominence, his chameleon-like versatil-
ity has made him a bit of an enigma in the photography world: it's not always
easy to define an Albert Watson image. However, this stunning debut volume
succeeds in capturing both the essence and variety of Watson's style and art in
every category, whether it be his fashion, portraiture, reportage, landscape, or
still life work. The range of his work is breathtaking: portraits of Louisiana
death-row convicts doing hard time in a maximum security prison; Keith
Richards enveloped in smoke; haute couture in an English country house;
ancient Scottish megaliths standing in silence; a female nude arched in ecsta-
sy; the simplicity and delicacy of a flower in a vase. His camera conveys the
kaleidoscope of human emotion with glamour, drama, and crystal clarity.
     AS A COMPLEMENT to his own photographs, Watson has written a
rich, revealing text, that draws the reader farther into the depths of the subjects
on which he chooses to focus. Richard Benson, the world's foremost authority on techniques of photographic, photomechanical, and digital reproduction
of fine imagery, has applied his unmatched skill to create pages that are faith-
ful to the original silver, platinum, or cyanotype prints.
     WITH THE PUBLICATION of this magnificent retrospective vol-
ume, Albert Watson—"the great unknown" in the words of *American
Photographer*—is destined to become a household name.

hitchcock with goose,
universal studios, ..., christmas 197.

Albert Watson, *Cyclops*, designed by David Carson (1995)

Commuter reading Penguin edition of *Lady Chatterley's Lover* (1960)

just zap
just rock it
just kick it
bounce it
just bou nce it

Neville Brody, T-shirt logo for Nike (1988)

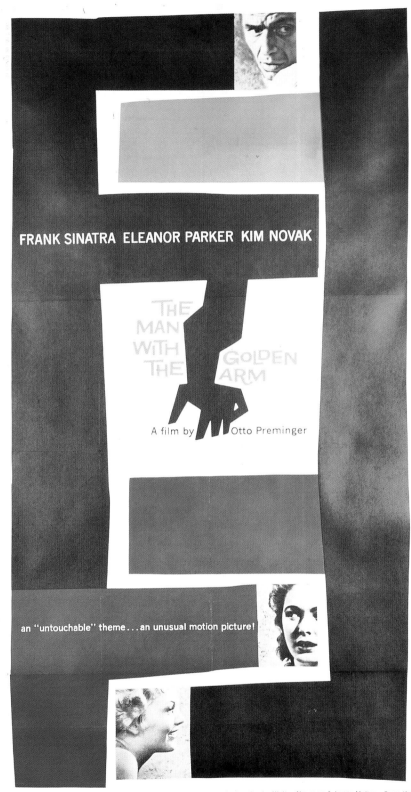

With Arnold Stang, Darren McGavin, Robert Strauss, John Conte, Screenplay by Walter Newman & Lewis Meltzer, From the novel by Nelson Algren, Music by Elmer Bernstein, Produced & Directed by Otto Preminger, Released by United Artists

Saul Bass, poster for *The Man with the Golden Arm* (1955)

New media create new visual languages. Saul Bass was one of the first designers to explore the graphic potential of film title sequences, using memorable images that cut to the heart of mood and plot. In a similar vein, the Polish poster for *Blow-up*, with its hugely enlarged detail, encapsulates the film.

The work of Neville Brody equates digital design with painting, 'except the paint never dries'. Brody exploits a loss of distinction between the traditional categories of product, film and print.

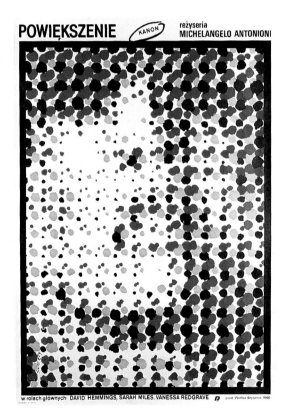

Waldimar Swierzy, poster for
Blow Up (Powiekszenie), Poland
(1967)

Tintin rocket and figures, based on illustrations by Hergé

Commercial art, as typified by the comic strip, has provided a fruitful source of inspiration for designers and artists. Pop art elevated logos and packaging styles into modern icons: accessibility and ease of reproduction allow such graphic styles to permeate many different areas of cultural activity. With the rise of merchandising comes a new twist. Books account for a mere 17 per cent of total Tintin sales, while the disposable, ephemeral comic book has become a collector's item.

'Signs and comic strips are interesting as subject matter. There are certain things that are useable, forceful and vital about commercial art'

Roy Lichtenstein

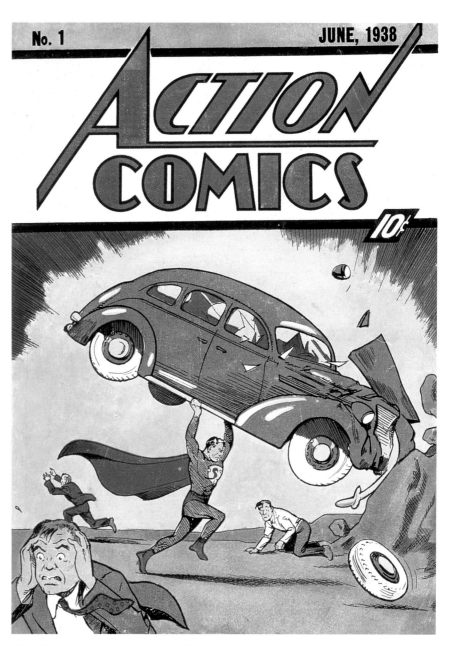

D.C. Publications, *Action Comics*, issue 1 (June 1938): the first appearance of Superman

Children reading comics, Square Saint-Lambert, Paris (1948), photograph by Willy Ronis

out

'Though human genius in its various
inventions with various instruments
may answer the same end, it will never
find an invention more beautiful or
more simple or direct than nature,
because in her inventions nothing is
lacking and nothing superfluous'

Leonardo da Vinci (1452-1519)

At the heart of design lies our relationship

with the natural world. From the earliest civ-

ilizations, landscapes have been shaped by

cultivation and industry; and our idea of

nature itself is no less man-made.

doors

The garden, the city park or the wildlife reserve place 'nature' in an enclave, superficially divorced from the manufactured or artificially created world. But nature in such forms is never free from human intervention, or from design. The most 'natural' gardens are still planned and created; the national park is overrun with visitors who in the act of appreciating what has been set aside threaten its survival. The inspiration that nature provides is not a simple exchange, but is framed by the way it has been interpreted in different cultures over hundreds of years.

The Japanese garden and the English park are both natural places that are nevertheless highly designed to reflect quite different views of the world. It is almost impossible for Westerners to appreciate the conceptual basis of Eastern garden design, however much we may enjoy the result. Temple gardens – with their sparse groupings of rocks surrounded by raked sand – distil nature into a symbolized expression of elemental forces. The English country-house park could not look more different, arranging nature in sweeping romantic vistas, an aesthetic composition of specially planted woods, artificial lakes and hills which is neither true wilderness nor productive land.

The landscape movement of the eighteenth century arose at a time when the working landscape had been transformed by the agricultural revolution and when the beginnings of the industrial revolution threatened far more radical changes. In the preceding centuries, when real untamed wilderness still existed in some parts of Europe, the garden and the farm were places where nature could be tamed and controlled in formal, geometric patterns, such as the knot, the parterre and the tilled field. The landscaped park was equally controlled, but it expressed a nostalgia for nature as a source of heightened feeling, rather than a desire to overcome.

Formal, stylized elements (raked gravel, rock and moss) are typical of Japanese temple gardens.

The great Victorian city parks added a moral dimension to the picture. Frederick Law Olmsted and Calvert Vaux – who planned and designed Central Park in New York as a microcosm of nature, complete with lake, meadows, 'wilderness' and winding trails – intended that the good life enshrined in the park would civilize and educate the poor out of drunkenness and violence. Octavia Hill founded the National Trust chiefly as a means of safeguarding the landscape – not large country houses – for the general edification,

The majestic sweep of an English landscape park designed by Capability Brown at Bowood House, Wiltshire (1760s).

health and spiritual uplift of the population. Victorian municipal parks were part 'outdoor sitting-room', part schemes for moral improvement. Urban green spaces have made many cities bearable and habitable for those with no garden of their own and limited access to the countryside. But they have largely failed as moral educators, as the dangers of walking in Central Park after dark vividly illustrate.

In the nineteenth-century expansion of towns and cities that followed industrialization, great chunks of countryside were systematically developed along railway lines to house the working population. But the backyard of the standard working-class, terraced house was treated more as a service area than an ornamental garden. In this country, it was not until the post-war building booms that the garden became an inseparable part of the 'ideal' average home. For the first time, gardening became a serious leisure pursuit for ordinary people rather than just a means of supplementing the larder.

The private garden, rather than the public park, is the way most people connect with nature today. In Britain alone, over one million acres of land are gardened for pleasure and the gardening business is now worth some £6 billion a year. But in most domestic gardens, nature is seldom allowed to get away with much. I love the story in which a rather grand Edwardian lady, visiting her rather less grand friend, went into ecstasies of admiration at the sight of golden autumn leaves scattered on the grass. 'We don't have that at home,' she remarked wistfully, blissfully unaware that her battalion of gardeners laboured long, hard and early to maintain the pristine perfection of her lawn.

Gardening may be a leisure pursuit, but it is one that people are increasingly unwilling to devote that much time to. The demand for plants which are low in maintenance but big on effect, and the development of motorized tools that substitute technology for the down-to-earth craft of digging and getting your hands dirty helps to promote this conformity. Plant varieties – and, indeed, whole species –are fast disappearing, as traditional horticulturalists and specialist nurseries are replaced by the garden centre which concentrates on hardy, reliable bestsellers.

Many domestic gardens are not conceived and nurtured with the future in mind, but have become the focus for more instant gratification. I am not convinced that many of us would have the generosity of spirit to plant an avenue of trees or carve the landscape as dramatically as Capability Brown and his clients did for the pleasure of later generations to walk through, even if we had the land to realize such a project. The upshot is that gardening is becoming another branch of commercial activity, subject to the same whimsical swings of fashion and taste.

You would think that the intense modern interest in gardening, not to mention the sheer acreage involved, would result in a wonderful diversity of garden design and planting. Sadly, this is far from the case. The dreary predictability of lawn, border and rockery is duplicated in countless suburban plots around the world. Suburbia itself – the featureless colonization of tracts of land, where each identical house has its own identical garden – stands the idea of nature on its head. In such mindless developments, the worthy aim of providing each household with access to outdoor space has resulted in communities utterly devoid of vitality or any natural quality at all.

There is no reason why housing estates cannot be planned and designed to be truly inclusive of nature. Eric Lyons' Span developments of the late 1960s – with their variation of house types, their common spaces and imaginative planting – demonstrate that it can be done. Far too often, however, what passes for commercial logic still prevails over sensitivity to site, layout and context. Nature, along with human needs, is designed out of the equation.

Brighton Pier (1866).

It isn't only in the sphere of the private garden that nature can be the loser. One of the things I really enjoy is the seaside, the spindly piers and small towns hugging the shore which seem to look so much better out of season. Like many people, I derive immense satisfaction from just walking by the sea, looking into rock pools and picking up shells and driftwood with the contour of the shingle or sandy beach unfolding in front of me. I love beach-combing, picking up *objets trouvés* from the flotsam and jetsam at the water's edge. I would contrast this with the experience of man-made seasides, such as the appallingly contrived Porto Cervo in Sardinia created by the Aga Khan. Such totally synthetic places only get worse as they get older.

Flowers have always inspired passionate appreciation: you have only to think of the tulip cult of seventeenth-century Holland, with bulbs exchanging hands for small fortunes, or the way in which exotic botanical specimens from halfway across the globe were avidly cultivated on home ground in the nineteenth century. Individual flowers sometimes symbolized a whole approach to life:

in the 1880s and 1890s, the lily, for example, was synonymous with the languid sensibilities of the Aesthetic movement. But what is relatively new is the way in which tastes in plants, shrubs and flowers have become a means of identifying lifestyles and aspirations. What your borders say about you has become just as revealing as the clothes you wear or the car you drive. Gardening features in popular magazines draw up lists of what's in and what's out, where plants provide the same kind of index of fashionability as the hemlines of skirts and dresses.

I like flowers that look naturally rather frail and fragile. However, there are few plants or flowers I actively dislike, although I must confess to a loathing for African marigolds, certain kinds of dahlias and pompom chrysanthemums. There are doubtless ways in which even these plants could be employed which might be appealing, but their association with dreary bedding schemes and their gaudy colours have kept them out of my garden. I used to dislike gladioli, too; there was a time when every aspiring socialite had a cut glass vase full of them. Now, somewhat to my surprise, I have grown to like them.

These are, of course, personal tastes. I cannot help feeling, however, that allowing fashion alone to dictate the choice of flowers and plants in the garden ultimately encourages an attitude of disposability which is at odds with the whole notion of gardening. Gardening takes time. The effect of climate and seasons and the varying patterns of growth are precisely what distinguishes nature from the man-made world. Without this mutability, gardening would be far less valuable and challenging a pursuit.

All gardens are designs. The whole Western convention of lawn and flower border – where one area is exclusively devoted to the cultivation of a single type of plant to serve as a foil for a careful composition of other specially selected ones – is hardly natural at all. But even within such conventions there are gardens which evoke the spirit of nature and those which do not. Where plants are chosen for immediate, predictable impact and shrubs and grass are neatly trimmed so that barely a leaf or blade is out of place, nature has all but been designed out of the picture. The garden just becomes a dull extension of the dull furnishings of the dull house to which it is attached. By contrast, the lack of 'perfection' in those gardens where nature is allowed to let rip – where climbers clamber and vines tangle, flowers self-seed and paths are softened by overgrown grass – is infinitely more evocative, and sympathetic: a sensual celebration of life and the changing seasons.

It is a modern cliché that the garden is an outdoor room. Certainly, many urban gardens are little more than room-sized, and given halfway decent weather, we all like to eat, snooze, sit, read and chat outside as much as in. Good garden design accommodates and promotes these activities, providing a quiet shady spot to get away from it all, an area in which to entertain – otherwise there would hardly be any point in having a garden at all.

Our tendency to view the garden as an extension of the home has been aided, ironically, by technology. It is unsurprising that the landscaped parks of the eighteenth century, with their carefully judged vistas, occurred at a time when such effects could be increasingly appreciated. When window glass was barely transparent and could only be manufactured in tiny panes, a sweeping view was largely irrelevant for people indoors. But as soon as the technology of glass manufacture had arrived at the point where larger, clearer panes were possible, and window design had altered from small, deeply embrasured leaded casements to tall elegant sashes, the world outside came into view. The principal living apartments which had maintained a lofty superiority on upper floors began to shift to ground level, with French windows permitting a free flow from house to garden.

In the latter part of the twentieth century, central heating has provided a temperate indoor climate year round. With little practical need for layers of drapery and carpeting as a means of insulation, furnishings associated with garden use have migrated indoors. Lightweight wicker furniture, slatted garden chairs and metal café tables are just as likely to be found in the living-room as on the terrace. The opportunity for house and garden to blend and merge is greater than ever.

If this increasing connection between indoors and out allows us to view the planning and furnishing of our homes in a different light, it also provides scope for new ways of approaching garden design. As in the interior, planning a garden means getting the basics right: the structure of paths, paved areas, walls, fences, borders and beds that provide a framework for the planting. This means thinking about scale and proportion, varying levels and contrast of surfaces, elements which enhance the pleasure of moving through a garden and provide a sense of vitality and interest. Nothing is more dispiriting than a garden which is static, designed to be seen from a single angle, where everything is laid out in full view. Such gardens seem to be designed with the picture window in mind, as two-dimensional 'views'. The garden that works in its own right, rather than as an element of interior decoration, must include elements of surprise, hidden vistas and corners, which encourage direct experience and appreciation – 'hazard and surprise', as John Soane would have put it. This quality does not depend on size or style, but can be achieved in the smallest, most confined area and within any scheme of design from the formal to the rustic.

It is almost instinctive to complement plants and turf, earth and rock with garden surfaces and equipment made from natural sources and materials. Plastics and other artificial materials often work better in a strictly functional sense. Plastic, for example can

'Go to the woods and fields for colour schemes'

Frank Lloyd Wright

A scene from *The Draughtsman's Contract* (1982) directed by Peter Greenaway.

be moulded to fashion more ergonomically shaped handles for gardening tools; plastic watering cans do not rust; plastic chairs can be wiped clean and won't split or swell in the heat. Yet the very qualities that make this material practical for garden use, its weather- and moisture-resistant properties, mean that it remains eternally out of step with nature. The ageing and weathering processes to which all natural materials are subject make us cherish them more. In the garden, materials which don't change in this way are glaringly obvious and obtrusive. The patina of age is very attractive, especially outdoors.

The natural aesthetic is currently enjoying something of a vogue indoors. This preference may be expressed in superficial fads, such as the trend for galvanized watering cans to serve as containers for flower arrangements, or it can extend to a deeper appreciation of the value of natural materials as flooring, at the window or on the walls. Seagrass or sisal underfoot, vegetable-dyed cotton furnishings that fade in the sunlight, paint recipes

composed of non-synthetic ingredients may be symptomatic of yet another passing decorative style, or they may hint at a more fundamental re-evaluation of our attitude to the natural world.

Nostalgia has always underpinned our relationship with nature, a kind of yearning for a lost Eden where people and nature co-existed in simple harmony. The truth is that human beings have always made their mark on the world, shaped it, used it, changed it and exploited it. Today, however, some of the marks we make look increasingly indelible as the pace of technology accelerates. With a hole in the ozone the size of Europe and the rapid shrinking of the world's rainforests and natural habitats, many people are acutely aware that there is simply less of the natural world than ever before. In this sense, the type of nostaglia evident in decorating trends may become a catalyst for change, and designers may find a role in making such changes not only practical but attractive.

By nostalgia I do not mean sentimentality; there's no reason why respect for nature should be incompatible with modern design any more than it should be synonymous with a cosy Beatrix Potter fantasy. Corbusier may have inspired some fairly meretricious imitators but he was always acutely aware of the importance of natural light, fresh air and green space, and his buildings were designed to bring these elements within reach of more people. While the ideas behind Corbusier's Unité d'Habitation came to be interpreted as soul-less high-rise blocks, they were conceived to bring green space to city sprawl. Done with sensitivity, they remain an admirable solution to enhancing the urban landscape.

Natural materials have time and variety built into them. No single piece of wood, for example, is like another; the living origin of wood can be seen in every pattern of grain or knothole. It ages in a way we find beautiful, preserving the memories of its use. But it also changes in a way we can trust, for ultimately its disposal does not harm the planet.

Consumers are demanding products that are environmentally friendly, both in their composition *and* their means of production. Voting at the sales checkout has had real impact, and manufacturers can no longer dismiss such concerns as those of a minority. Designers could become essential intermediaries, reconciling the demands of consumers and industry with the needs of the planet.

The quotation by da Vinci at the beginning of this chapter is incorporated in the sculpture by Eduardo Paolozzi which stand s outside the Design Museum. Da Vinci was one of the world's greatest innovators, visionaries and designers, but he was also one of its most sympathetic students of nature. His work is a reminder that design and nature need not be seen in opposition to one another.

Creative recycling: upturned boats transformed into sheds, Holy Island, Northumberland.

Nature is embedded in our cultural history. Medieval cathedral naves display in stone the interlaced branches of the forest canopy, and to such direct references can be added many more abstract expressions of inspiration from natural colours, textures and forms. In Andy Goldsworthy's work, for example, there's an exquisite tension between the ephemeral beauty of nature and our creative appreciation of it. Nature, design and aesthetics come full circle.

Design is not merely about the way things look, feel or work; it is about the emotions and associations they arouse, and it is about how things are made. Necessarily, it is also about the way in which that process of making things shapes and changes the world and our expectations. If design is to improve the quality of everyday life in any meaningful way, it must improve not only our immediate world, but also the future.

Every year, thousands of visitors flock to Sissinghurst Castle, Kent, to admire the gardens created by Vita Sackville-West and her husband, Harold Nicolson. For many people, the White Garden at Sissinghurst has come to symbolize the height of gardening good taste, a scheme which relies on the refined subtleties of leaf-shape, texture and pale, cool tones for its impact. There have always been fashions in gardening; the countless suburban white gardens that Sissinghurst has inspired are only a recent example. What is relatively new is the ease with which such ideas can be turned into reality. Sissinghurst may have been created and maintained with the aid of a large staff, but it was first planted and laid out in the days before garden centres offered virtually instant gratification.

'A large rose-tree stood near the entrance of the garden: the roses growing on it were white, but there were three gardeners at it, busily painting them red'

Lewis Carroll, *Alice's Adventures in Wonderland*

Vita Sackville-West and Harold Nicholson, Sissinghurst Garden, Kent (1930s)

Le Notre, south parterre, garden at Versailles, France (17th century)

Moving palms trees inside for winter, Versailles, France

All gardens are designed, but the formal garden is more obviously designed than most. The gardens at Versailles were created in the seventeenth century for Louis XIV by Le Notre, who also laid out St James's Park in London. Nature is treated architecturally, as a means of expressing aesthetic principles of harmony, proportion and symmetry: in the south parterre, over 1200 orange, pomegranate, myrtle, bay and palm trees, potted in wood and cast-iron tubs, are arranged in strict order on gravel paths radiating from a central pool. Every autumn they must all be brought indoors for the winter, an exercise once accomplished by the army with the aid of special horse-drawn carts, nowadays with fork-lift trucks.

Formal garden design need not be so arch, however: the enchanting eighteenth-century garden of Beloeil, near Brussels, consists of a series of interconnecting 'rooms' created by lines of beech trees and hedging, once the setting for balls, fetes and outdoor entertainments.

OVER: Beloeil gardens, Belgium (18th century)

'Any landscape is a condition of the spirit'

Henri-Frederic Amiel (1821-1881)

The eighteenth-century landscape designer treated nature architecturally, creating suites of outdoor rooms, promenades and walkways that echoed the enfilade of a palace or grand manor. In the twentieth century, technological developments in plate-glass manufacture and structural engineering have made it possible to dissolve the boundaries between indoors and out, yet often the result is no less formal or architectural.

At the Singleton House, the influence of the formal Japanese tradition is apparent – the garden features rocks specially placed by Isamu Noguchi in a highly ordered composition that extends the architectural style of the interior into the land-scape. Window walls which slide open or lift up allow outdoor areas to be annexed as living space, complete with decked flooring and furniture.

OUTDOORS

Henry Smith-Miller and Larry Hawkinson, house for a film producer, California (1991)

266

"Now, there's a nice contemporary sunset!"

Drawing by Stevenson, © 1964, 1992 The New Yorker Magazine, Inc.

Richard Neutra, Singleton House, Los Angeles (1957)

TBWA ABSOLUT COUNTRY OF SWEDEN VODKA & LOGO, ABSOLUT, ABSOLUT BOTTLE DESIGN AND ABSOLUT CALLIGRAPHY ARE TRADEMARKS OWNED BY V & S VIN & SPRIT AB. © 1989 V & S VIN & SPRIT AB.

ABSOLUT MANHATTAN.

INSIST ON ABSOLUT. THERE IS NO PURER VODKA. DRINK IT NEAT AT 0°C.

The gardener's impulse is to create order out of chaos. The garden created by architectural theoretician, Charles Jencks, and his wife, Maggie Keswick, in southern Scotland features a spiral mound and a series of 'twisting snakes' that sculpt the landscape into curving contours. The design has been inspired by Jencks's interest in developments in cosmology, which suggest that 'order' in the universe is curved, folded and wave-like.

The French golf-course designer, Robert Berthet, treats nature equally graphically, as a huge canvas for what he calls 'the epitome of Land Art'. The green at the 10th hole at La Salle golf course near Macon is a giant foot, with bunkers in the form of toe prints. Other fairways, greens and bunkers are shaped in the form of rather more explicit body parts.

One of the recent advertisements in the campaign for Absolut vodka makes graphic play of the green space of Central Park inserted into the New York city grid. Vodka, colourless and odourless, is a challenge to advertise; this campaign makes a positive use of the anonymity of the drink by focussing on the distinctive shape of the bottle.

Charles Jencks and Maggie Keswick, garden, Scotland

Robert Berthet, erotic golf course, Macon, France

Tom McManus, Absolut Manhattan (1986)

'Nature goes
beyond what is
called countryside –
everything comes
from the earth'

Andy Goldsworthy

Andy Goldsworthy, 'Balanced rocks brought down by the incoming tide', Porth Ceiriad, Wales (23 July 1993)

Dr Georg Gerster, Meiji Shrine, Tokyo, Japan

Dr Georg Gerster, Labbezanga village, Nigeria

The Swiss photographer, Dr Georg Gerster, specializes in capturing the patterns we have created on the face of the earth. From the air, farmlands, villages or urban centres are revealed as compositions of colour and form. The rigid geometries and grids of modern urban developments may have a graphic beauty from an aerial viewpoint, but down on the ground the everyday reality can be less sympathetic.

Ordnance Survey map

Ramblers outside Alpine chalet

As well as fresh air and fine views, ramblers and back-packers who take to the hills at weekends and on holidays seek the opportunity to experience nature directly. Today true wilderness is fast disappearing, and those who answer the call of the wild are liable to find they have plenty of company. The popularity of such pursuits may owe something to the fact that nature has increasingly been designed out of our immediate surroundings.

Martin Parr, ramblers in Switzerland (1995)

Terence Conran, sketch for design of the Imperial War Museum's Victory Garden, Chelsea Flower Show, London (1995)

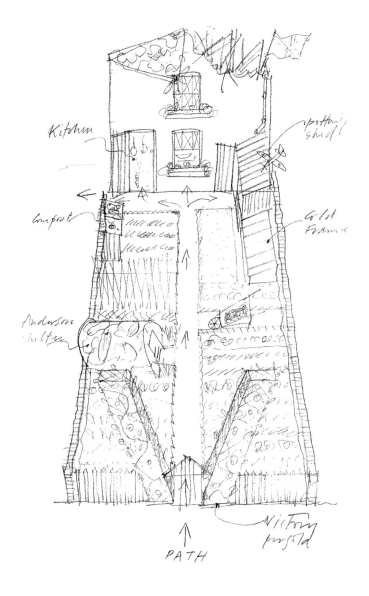

Vegetables growing on top of Anderson shelter in the Imperial War Museum's Victory Garden, Chelsea Flower Show, London (1995)

British, American and Japanese seed packets

During the Second World War, the British were
constantly exhorted to 'Dig for Victory'. It's a
cliché, but the result of a diet low in meat, butter
and sugar and high in fresh vegetables and pulses
was a population fitter on V.E. Day than ever
before or since. I certainly have no nostalgic
yearnings for much of what we ate in those days;
those who have never tasted snoek or powdered egg
have not plumbed the depths of culinary nastiness.
But I can well recall the freshness and flavour of
vegetables just picked from the garden. It's a
pleasure I have never foregone – my gardens in
Berkshire and Provence supply much of the fresh
produce we eat at the table. Growing your own is
satisfying, economical and provides a new
experience for those used to supermarket
greengrocery. It is estimated that we have lost
97 per cent of our vegetable varieties since the
beginning of the century, a sad consequence of the
move from home-grown to shop-bought.

I love the effects of time, use and weather on natural materials. There is something incredibly depressing about artificial materials outdoors – plastic may be practical, but it remains immutable while everything around is growing and changing.

Gardening tools

Ironically, now that traditional gardening equipment such as galvanized watering cans, wooden trugs and terracotta pots have become fashionable indoor accessories, they may find new popularity in the garden again, where their beauty can be fully appreciated.

Galvanized watering cans

Terracotta flower pots

OUTDOORS

Derek Jarman understood how design can make a difference to the quality of life. His beautiful garden, in such an unpromising location, is a perfect demonstration of the art of the possible.

On the bleak Kent coastline in the shadow of Dungeness nuclear power station, the garden at Prospect Cottage is memorable both for its originality and its powerful sense of defiance. The extreme conditions of the eerie, inhospitable site – plants have to survive dryness, salty air and exposure to winds – are matched by the circumstances of the garden's creation during the final years of Jarman's life. The garden grew from a single planting – a dog rose staked with a piece of driftwood – into a sculptural assembly of old tools, rusting metal, flotsam and jetsam interspersing clumps of santolina, poppy, mallow, seakale, samphire, roses, cistus and lavender, some brought in and carefully cultivated, others self-seeded native wild species. In the winter, when the plants die back, the strange posts looped with holey stones threaded on twine and squiggles of metal stand as markers in a landscape where the man-made and natural come face to face in harmony.

OUTDOORS

280

Derek Jarman, garden at Prospect Cottage, Dungeness, Kent

Page numbers in **bold** type refer to the illustrations

A La Mère De Famille, Paris **144**
Aalto, Alvar **44**, **45**, 58
Absolut vodka **268**, 269
Achirivolto **59**
Adam, Robert 16
Adirondack chairs **3**
'admass' 228, 229
advertising 97, 228, 229
AEG 196, 197
Aeroflot 168
'Aeron' chair 202
Aesthetic movement 256
aesthetics 14, 28
Aga 65
Aga Khan 256
airports 165-8, **166**
Airstream trailer **174**
Alessi 66-7, **80**
Alexander, Christopher 31
Alfa Romeo **180**
Allen, Woody 164
American folk art **54**
Amiel, Henri-Frederic 266
Anglepoise lamp 34, 82, **217**
Apple Macintosh computers 200, **212-13**
Arab Institute, Paris **2**
Arcimboldo, Giuseppe 151
Armani, Giorgio 94, **94**
Arribas, Alfredo 225
Artemide **82**, 196
articulation **82**
artificial fibres 94-5
Arts and Crafts Movement 27, 63, 194, 203
Arup, Ove & Partners **233**
Ascher, Zika 93, 112, **113**
assembly lines 194-5, **195**
Aston Martin 229
Auchett House, Hertfordshire **77**
Aulenti, Gae 196
Austen, Jane 227

Babygro **100**
Balenciaga 94
Ball, Douglas 204, 205
balls **240-1**
Bang & Olufsen 196
'Bap' back protector **184**
Barcelona 225
Barfield, Julia **233**
Bari Stadium **243**
Baron, Fabien 110, **111**
Bartle Bogle Hegarty 96
Bass, Saul **249**
Batman films **202**, 229
Bauhaus 27, **28**, **59**, 102, 194, 196, 197
Bayley, Stephen **161**
Bayliss, Trevor 11-13, **12-13**
BBC2 20
beanbags 56, **57**
Beck, H.C. **172**
Behrens, Peter 197
Bel Geddes, Norman 224
Bell, Alexander Graham 13
Bell '300' telephone 200, **200**
Bellini, Mario 196
Beloeil gardens, Belgium **264-5**
Benetton **110**
Berthet, Robert **269**
Bertoia, Harry **58**
Bertoni, Flamineo **15**
Betjeman, John 170
Biba 71, 97
bicycles **160**
'black box' aesthetic 223
Bladerunner 191
Blow Up **249**
BMW 21, 162, 164, 196
Boeing 168
Boilerhouse, London 192, 227
Bookbinder, Lester **120**
boots 96
bottles **16**, 129-30, **147**
Boulanger, Pierre **175**
Bow, Clara 94, 114
Bowood House, Wiltshire **254**

brands 68-70, 130-1, 197, 228
Braun 66, 196, **210**
Brenta, Luca **181**
bridges **179**
Brighton Pier **256**
Brillat Savarin, Anthelme 128, 143
Bristol University 13
British Airports Authority 167
British Airways (BA) 168, 229
British Fashion Council 98
British Home Stores 198-9
British Leyland 21
British Telecom 229
Brody, Neville **248**, 249
Brooks, Louise 114
Brown, Capability **254**, 255
Burberry 14, 95
Burnett, Mieajah 38
Burton, Tim **202**
Butlers Wharf 'Gastrodrome' 136

cabinets **86**
Cadillac Coupe de Ville **177**
Café Metropol, Vienna **244**
cafés **244-5**
cafetières **217**
Calatrava, Santiago **179**
Calvert, Margaret 183
cameras 238-9
Campbell, Malcolm **230**
Campbell, Naomi **110**
Cardin, Pierre 32, 93
Carroll, Lewis 260
cars **15**, 21, 158, 160-1, 162-5 **164-5**, 168-9, **170-1**, **174-7**, **180**, **184-5**, **209**
Carson, David **132**, 201, 246, **247**
Carwardine, George 82
Case Study House Number 8, Pacific Palisades **48-9**
cashmere **104**
Cassandre **189**
Cassina 33, 196
Casson, Hugh 29

Castella, Xavier de **43**
catamarans **176**
C.D. Partnership **140**, 225-6
Central Park, New York 254, 255, **268**, 269
Chadwick, Don 202
chairs 58
  Adirondack chair **3**
  B3 chair **59**
  Diamond chair **58**
  DKR chair **35**
  Eames chair and ottoman **56**
  Ginger chair **59**
  Karuselli chair 56, **57**
  Louis XX chair **33**
  office chairs 202, **216**
Chanel, Coco 89, 92, 93, **106-7**
Chanut, Ferdinand **108**
Charbonnier, J.P. **211**
Chareau, Pierre **32**
Chartier, Paris 138, **140**
Chedanne, Georges **108**
Chelsea Flower Show **276**
Chermayeff, Serge **39**
Christiansen, Ole Kirk 230
Christo 229, **236**
Citroën DS 14, **15**
Citroën Dyane 174, **175**
Citroën 2CV 163
Clipper CS-1 workstation 204, **205**
clothes pegs **79**
clothes rails **87**
Coakley, Sheridan 33
Coates, Nigel 94, **109**
Coates, Wells 224
Coca-Cola **154-5**, 197, 227
Cocteau, Jean 93
coffeepots 66, **80-1**
Cole, Henry 623
Columbo Design **85**
comfort 35, **56-7**, 94-5, **104**
comics **250-1**
computers 199, 200-1, **210**, **212-13**

Concorde 14, **14**, **180**
Connolly Limited **189**
Conran, Terence **4**, **86**, **276**
Conran Design Group 130, 131,
 163, 167-8, 198, 202
Conran Foundation 227, 231
Conran Shop, The 71
convenience foods 131-2
cookbooks 134-5
cookers 63-4
Le Corbusier 24-5, 26, 28-9,
 40-1, 58, 194, 258
corporate identity 131, 196-9
corsets **101**
cosmetics **17**, 94, **114-16**
Costin, Frank 161
country style **54-5**, 65-6
couture 92-4
Coward, Noel **211**
Cox, Patrick 112
craftsmanship 45, 194
Cream **244**
Cruise, Tom **123**
Cubic Corporation 160

Dalen, Dr Gustaf 65
Dali, Salvador 58, 93
Dalisi, Riccardo **80**
Dark Room photography shop,
 Beverley Hills **239**
d'Ascanio, Corradino **174**
Davey, Andy 13
David, Elizabeth 74, 134, **134**
D.C. Publications **251**
De Havilland Aircraft Company
 161
De La Warr Pavilion, Bexhill-on-
 Sea **39**
Dean & DeLuca **145**
Delaunay, Sonia 93
denim 95-6, 104, **105**
Department of Trade and Industry
 98
Design Museum, London 227-8,
 228, 231, 259

Dessau Bauhaus **28**
Deux Magots, Paris **245**
Dior, Christian 92, **98**
'Discovery' Range Rover 163
Doc Marten's 96
Doisneau, Robert **137**
domestic appliances 63-4, 66-7,
 75-7
Dominic, Peter 131
door handles **84-5**
Doyle Dane Bernbach 164
The Draughtsman's Contract **258**
dress codes 90, 119, 125
dressing-tables 86
Drevost, Laurent **176**
Dreyfuss, Henry 64, 200, **200**
Dunlop, John 160
Dyson vacuum cleaner **66**

Eames, Charles and Ray **35**, **48-9**,
 56, 58, **216**
Earl, Harley **177**
Easisteer trolley 132
Eastman Kodak **238**
egg boxes **146**
Eiffel Tower, Paris **233**
electric light 64
electronics 222-4
Emerson, Ralph Waldo 202
ergonomics 65, 201
espadrille **108**
ethnic influences **50-3**
Eurostar terminal, Waterloo
 station 166, **178**, 179

Fallingwater House, Bear Run,
 Pennsylvania **46-7**
Festival of Britain (1951) 18
Fiestaware crockery **78**, 79
films 16-17, 96, **222**, 229, 231, **249**
Filofax 200, 202, 216, **217**
Fire Station, Dallas **214**
fireplaces **73**
Fisher, M.F.K. 136
fitness of purpose 10-11, 16

flowers 256
food 126-36
 convenience foods 131-2
 cookbooks 134-5
 fresh food 133, 134
 packaging 23, 129-30, 131,
 146-9, **152-3**
 photography **150-1**
 restaurants 135-6, **136**, **138-43**
 seasonality 133
 shops and supermarkets 128-9,
 130-1, 132-4, **133**, **144-5**
food processors **75**
Forbo-Kromely 33
Ford, Henry 161, 162
Ford Motor Company 162, 164,
 194-5, 227
Formula One racing cars 161
Fortuny, Mario 93
Forty, Adrian 36
Foster, Norman 166
Frascio **85**
Frederick, Christine 65
Freeplay clockwork radio 11-13,
 12-13
French House, London **223**
Freson, Robert **151**
fridges 64, 66, 76, **77**, 129
Frisch, Max 209
furnishings 31-5
furniture 19, 33-5, 257

Gabellini, Michael & Associates
 109
Gable, Clark 94
gadgets 75
Galeries Lafayette, Paris **108**
Games, Abram 170
Gap 89, 91, 97
Garbo, Greta 94
gardens 253, 254, **254**, **255**,
 256-8, **260-9**, **276-81**
Garouste and Bonetti 94
Gatwick Airport 167-8
Gaudi, Antonio 225

Gehry, Frank 58, **138**
Gellert Hotel, Budapest **234**
Gerster, Dr Georg **272-3**
Gestetner duplicating machine
 195
Gigli, Romeo 50, **51**
Gilbert, Thomas Wallis **65**
Givenchy 94
Glasgow School of Art **206-7**
Glass House, New Canaan 29, **29**
Glyndebourne Opera House **243**
Goetz Gallery, Munich **236**
Golden Section 16
Goldsworthy, Andy 259, **270-1**
golf courses **269**
Goodgrips paring knife **85**
Gopnik, Adam 111
Gough, Piers 68
Gowrie, Lord 202
Grahame, Kenneth 176
Grand Central Station, New York
 186-7
Grantham, John 132
Graves, Georgia **101**
Gray's Anatomy **38**
Great Exhibition (1851) 62
Greenaway, Peter **258**
Grimshaw, Nicholas 166, **178**
Gropius, Walter 197
Guggenheim Museum, New York
 236
Guinness 229

Habitat 19-20, 50, **57**, 70-1, **70**, 97,
 197
Halliburton cases 216, **217**
hammers 192-3
Hancock Shaker Village,
 Massachusetts **84**
hand tools 192-4
Haring, Keith **112**
Harper's Bazaar 110, **111**
Harvey's of Bristol 198
Hasuike, Makio **85**
hats **124-5**

Hawkinson, Larry **266**
Heath-Robinson, W. **11**
Heathrow Airport 167
Hegarty, John 96
Heidenheim Public Baths **234**
Heinz **215**
Hennigsen, Poul **45**
Hepburn, Audrey **94**
'heritage' 21, 30, 227
Heron, Ron **204**
Herzog and de Meuron **236**
high-tech style 48, 202
Hill, Octavia 254
Hill House, Glasgow **42**
Hilton, Matthew 33
Hitachi 223
Hoffmann, Josef 194
Holden, Charles **173**
Holy Island **259**
Honda 21, 165
Hoover Building, London **65**
Hopkins, Michael 226, **243**
Hopper, Edward **199**
housing 26, 28-31, **36-7**, 37,
   40-9, 255

IBM 197, **197**
ICI 197
IKEA 33, **44**
image:
   clothing and 95
   corporate identity 196-9
   lifestyle 32
Imagination Building, London **204**
Imperial War Museum, London
   276
India **50**, **52-3**, **100**
industrial design 195-6
Industrial Revolution 26-7, 62,
   203, 254
'innovators' 223
International Stores 130
Internet 14, 203
inventors 11-13
Issigonis, Alec **164**

Jacobsen, Arne 45, 58, 231
Jaguar E-type 161
Japan Air Lines (JAL) 168
Japan Railways **191**
Jarey, Paul 161
Jarman, Derek **280-1**
Jeanne-Claude **236**
jeans 95-6, **105**
Jencks, Charles **269**
Jensen, Georg 45, 231
Jigsaw **109**
'Jim Nature' television 224, **224**
Jiricna, Eva 94
Jobs, Steve 213, 231
Johnson, Philip 29, **29**, 30
Johnson Wax building **195**
Johnston, Edward **173**
Jones, Stephen **125**
Joseph 93
Juhl, Finn 45
Just Imagine **191**

Kabuki actors **114**
Kansai Airport **166**
Kartell 196
Karuselli chair 56, **57**
Kauffer, E. McKnight 170
Kawabata, Kenji 43
Kawase, Shinobu 22, **22**
Kelly, Ben **244**
Kelmscott House, Oxfordshire 63
Kenwood food processor **75**
Kenzo **99**
Kenzo House, Paris **43**
Keswick, Maggie **269**
kettles 66
keyboards **210**
Kinnier, Jock 183
Kirkwood, Ken **150**
kitchens 65-7, **65**, **73-7**, 201
   restaurants 136, **136**
kitsch 32
Klein, Bernat 93
Klein, Calvin 32, 43
K'nex 230

knives **85**
Knoll **209**
Kubrick, Stanley 231
Kukkapuro, Yrjö 56, **57**

Labbezanga village, Nigeria **273**
labels 94
labour-saving appliances 63-4
Lacoste **123**
Lagerfeld, Karl 106
Lambie-Nairn, Martin **20**
Landor, Walter 168
landscape movement 254, **254**
Lane, Allen 246
Lane, Danny 226
Lauren, Ralph 32, 93, **108**
Le Creuset 68
Le Nôtre, André **262**, 263
Lee, Sister Ann 206
Lego 230, **231**
Leith 225-6
Lelong **101**
lemon squeezers **18**, 66
Leonardo da Vinci 252, 259
Lethaby, W.R. 27, 215
Lever, W.H. 68
Levi's 96, **105**
Lexicon 80 typewriter 196
Lezénès, Gilbert **2**
licensing 32, 93
Lichtenstein, Roy 251
lighting 64
   Anglepoise lamp 82, **217**
   PH-5 hanging lamp **45**
   in shops 71
   Noguchi **102**
   Tizio desk lamp **82**
Lillie, Bea 96
linen **76**
linoleum 33
lipstick 114, **116**
Lloyds Building, London **218**
loafers **112**
Loewy, Raymond 64, 162, **163**,
   195, 196

Löfstad Castle **73**
lofts, urban **26**, 30-1
London Underground **172-3**
Loos, Adolf 26, **244**
Lorenz **43**
Lotus Elite 161
Louis XIV, King of France 263
Louis XX chair **33**
Louvre, Paris 225
Lovegrove, Ross **189**
Lubs, Dietrich **210**
Lycra 95, 100, 123
Lyon train station **179**
Lyons, Eric 255

McCardell, Claire 123
machine aesthetic 27
Mackintosh, Charles Rennie **42**,
   47, 58, 76, **206-7**
Mackintosh, Margaret Macdonald
   80
Maclaren, Owen 160
Maclaren buggies 160
McManus, Tom **268**
Mae West Hot Lips sofa **59**
magazines **246-7**
Magistretti, Vico 196
Magritte, René **118**
Mainbocher **101**
Maison de Verre, Paris **32**
make-up **114-16**
Malton sofabed **83**
The Man with the Golden Arm **249**
Maragall, Pasqual 225
Marimekko 196
Mariscal, Javier 225
markets 127, 128, **128**, **145**
Marks, David **233**
Marks and Spencer 91, 130, 132
Marriott, Michael **86**, **87**
mass-production 62, 64, 194-5,
   195, 228
Matisse, Henri 93
Maugham, Syrie 76
Mazda MX-5 165

Meccano 230, **230**
Meier, Raymond **111, 116, 121**
Meiji Shrine, Tokyo **272**
Mendelsohn, Erich **39, 77**
Mendini, Alessandro **85**
Mercedes-Benz 196
merchandising 229-30, **250**
Mezzo, Soho 39, 136, 138, **140**
Michelin **170**
Michelin, Edouard 160
Microsoft **210**, 229
Mies van der Rohe, Ludwig 58,
  197
Millennium Wheel, London **233**
Miller, Herman **35**, 56, 202
Milne, A.A. **37**
minimalism 29, 43
Mr Chow's Chinese restaurant **75**
Mitterand, François 225
Miyake, Issey 102, **103**
Model-T Ford 161, 162, 164, 195
Modern Movement 26, 28, 29-30,
  34, 194
'Modulor' **40**, 41
mohair **104**
Monster House, New Canaan **30**
Mont Blanc fountain pen **216**
Morris, William 16, 22, 26, 27, 30,
  55, 63, 194
Morris Mini Minor **164**
Morrison, Jasper 33
Moschino **156**
Moser, Koloman 194
Mothercare 71, 198
Muir, Jean 93
Muji 71, 89, **97**
Museum of Modern Art (MOMA),
  New York 196, 197, 227
museums 226-8, **236-7**

Nash, Paul **171**
National Trust 73, 225, 254-5
natural materials 258-9, **278-9**
Neutra, Richard **267**
New York City Transport 160

News Bar, New York **244**
Newton, Helmut **116-17**
Nicholson, Ben 93, **113**
Nicolson, Harold **260**
Nike 96, **248**
Nissan **123**, 164
Nizzoli, Marcello 196
Noguchi, Isamu **102**, 266
Nokia mobile phones **217**
Nordiska Kompaniet **45**
Nouvel, Jean **2**
Noyes, Eliot 197
nylon 95

obsolescence 66
office design **198**, 199-200, **199**,
  201-3, **202, 204-5**
Olivari **85**
Olivetti 196, 197, **210**
Olmsted, Frederick Law 254
Olympus 238, **239**
Orrefors 196
Oyster Bar, Grand Central
  Station, New York **138-9**

packaging **23**, 71, 129-30, 131,
  146-9, 152-3
paint 31, **31, 52-3**
Panhard et Lavassor 161
Paolozzi, Eduardo **187**, 259
paperclips **10**
parks 254-5, **254**, 257
Parr, Martin **238, 275**
Pascal, David **204**
pasta **129**
patchwork quilts **54**
Pawson, John **42**, 43, 94
Peclair, Dominique 90
Pei, I.M. 225
Penguin Books 246, **247**
Pennsylvania Railroad **163**
period styles 16-17, 33, 90
Perrier mineral water 130
pestles and mortars **74**
Peterghen, Van **176**

Peugeot 160, 194
Philco 224
photography **150-1, 238-9**
Piaggio 161
Piano, Renzo **166, 243**
Picasso, Pablo **137**
Pick, Frank 173
Pitchford Hall, Shropshire 37
platform shoes **110**
pneumatic tyres 160
Polartec 123
pop culture 229
Porsche 161, 165, **176**
Porsche, Dr Ferdinand 161, 164,
  184
Porsche, Ferdinand-Alexander
  176
Porto Cervo 256
Premier Vision 90
Priestman Associates 223
Prospect Cottage, Dungeness
  280-1
Prunier **131**
pushchairs 160
Putman, Andrée 94

Quaglino's, London 39, 135, **215**
Quant, Mary **17**, 97

radios 11-13, **12-13**, 224
railways **163**, 169, **178-9, 186-7,**
  191
Rams, Dieter 66, **210**, 223
Rand, Paul 197, **197**
Range Rover 21
Rawsthorn, Alice 231
Ray, Man **172**
Raybans **123**
Rebecca's Restaurant, San
  Francisco **138**
record labels **229**
Remington 200
Renault 164, **165**
restaurants 126, 135-6, **136,**
  138-41, 215

revivalist design 224
Ricard, André 225
Ricci, Nina 94
Richards, Penny 226
Rietveld, Gerrit 58
Roberts radio 224
robots **209**
Rockefeller Center, New York
  234
Rogers, Richard **218**
Rolling Stones 229
Rolodex 202, **216**
Ronis, Willy **55, 145, 251**
Rootes 164
Rootes, Lord 164, 184
Rossi, Aldo 66, **81**
Routemaster bus **182**
Rover 21, 164, 165
Rover safety bicycle **160**
Royal College of Art 97-8
Rubenstein, Helena 114
Ruskin, John 203

S-Cargo van 164
Saarinen, Eero 58, 165, **177**
Saatchi and Saatchi 229
Sackville-West, Vita **260**
Sadler, Marc **184**
Salt, John **169**
Sampe, Astrid **45**
Samso, Eduardo 225
Sander, Jill **109**
Sapper, Richard 66, **82**
saris **100**
Saunders, Clarence 128
Scandinavia **44-5**, 196
scarves 112, **113**
Schiaparelli, Elsa 93, 125
Schlemmer, Oskar **59, 102**
scissors **85**
scooters 161-2, **174**
Scott, Ridley 191
SCP 33
Scrimenger Kemp Gee 98
Sears Roebuck 71

'Seven Series' sardine tin collector's cabinet **86**
Shakers 34, 35, **38**, **84**, 206
shaving mirrors **82**
Shaw, Bernard 63
Shell 170, **171**, 197
Shepard, E.H. **37**
shoes 96, **98**, **110-13**, 125
shopping, as leisure activity 230-1
shops 68-71, **108-9**
  food 128-9, 134, **144-5**
  in museums 227
  supermarkets 128, 129, 130-1, 132-4, **133**
Shrimpton, Jean 94
signage 167, **182-3**
Singleton House, Los Angeles 266, **267**
Sissinghurst Castle, Kent **260-1**
Smart Design **85**
'smart' fabrics 95
'smart house' 67
Smith, Paul 20-1, **21**, 57
Smith-Miller, Henry **266**
Smithson, Peter 58
Soane, John 257
soap 68
Socrates 60
sofa, Mae West Hot Lips **59**
sofabeds **83**
Sokolsky, Melvin **114**
Sony 196, 224, **225**, 227
Soria, Pierre **2**
Sottsass, Ettore 196, **210**
Soup Kitchens 135
Space Shuttle **160**
Sparke, Penny 62, 222
sport **122-3**, 228, **240-1**
staircases **38-9**, 199
Stansted Airport 166, 167
Starck, Philippe **18**, **33**, 66, 67, 224, **224**
Stein, Gertrude 123
Stevenson **267**

Stewart, Dave 229
Stewart, Martha 32
storage 29, **86-7**
Strauss, Levi 95-6
streamlining 161-2, **176-7**
Studio BCF **85**
Stumpf, Bill 202
styling 17, 64, 65, 162, 195
suburbia 255
Sudjic, Deyan 65
Summers, Kevin **150**
Sunbeam cars **188**
supermarkets 128, 129, 130-1, 132-4, **133**
Sutherland, Graham 170
Swatch **112**
Swierzy, Waldimar **249**

taste, aesthetics 14-15, 32
Tatra 161
Teague, Walter Dorwin 64, 162
technology 26, 27, 29-30, 67
  clothing 91, 95
  electronics industry 222-4
  home working 203
  'user-friendly' 21, 200
  at work 199-201
Tecnolumen **85**
Teflon 13-14
telephones 13, 200, **200**, **217**
television 223, 224, **224**, 228
Tetrapak containers 129
Thomson, Robert 160
Thonet 194
Thornton, Peter 34
Thurber, James 200
Timberland boots 96
Tintin **250**
Tizio desk lamp **82**
TKO 13
tools 192-4, **279**
toothbrushes 79
Toscani, Oliviero **110**
Tottenham Court Road station, London **187**

tourism 224-6, 238
Toyota 165
toys 229-30, **231**
tradition 21, 30, 165
Traeger, Tessa **150**
Tredegar House, Cornwall 73
tree houses **37**
trenchcoats 95
Triadic Ballet 102
trolleys, supermarket 132, 146, **147**
Tupper, Earl S. **62**
Tupperware **62**
Turrett Collaborative Architects **244**
Tusquets, Oscar 225
TWA terminal, Kennedy airport 165-6, **177**
2001: A Space Odyssey 231
Ty Nânt mineral water **16**, 129-30
typefaces 201
typewriters 200, **210-11**
tyres, pneumatic 160

Unarco 132
Ungaro **90**
Unité d'Habitation, Berlin 41
Unité d'Habitation, Marseilles 28, **40**, 41, 258
Unwerth, Ellen von **156**
'user-friendly' technology 21, 200

vacuum cleaners 63, **66**
Vanhall 161
Vaux, Calvert 254
vegetables **276-7**
Venturi, Robert 58, **80**
Versace **93**
Versailles **262-3**
Vespa 161-2, **174**
Victoria and Albert Museum, London 62-3, 192, 226-7
Victorian period 27, 201
video recorders 223

Villa Mairea, Finland **44**, **45**
Villa Savoy, Poissy **41**
Vitra Design Museum 58
Vitruvius 16
Vivier, Roger **98**
Volkswagen Beetle 161, 164, 165, **184**
Volkswagen Concept 1 165
Volkswagen Golf GTi 162
Voysey, C.F.A. 43, 68
Vreeland, Diana 91, 156

Wagenfeld, Wilhelm **85**
Walkman 224, **225**
Wally Gator yacht **181**
Wannabe loafers **112**
Warhol, Andy 79
Warren & Wetmore Architects **138**, **186-7**
washing-machines 63, 67
waste bins **87**
watches **112**
Watson, Albert 246, **247**
Wegner, Hans 45
Weil, Daniel 224
Welles, Orson 231
West, Mae 58, **59**
Westwood, Vivienne **110**, **118-19**
Whitcomb Judson **101**
wicker furniture 34, 257
Wickham, Michael 67
Wiener Werkstätte 27, 194
Wilde, Oscar 234
wooden spoons 68, **74**
Worth, Charles 92
Wright, Frank Lloyd **46-7**, 58, **195**, **236**, 257

yachts **181**
YRM 167

Zen Buddhism 43
Zeppelins 161
Zippo lighters 14, 95
zips 95, 100, **101**

ACKNOWLEDGEMENTS

The publisher would like to thank the picture researchers Nadine Bazar, Gareth Jones and Clare Limpus for their invaluable contribution to this book.

Conran Octopus would also like to thank Dinah Hall and Victoria Davis for reading and commenting on the text; Sarah Pearce, Tomoko Hori and Claire Taylor for their assistance with picture research; Nato Welton and Kirsty O'Leary-Leeson for organizing material for special photography; Hilary Bird for the index.

The publisher thanks the following photographers and organizations for their kind permission to reproduce the photographs in this book:
2 Antonio Martinelli; 3 Mark Fiennes; 4 Harry Borden/Katz Pictures; 6 New York Bound Bookshop; 10 Jared Fowler; 11 *Absurdities* published by Gerald Duckworth & Co. Ltd,1975/©Mrs J. C. Robinson; 12-13 Ian McKinnell/design: TKO Product Design Consultants; 14 Adrian Meredith Photography; 15 Niepce/Rapho; 16 Jared Fowler; 17 Advertising Archives; 18 Hannah Lewis; 20 ©1991, BBC Television, Broadcasting and Presentation Department; 21 Design Museum; 22 above Brian Ma Siy; 22 below Ken Adlard; 23 Richard Foster; 26 Max Jourdan, courtesy of Manhattan Loft Corporation; 28 Bauhaus-Archiv, Berlin; 29 Ezra Stoller/©Esto; 30 Michael Moran; 31 Jared Fowler; 32 Jordi Sarra Arau; 33 Hans Hansen/Vitra Design Museum; 35 courtesy of Herman Miller, Inc.; 36 above Christian Sarramon; 36 below left Fritz von der Schulenburg/The Interior Archive; 36 below right Mary Evans/Institution of Civil Engineers; 37 left from *Winnie The Pooh* by A.A.Milne, illustrated by E.H.Shepard. Copyright the Berne Convention & 1926 by E.P.Dutton, renewed 1954 by A.A.Milne. Reproduced by permission of Curtis Brown, London and Dutton Children's Books, New York, a division of Penguin Books USA Inc; 37 right Jerome Darblay; 38 left Chancellor Press; 38 right Paul Rocheleau/Trustees Office, Pleasant Hill, Kentucky; 39 left Peter Cook; 39 right Graeme Harris/The Special Photographers Library; 40 above René Burri/Magnum; 40-41 © Fondation Le Corbusier; 40 below: Le Corbusier et Pierre Jeanneret *Oeuvre Complète*, edited by Willy Boesiger, Girsberger, Zurich; 41 above left Martin Jones/Arcaid; 41 above right Martin Charles; 41 below Peter Cook; 42 above left Fritz von der Schulenburg/The Interior Archive; 42 above right Mark Fiennes; 42 below Richard Glover; 43 above Eric Morin; 43 below *The New Yorker* Magazine, Inc; 44 left Ikea; 44 right Simo Rista/Phaidon Press; 45 above left Jared Fowler; 45 above right Sotheby's, London; 45 below left Fritz von der Schulenburg/The Interior Archive; 45 below right courtesy of the Board of Trustees of the Victoria and Albert Museum/photograph: Daniel McGrath; 46 left N.A. Callow/NHPA ; 46-7 Peter Cook/Phaidon Press; 47 above Ezra Stoller/©Esto; 47 below Avery Architectural & Fine Arts Library, Columbia University; 48 above Tim Street-Porter; 48 below Lucia Eames Demetrios dba Eames Office ©1989.1995; 49 Julius Shulman; 50 above left Christian Sarramon; 50 above right Guy Bouchet; 50 below Paul Ryan/International Interiors; 51 Santi Caleca; 52-3 Stephen P. Huyler; 54 above Jennie Woodcock/ Reflections; 54 below reproduced by permission of the American Museum in Britain; 55 left Rapho; 55 right Sylvie Lancrenon/Stylist: Marion Bayle/Marie Claire Maison; 56 Hans Hansen/Vitra Design Museum; 57 above Habitat UK; 57 below Avarte Oy; 58 Richard Bryant/Arcaid; 59 above left Henry Bourne/The Conran Shop; 59 above right Erich Consemüller/Bauhaus-Archiv, Berlin; 59 below Royal Pavilion, Art Gallery and Museums, Brighton/©Demart ProArte BV & DACS 1996; 62 below Archive Photos; 65 above Peter Mackertich; 65 below Robert Harding Picture Library; 66 Dyson Appliances Ltd; 69 Richard Caldicott; 70 Habitat UK; 72 Fritz von der Schulenburg/ World of Interiors; 73 James Mortimer/World of Interiors; 74 above Jared Fowler; 74 below Phillips Fine Art Auctioneers; 75 left Marianne Majerus; 75 right Jared Fowler; 76-7 Jacques Boulay; 77 above Tim Street-Porter; 77 below Peter Cook; 78 ©Paul Warchol; 79 left Björn Keller/Faragstudi Avanti; 79 right Sandro Sodano; 80-1 Alessi; 82 left Mann & Man/Options/Robert Harding Syndication; 82 right Jared Fowler; 83 left Jared Fowler; 83 right Henry Bourne/The Conran Shop; 84 Paul Rocheleau; 85 left Abitare/Leo Torri; 85 centre Jared Fowler; 85 right Smart Design; 86 above left Jacqui Hurst; 86 above right Steve Rees/Crafts Council; 86 below David Brittain/Stafford Cliff; 87 above left Contemporary Applied Arts; 87 above right Fritz von der Schulenburg /The Interior Archive; 87 below left & below centre James Johnson/ES Magazine; 87 below right Jared Fowler; 90-2 Abbas/Magnum; 93 Marineau/Stills/Frank Spooner Pictures; 94 Henrietta Butler/Camera Press; 97 left Michel Brodsky in collaboration with Roger Vivier; 97 right Muji; 99 Roberto Badin/Kenzo; 100 above Christophe Boisvieux; 100 below Jared Fowler; 101 left Hamilton's Photographers Ltd; 101 above right Hamilton's Photographers Ltd; 102 above courtesy of the Isamu Noguchi Foundation, Inc; 101 below right Chancellor Press, 1985; 102 below ©1996 The Oscar Schlemmer Theatre Estate, courtesy photo Archive C. Raman Schlemmer, Oggebbio, Italy; 103 Issey Miyake (UK) Ltd; 104 left James Martin for *Arena*; 104 right Hannah Lewis/Elle Decoration; 105 Jared Fowler; 106 left: Henry Clarke/©Vogue, The Condé Nast Publication Ltd; 106-7 Chanel; 107 above right Michael Freeman; 107 centre right Cecil Beaton, courtesy of Sotheby's London; 107 below right: Pierre Sabatier/Marie Claire Maison; 108 above left Guy Bouchet; 108 below left Michael Moran; 108 right Hervé Champollion/Agence Top; 109 above © Paul Warchol; 109 below Chris Gascoigne/Arcaid; 110 above courtesy of United Colors of Benetton; 110 below Arnal Garcia/Frank Spooner Pictures; 110-11 Baron & Baron; 112 left Jean-Pierre Masclet/Katz Pictures; 112 right Swatch; 113 ©Ascher, courtesy of Ascher Collection, Peter Ascher, New York; 114 left Rafael Wollman/Frank Spooner Pictures; 114 right J.Perno/Explorer; 115 Fahey/Klein Gallery, Los Angeles; 116 left ©Vogue, The Condé Nast Publication Ltd; 116-17 Hamilton's Photographers Ltd; 118 above left Popperfoto; 118 above right Chris Moore; 118 below Hickey Robertson/The Menil Collection, Houston/©ADAGP, Paris & DACS, London 1996; 119 Hamilton's Photographers Ltd; 120 Vogue, ©Condé Nast Publications Ltd; 121 Raymond Meier; 122-3 Pentagram Design Ltd; 123 above centre Stuart Franklin/Magnum; 123 above right Lacoste; 123 below Paramount/courtesy The Kobal Collection; 124-5 The Times, London; 128 Robin Smith/Tony Stone Images; 129 Jared Fowler; 132 David Carson Design; 133 Chris Steele-Perkins/Magnum; 134 *French Country Cooking* by Elizabeth David, published by Penguin, illustrated by John Minton; 136 Eric Morin; 137 Rapho; 138 left Tim Street-Porter; 138-9 Andrew Bordwin; 140 Christian Sarramon; 141 David Brittain; 142 Greg Barrett/Vogue Entertaining; 143 above left Gentl & Hyers; 143 above right & below Kijuro Yahagi Co. Ltd; 144-5 Alex Bartel/Arcaid; 145 centre Willy Ronis/Rapho; 145 above right

M.J. Jarry/J.F. Tripelon/Agence Top; **145** below right: Peter Cook; **146** left *How to Wrap Five More Eggs* by Hideyuki Oka, published by Weatherhill Inc.; **146** right Jared Fowler; **147** above Stephen Wilkes/The Image Bank; **147** below Hulton Getty Picture Collection; **148-9** Kevin Summers; **150** above left Kevin Summers; **150** above right Tessa Traeger; **150** below Ken Kirkwood; **151** Robert Freson; **152-3** Jared Fowler; **154** above Hannah Lewis; **154-5** 'Coca Cola' and 'Coke' and the design of the Contour Bottle are registered trademarks of The Coca-Cola Company; **155** above courtesy of Bartle Bogle Hegarty/The Coca-Cola Company; **156** Smile Management; **157** Borse Moschino; **160** above US Postal Service; **160** below The Science Museum/Science & Society Picture Library; **163** Corbis/Bettman/UPI; **164** British Motor Industry Heritage Trust; **165** left Renault UK Ltd; **165** right Mercedes-Benz, Germany; **166** Dennis Gilbert/Arcaid; **169** courtesy O.K. Harris Works of Art, New York; **170** above Mclean/Bailhache/Marie Claire Maison; **170** below Michelin Tyre PLC; **171** The National Motor Museum, Beaulieu; **172** above left London Transport Museum, Man Ray Trust/©ADAGP, Paris & DACS, London 1996; **172** below left courtesy of the Board of Trustees of the Victoria and Albert Museum; **172-3** London Transport Museum; **174** above left Wernher Krutein/Liaison International; **174** above right René Burri/Magnum; **174** below Piaggio; **175** Citroën; **176** left Gilles Martin Raget/Kos Picture Source Ltd; **176** right Porsche; **177** above Ezra Stoller/©Esto ; **177** below Martyn Goddard/Tony Stone Images; **178** Peter Cook; **179** above Luc Boegly/Archipress; **179** below Paul Raftery/Arcaid; **180** left courtesy of British Airways; **180** right Tim Wren; **181** Guy Gurney; **182** above left Nacäsa & Partners; **182** above right R.J.B. Goodale/Oxford Scientific Films; **182** centre left Nacäsa & Partners; **182** centre & centre right Christian Sarramon; **182** below left Department of Transport; **182** below right Syndication International/Hulton; **183** above Roy Gumpel/Liaison International; **183** below: Peter Aaron/©Esto; **184** Marc Sadler/Dainese S.p.A; **185** ©Cindy Lewis 1984; **186** Samuel Kravitt/Archive Photos; **187** above Peter Cook; **187** below Tim Crosby/Liaison International; **188** BFI Stills; **189** left (GB) Ross Lovegrove: Dragtpose/Connolly Leather; **189** right Musée de la Publicite, Paris/©ADAGP, Paris & DACS, London, 1996; **190-1** Peter Seaward/Tony Stone Images; **191** right: PROD/Daniel Boutellier; **194** Stefan Kirchner/Soldi & Donadello; **195** left Popperfoto; **195** right SC Johnson; **197** IBM; **198** Ezra Stoller/©Esto; **199** Collection Walker Art Centre, Minneapolis, Gift of the T.B. Walker Foundation, Gilbert M. Walker Fund, 1948; **200** Henry Dreyfuss Associates; **202** Warner Bros/DC Comics/courtesy The Kobal Collection; **204** above *The New Yorker* Magazine, Inc.; **204** below Peter Cook; **205** above left Gilles de Chabaneix; **205** above right Design Museum; **205** below Goursat/Rapho; **206** Anne Von Brömssen/Andrew Massey; **207** Mark Fiennes/Arcaid; **208** Elliott Kaufman; **209** above Toyota Motor Corporation/International Society for Educational Information Inc, Japan; **209** below Eric Morin; **210** above left Philippe Garner; **210** above right Simon Lee; **210** below Text 100; **211** Agence Top; **212** above left Apple Computer UK Ltd; **212** below left & right, Giampiero Benvenuti; **213** left, below centre & below right Giampiero Benvenuti; **213** above right D. Sorey/Liaison International; **214-5** Ed Lallo/Liaison International; **215** above Robert Mort; **215** below Ezra Stoller/©Esto; **216-17** Jared Fowler; **218** Peter Cook; **219** Lyle Leduc/Liaison International; **222** Christie's Images; **223** Willy Ronis/Rapho; **224** Thomson Multi-Media; **225** David Gill; **228** Peter Cook; **229** left & centre Sylvia Pitcher Photo Library; **229** right Conran Octopus; **230** Jared Fowler, courtesy of S Martin Summer; **231** Jared Fowler; **232** photomontage by Hayes Davidson/Nick Wood; **233** Ministière de la Culture, Paris; **234** above Dieter Leistner/Architekton; **234** below Sandra Baker/Liaison International; **235** Peter Korniss; **236** above Volz/Grossmann/Bilderberg; **236** below Margherita Spiluttini; **237** ©Esto; **238** left Magnum; **238-9** Advertising Archives; **239** above right design by Shozo Toyohisa, manufactured by Olympus Optical courtesy of Yasuo Satomi; **239** below right Peter Mackertich; **240-1** Jared Fowler; **242-3** Peter Cook; **243** above Peter Cook/Arcaid; **243** below Guy Bouchet; **244** above left Christian Sarramon; **244** above right ©Paul Warchol; **244** below left courtesy of Tony Wilson/Factory Too; **244** below centre Dennis Gilbert/Arcaid; **244** below right Roger Sinek/design: Fab; **245** Eric Morin; **246** Archive Photos; **247** above David Carson Design; **247** below Hulton Getty Picture Collection; **248** *The Graphic Language of Neville Brody II* published by Thames & Hudson, 1994; **249** Christie's Images; **250-1** Rapho; **250** left Sundancer; **251** right 'Superman' is a trademark of DC Comics copyright ©1938. All rights reserved. Used with permission. Cover artist: Joe Shuster, courtesy of Christie's Images; **254** above Jerry Harpur; **254** below Nick Meers/Arcaid; **256** REX Features; **258** BFI Stills; **259** Steve Lyman/Arcaid; **260** Jared Fowler; **260-1** David Bowie/Collections; **262-3** Roland Beaufre/World of Interiors; **264-5** Marijke Heuff; **266-7** ©Paul Warchol; **267** above *The New Yorker* Magazine, Inc.; **267** below Tim Street-Porter; **268** TBWA; **269** above Charles Jencks; **269** below Richard Ansett; **270-1** from *Stone*, ©Andrew Goldsworthy courtesy of Michael Hue-Williams Fine Art Ltd; **272-3** ©Georg Gerster; **274** Magnum; **275** left Jared Fowler/'Reproduced from the (1993) Ordnance Survey 1:25 000 Outdoor Leisure Map with permission of The Controller of HMSO ©Crown Copyright, Licence No MC85766M'; **275** right Jerome Darblay; **276** left Terence Conran; **276-7** Clive Nichols/design: Terence Conran; **277** right Conran Octopus; **278** Kate Gadsby; **279** left Derek St Romaine; **279** right Jacqui Hurst; **280-1** John Glover.

Special thanks to the following for lending material to be photographed: Artemide (GB) Ltd, Terence Conran, The Conran Shop, The Conran Shop Contracts, Factory Too, Filofax, Mike Frankel, Gilbert Makers, Halliburton, Kenwood, Montblanc Pens, Nick Neads, Nokia Phones, George Powell, Martin Summer.

Quotations originally appeared in the following: 10, 14, 165 *Definitions of Design* (Design Council, 1995); **24, 28, 40** Le Corbusier, *Towards a New Architecture* (1923); **31** Christopher Alexander, *A Pattern Language* (OUP, 1977); **36** Adrian Forty, *Objects of Desire*; **56** Paul Smith quoted in 'Body-formed for who?' by Kathryn Flett (*Observer*, 12 December 1995); **64** Deyan Sudjic, *Cult Objects* (Paladin, 1985); **66** Philippe Starck quoted in 'Starck Raving' by Peter Lennon (*Guardian*, 17 September 1994); **110** Adam Gopnik, *The New Yorker*; **128** Brillat Savarin, *Physiologie du Gout* (1825); **176** Kenneth Grahame *The Wind in the Willows* (1908); **202** Ralph Waldo Emerson, *Ode, Inscribed to W.H. Channing*; **203** John Ruskin, *The Stones of Venice* (1851-3); **226** Jane Austen, *Emma* (1816); **231** Steve Jobs quoted in *Wired* (February 1996); **257** Frank Lloyd Wright, *In the Cause of Architecture* (1894); **260** Lewis Carroll, *Alice's Adventures in Wonderland* (1865); **270** Andy Goldsworthy, *Stone* (Viking, 1994).

Every effort has been made to trace the copyright holders, architects and designers and we apologise in advance for any unintentional omission and would be pleased to insert the appropriate acknowledgement in any subsequent edition.

ecorbusiergrandcentralstationjamesdy

nelvespacomfortmujifrankgehryconco

meccanogiorgioarmanivitasackvi

tofiestawaremontblancfountain

arnejacobsentheshakerstheeiffelt

azeslevi'splasticirvingpennmarcel

ouchcomicsderekjarmanthebauh

enguinbookshenrydreyfussmohair

streamlininganglepoisenevillebrodyson

oshergonomicsshellbicbiroeliz

dieterramsfilmposterscadillacthesixties

rthyviviennewestwoodraymondlo

paulsmithphilippestarckmaryquantreco

bienbaronolivettisportsballsdavi

franklloydwrightrenzopianonewyorker

obertdoisneauthezipdianavreelan